COMFORTABLY NUMB

Mike Casey

VicToria Freudiger: Publisher and Editor-in-Chief
Marketer/Brand Developer: Digi-Tall-Media .com
editorshepherd@gmail.com

~

Special thanks to John & Noelle Ehab
for helping to write this book.

~

Proofreader: Jody Amato

~

Cover Design: Bernhard Klingenberg

~

Social Media Director: Marguerite McCurry

~

Special additions/edits: Heather Hansen

ISBN: 1519397747

Dedication

This book is dedicated to Bob Stewart and Skip Joannes and all those who helped me along the way and unselfishly gave of themselves.

Acknowledgment

A special thanks to Fred and Regina Amoroso who made this book possible.

The two most important days in
your life are the day you were born
and the day you find out why.

~ Mark Twain

Sarah Casey, English 111
February 5, 2010

Foreword
Moment of Power

My moment of power occurred when I was a sophomore in high school. I was sitting on the counter in the bathroom putting on my make-up as I did every morning while getting ready for school. I looked over to see my step dad standing in the doorway. He had come to deliver bad news. "Your dad has suffered a major stroke," he told me. I replied, "Okay, thank you, I understand." I didn't know what else to say. I didn't begin crying nor did I panic. I just wanted to be alone to reflect on what I had just been told. It was weird to hear from one dad that my other dad might die. I didn't know what a stroke was exactly, but I knew it was life threatening. I also knew that there was nothing much I could do and I felt powerless. I hated the thought of staying home with my family worrying and I wanted to be around my friends and pretend that it was a normal day. My mom said that she would call if she got an update on my dad's condition. So my older brother and I went to school and attempted a normal day.

It was almost lunch time when my principal pulled my brother and me out of class and took us into his office; we knew it couldn't be good news. I was nervous as we sat in the chairs across from Mr. Johannes. He told us that he had spoken to my mom and that the doctors expected my father to die within hours. By the time my mom picked us up, I was numb. The thought of my dad dying was surreal and it couldn't sink in. I felt even more powerless.

The hospital in Salinas was at least 30 minutes away which seemed much longer. My dad had been there for two weeks prior as a result of his years-long heroine addiction which caused him to develop a skin eating bacteria from the repetitive use of needles. During his treatment, a nurse made the mistake of inserting the IV needle into a major artery instead of a vein where it should have gone. This caused the imperiling stroke. As I was driving in the car antici-pating what I would see, I somehow knew this wasn't the end for my dad. He couldn't die because my prayers for him had not yet been answered. My prayers were that my dad's life would be changed no matter what it took. I prayed that very thing for almost as long as I could remember. Although I may not have felt it at the time, I knew that there was power in prayer.

My father's story of addiction is similar to many others. He was a successful paramedic, saving the lives of others. His marriage with my mother thrived and all was well. By the time he was given a death sentence by the doctors, his addictions had stripped him of his job, money and marriage. Now he was about to lose it all. It was awful. I prayed for so many years because I needed my dad to change for us.

At the hospital, my father was unrecognizable. He looked like the same man to me, but it wasn't him. The stroke left him unable to read, write, tell time, speak and even walk. The doctors said that if by some miracle he made it through the night he would never be able to do those things again. Saying good bye to my dad wasn't really possible because he didn't even know who I was. As I sat in the waiting room I felt nothing. I couldn't cry because I refused to believe that it was the end.

Despite the doctor's prognosis, my dad did make it through the night. One day became a week, and then a week became a month and he never died. I went to visit my father in the hospital as he recovered. When I had my first conversation with him since the stroke, I realized that my prayers had been answered. There sitting on the hospital bed was my dad talking to me! I had my power moment because my dad could talk to me and my prayers had been answered.

The extent of my power moment reaches far beyond that conversation and continues to this day. He now leads a recovery home for men that have also struggled with life dominating addictions. He is indeed a changed man and a fully functioning member of our society.

My prayer was that God would save my dad and bring him back to me. In my desperation to see my dad be better, I was powerless. However, I saw with my own eyes the power of prayer and learned from that day forth that there is nothing which prayer can't help.

Sarah

[This is a paper that Mike's daughter Sarah wrote as an English assignment while in college.]

Out of sufferings have emerged the strongest souls;
the most massive characters are seared with scars.

~ Khalil Gibran, *The Prophet*

Table of Contents

Introduction

It's a beautiful sunny day as I pull into the parking lot of the Monterey County jail. I can't help but wonder about the two men I will visit today. Walking toward the front door I scan the horizon, admiring the beauty of the day; from my perspective things are great. Those on the inside looking out through the chain-link fence and razor wire probably don't share the same opinion. I guess it's all a matter of perspective.

As I walk into the reception area there is the usual flurry of activity: bail bondsmen posting bonds; attorneys, parole, and probation officers visiting; as well as a trail of inmates coming back from cleaning the grounds. As I approach the window, the deputy activates the speaker and asks in a loud voice, "Can I help you?" I step back and take a deep breath. "I'm here for a clergy visit," I reply. This whole thing still seems surreal to me—after all, it hasn't been that long since I was an inmate here at the Monterey County jail. I know nothing about the men I will visit today other than they've reached out for help.

The deputy hands back my ID and motions for me to head back. As we approach the first large blue steel door I hear a loud click as the locking mechanism disengages; I look up to see a video camera is watching my every move. The door slams behind me and I move down the hall, still uneasy about being inside a jail.

There is no doubt in my mind that the reason I have so much compassion for these incarcerated men is that I've been there and I've made a lot of bad choices in my life. As my thirty-year high school reunion approaches, I can't help but look back and think about old friends and places, and the things that helped to shape my life.

One of the things that stands out the most is my time in high school running track and cross-country. I didn't realize until later that I was really running from my life. Running for me was the only normal thing in a totally dysfunctional life. It was the dysfunction in my life that motivated me to run. My reactions were different ways to get away from my dad as he would consume his nightly allotment of beer and whatever medication he had on hand. It became my way of escape.

Lately I've felt a definite need to encourage those who are out there still struggling. But it must be a message of hope; I want to emphasize that what doesn't kill you makes you stronger. I should know: I just dropped my brother off at rehab, my sister is in prison, and I was molested multiple times by several different people. I was also kidnapped from the school playground by my stepmom in order to protect me from my dad.

***

Chapter One
A Bumpy Takeoff

Back in the 60s in my home town of Norwalk—a suburb of Los Angeles—the streets and front lawns were a safe place to play. It was the perfect kind of warm sunny day to wait outside for the ice cream truck. As a six-year-old having fun kicking a ball in the yard outside our house, I could hear the familiar jingle on the next street. I scrounged up what change I could and, realizing that I didn't have enough, headed back into the house looking for Dad.

The door to his room was slightly ajar. *Dad doesn't like to be bothered in his room*, I reminded myself, but I really wanted that ice cream. *It'll only take a second to ask for change.*

Timidly I knocked on the door, my heart stopping as the door swung open and I saw his furious eyes. I was in serious trouble. As Dad towered over me, my gaze settled on the tattoo on his left bicep: a terrifying devil he had picked out during his first time he got drunk.

From time to time Dad would brag... "One night a bunch of us—me, Tom and Ralph, got drunk and went to the Long Beach Pike looking for pussy." Also Dad would add, "Like I told you before, and I'll tell you again, never, never pass on a piece of ass; 'cause as hard as you try you can never make up for the piece you pass up." He'd take a swig of beer before continuing, "Well, the longer we looked, the drunker we got. That night all of us went into this nasty little tattoo joint and I decided, 'What the heck.' Looking through the books I saw the devil and I knew that was the one. He said that when the girls saw it they liked the tattoo, because it was a "bad boy" thing to do. After all, when I die I'm going to hell 'cause that's where all my friends will be."

The choice of the devil must have been prophetic for him, because that's what Dad seemed like to me. His tat paired well with a blacklight poster he had bought at a swap meet, which was proudly displayed on the wall. It was a picture of the Tasmanian devil with the caption, "Yea, though I walk through the valley of the shadow of death, I will fear no evil, 'cause I'm the meanest son of a bitch in the valley." Dad really got a kick out of this. He told me the quote was from the Bible.

So there I was, standing before the meanest son of a bitch with his bad-boy Lucifer tattoo, wide-eyed and knees knocking. Before I even had the chance to ask for change, he gripped my neck and began violently shaking me. *I should have known better*, I scolded myself, trying not to cry.

"Suck it up, you pussy!" He saw my tears and tightened his grip.

I scolded myself again, *why do you always show him your weakness?*

"Dad, I just wanted to ask for change to get some ice cream," I managed to whimper.

"You're going to cry like a fucking girl over a Popsicle?" he mocked.

By now, my tears were flowing. The more I cried, the tighter his grip became and the more violently he shook me. His strong hand bore into my neck, gagging me and stifling my breathing. I couldn't even choke. For a second his man-handling felt as if this was it for me. *He's gonna kill me here and now,* I thought, knowing he could do it, too. One time I'd overheard Dad telling my Uncle Ralph that he could kill someone and then sit down to eat his lunch over the dead body. Hearing these sorts of things always terrified me.

The ice cream truck pulled onto our street and its music grew louder. My dad's grip loosened around my neck, his muscles relaxed, and he broke down sobbing like a baby. As I struggled to catch my breath, he threw his arms around me.

"I love you, Mike," he bawled. "You just want some ice cream? Of course you can get yourself some ice cream. You know I love you." Dad grabbed the change jar from on top of his dresser and poured it out on the bed, change spilling everywhere, it looked to me like a thousand dollars in dimes, nickels and quarters.

A warm feeling of crazy love swept over me as he handed me the change, tears running down his cheeks.

***

I hadn't always lived with my dad. For the first couple years of my life he was in and out of jail, and barely a part of my life. During that time—my older brother, also named Paul after our dad, and I lived with Dad's parents. We didn't really know anything about our mom. I had no real memories of her. Unfortunately by the time I learned the truth about her absence in my life—I was 33 with a family of my own.

Grandpa was a gentle giant who stood nearly six foot four and weighed close to three hundred pounds. He worked at a company called L & F Industries cutting heavy-gauge steel, which eventually gave him black lung disease and congestive heart failure. After work and on the weekends Grandpa enjoyed relaxing at home in front of a baseball game with a beer in hand, though sometimes we would go fishing.

Grandma was a typical Donna Reed housewife who kept the house tidy, with dinner on the table. She went to church on Sundays, but also had a rather lewd sense of humor. Whenever Grandma had the opportunity to take a break from house-work, she'd be found sitting in her armchair buried in either a raunchy romance novel or her King James Bible.

However ironic, to my young eyes and limited experience, my grandparents were the model of a perfect family. It was only with the perspective of years that I realized they were far from it. Still, my grandparents were the best example I was given and they provided me with a certain amount of stability I wouldn't have had otherwise.

Every once in a while Dad would show up and then disappear again. Although I dreaded being the target of his anger, I always looked forward to the intervals of time we would spend with him. He would let us get away with things that Grandma never let us do, like stay up late and watch TV.

Whenever Dad wasn't around, his older brother, Ralph, filled in for him. Uncle Ralph was my childhood hero, mostly because he was funny and warm, and always made me feel important. Uncle Ralph had his own kids, about the same ages as Paul and me, but they were in Michigan with their mother— whom I never knew—and they only came to visit one week every summer. My uncle treated me like a son, and I felt safe around him—which made me wish that he could have been my father. He may not have been the been the best role model— he was the one who taught me how to break into vending machines and hotwire cars, among other vices—but all that seemed normal to me. It didn't matter that he and my dad were cut from the same cloth; it was the way Uncle Ralph related to me on a human level that made all the difference.

When Dad was home, he and Uncle Ralph would hang out in the garage building radio-controlled model airplanes. My brother, Paul, wasn't that interested, but I loved to watch them work. I was far too young to help. Nonetheless, Uncle Ralph would come down to my level and explain things to me as best he could. Dad didn't mind me being there as long as I didn't try to interfere. After all, he was so focused on what he was doing. If Dad found a tool in my hand he would get frustrated and pry it away, yelling at me.

"Calm down, Paul," Uncle Ralph would say. "It's just a plane."

Dad would usually take me out for ice cream afterward to make up for the yelling.

When Dad and Uncle Ralph had finished building one of their planes, we would all drive out to the radio control club at Lake Elsinore and watch it fly. Then we would celebrate by stopping at McDonald's on the way home.

***

Our lives changed completely in 1966, when Dad cleaned up his act and married Geri. At the ages of five and seven, Paul and I suddenly found ourselves in a real family with a step-mom and three step-sisters. Dad bought a big house for all of us to live in together, not far from Grandma and Grandpa in Norwalk. Strawberry fields and dairies surrounded us with miles of pastures and old barns where we could play and explore, and in the evenings we would have dinner together around the table. Don't get me wrong—I liked my new family but I often wondered what my real mom was like and wondered, did she know I longed for her even though I had no real memories of her? Was she somewhere else with her other family?

Geri entered into my life early enough to assume the role of step-mother seamlessly. She was tender and loving, and treated Paul and me no differently than her own three girls. It was a lot of fun to have stepsisters, too. Her daughter Micky and I were the closest; she was just a year and a half older than me, though she was two years ahead of me in school. Becky was not much older than Paul, and Linda was the oldest. We were not quite the *Brady Bunch*.

All of us would do fun things together as a family, like spend the afternoon at the city park in Norwalk, California. On the way to the park we would stop at Pioneer Chicken to pick up some lunch, and then we would spread out a picnic blanket where *Mom* (as I learned to refer to her as) and Dad would sit, sipping rum and coke and watching us chase each other around and often we would all swim in the pool.

Every Sunday morning the colorful Pied-Piper Sunday school bus would wheel through the neighborhood with loudspeakers announcing, "Come to church today! Watermelon! Prizes! Get on the bus!" In all actuality, Mom and Dad could have cared less about church, but the offer of a free, reliable source of childcare and a couple of extra hours of alone time were irresistible. The bus would stop in front of our house, and us kids would all jump on together on it. At Sunday school, we played fun games, heard interesting stories, and won prizes for completing activities.

One Sunday, a kite was sitting on the prize table caught my eye. The kite was enticing me, and the whole morning I found myself staring at it, hoping for a chance to take the kite home. I won the activity and was up for a prize, but there were a couple kids ahead of me who were each given the option to choose a prize first. I kept my fingers crossed. When my turn came, the kite was still up for grabs, but for some reason I found myself walking away with a pocket-size Bible.

I couldn't understand why I hadn't picked the kite, but afterward, I treasured that Bible. Often I found myself flipping through the pages. It didn't make any sense to me, but I read it anyway.

***

Paul, our stepsisters, and I all together attended Dolland Elementary School. Mom would pack us lunches and lick her fingers to smooth our hair before we headed off for school together—still not *The Brady Bunch*.

***

By the time I reached third grade, I had developed a bit of a reputation for being a troublemaker. My teacher, Mrs. Wright, was tall and skinny; with gray hair and a wrinkly face, she looked way older than Grandma. Sadly, it seemed I could never get out of her bad book.

During one of her classes, Mrs. Wright turned from the blackboard and dropped her horn-rimmed glasses to let them swing on a chain over her slim chest. "Sit still Mike!" she had yelled. Perhaps I'd been a bit restless. I'd turned to look at her with a fright that dissolved as soon as I leaned over to the boy next to me to whisper.

Time ran slowly in our teacher's class, and I inevitably attracted her attention again. The next time Mrs. Wright called me to come sit in the corner chair. She peered at me through her glasses and said, "Your parents should see this note and sign it." The dreaded note was pinned to my shirt with her tiny, shaky, but strong hands. "Don't even think of taking it off. Believe me, I will know if you do." There was no way I would ever take this note off, or any others, until my parents could read it, but the last person on earth I wanted to see any of the notes was my dad.

Later that day, I rushed home, entering through the front door, praying my dad wouldn't be home.

"Another note, Mike? Show me," Mom grabbed the note and read, "Disruptive in class. Mrs. Wright."

Mom signed it for me quickly and then hid it in her pocket just as Dad entered through the garage door.

"Did you get into trouble again today, Mike?"

The question terrified me, leaving me speechless, but Mom broke the silence. "Mike's teacher, Mrs. Wright told me that he's very well-behaved in her class."

I smiled.

The following day Mrs. Wright's note was signed and put back in my lunch box.

It felt good to have someone around to defend me. I fully believe that she did this to the best of her ability, but my step-mom had her own demons to deal with and was not always able to see past them. This was the case when it came to her own parents, who lived not too far from us.

Her parents, our step-grandparents, lived at the end of an old dirt road, tucked in behind a grocery store and surrounded by vacant lots. Going to their house always felt like an adventure because there were lots of things to explore. It was a great place to ride bikes and build forts.

As long as I could remember, Grandma Murphy had been ill. She was in and out of the hospital a lot, and was eventually put in a nursing home. After that, whenever we'd go over to their house, we'd hang out with Grandpa for a bit, and then head over to the nursing home for a visit with Grandma Murphy. I was not thrilled. I hated the way that place smelled like it had the stench of death.

On one particular day, when I was whining and complaining as usual, Grandpa extended a tempting offer. "Look, if you don't want to go today, that's fine. Why don't you and I just stay back this time and watch TV?" Grandpa Murphy smoked huge cigars, which to me smelled great.

As the car rolled away carrying everyone else to the nursing home, I followed my step-grandfather into the dark living room where the shades were pulled. He invited me to sit in his armchair, where a chill ran down my spine as his fat, yellow, smoke-stained fingers fumbled with his belt buckle. That day, under the dim light and the barely audible sound of the television set, I learned firsthand the sort of things perverted old men do to destroy the innocence of young boys. Things that can never be undone. I was eight years old.

Many don't tell anyone after they've been molested, for whatever reason, but I wasn't one of them. I knew that what had happened with Grandpa Murphy had been wrong, and I wasn't willing to stay silent. After we got home, I waited for a moment alone with Mom before divulging the events of the day.

The look of disgust on her face as I described the horrific things her father had done made me feel justified.

"That is repulsive," she said, mouth curled. It took me a moment and a half to understand from the way her eyes were probing me that the word "repulsive" was directed toward me and not her father. "Do you want me to slap your face?" she asked, her hand already in motion.

"What did I do?" I muttered, while rubbing my cheek.

"What did you do?" she mocked. "How dare you go telling lies about my father!"

"But they're not lies...." Before I could complete my sentence, she grabbed me by the ear and dragged me to the bathroom.

"I'm going to wash that filthy mouth out with soap," she howled.

As I tried to spit out the relentless lingering taste of Ivory soap from my mouth, her voice calmed and she attempted to reason with me. "Mike, that is a very serious accusation that you made just now, do you understand that?"

"Yes, I do."

"Good. Now you need to apologize and promise me that you'll never, ever say something like that again."

"I can't," I dared to rebut, "what I said was true." *The truth shall set you free, right?* At least that's what Grandma had always told me.

Next was the wooden spoon to my behind, which sent me wailing, but the punishment still did not produce the desired confession my step-mom was wanting from me. So, I was sent to my room to think it over until I was ready to recant.

I didn't want to think it over. I wanted to forget what had happened to me, but sitting alone in my room, that was all I could think about. *Dad will come home soon, and he'll believe me,* I thought.

When Dad finally did come home, Mom greeted him at the front door.

"Do you want to tell me now or after I've had a few drinks?" I heard him say. I guess she chose the second option because I had been banished to my room for several more hours by the time I heard my dad roar my name. My hopes were licked as quickly as a lizard snatches a fly. I sat on my bed hugging my knees tightly to my chest as my door was kicked open with enough force to leave an impression in the drywall where it came in contact with the door handle.

Dad was not an inch more sympathetic than Mom had been, and over the next couple of days I was subjected to opportunities to recant in-between spankings and time alone in my room. The time alone was as painful as the beatings, if not more so.

Pretty soon it was clear that I wasn't going to win this match, so I threw in the towel and told them that the whole story had been a hoax.

"That's my boy," said Dad. I felt pummeled. It felt as though I'd been stripped naked and hung out to dry. *It's the only way to keep the peace,* I thought.

It wouldn't be until some fifteen years later that I would discover that Dad had known all along I was telling the truth. "I didn't want to cause problems with Geri," was his excuse; "I was trying to keep my marriage together."

Dad's motto was always: "don't get mad, get even," and he did make some attempt to do that, in his own way, although Grandpa Murphy had been in the grave for about five years by the time it happened. We had been driving around in our old neighborhood, talking about those days. Dad always had the unsettling ability to laugh at things that most normal people would consider disturbing. As a "Yes" man, who had learned to keep the peace at all costs, I would always laugh along, too. All of a sudden, a mischievous smile spread on his face.

"Okay, Dad, where are you taking me?" I asked.

"You'll see."

He pulled up next to a cemetery, jumped out of the car, and started running.

"Hey!" I called, but he was already over the hill. When I caught up to him, panting, he was already squatting with his pants pulled down, taking a dump on the gravestone that read, "Samuel Murphy".

Chapter Two
Boiling Point

At the age of seven, Halloween was a time for telling scary stories, and our street was teeming with them. Excited whispers passed between the neighborhood kids as we circled the blocks, costumed as superheroes, ghosts, and princesses, clutching pillowcases for candy.

"Did you know that a guy was shot in that driveway last Halloween?" The house he was shot in was a tract house just like ours.

"Joey saw the whole thing. He said there was blood spattered all over the garage door."

"Let's go knock on the door."

"No way, that's so creepy. Anyway, the lights are off."

I shivered just thinking about the man's looming ghost, or his vengeful widow dressed like the Wicked Witch of the West, who was handing out razor-blade-laced candies or brownies mixed with broken glass.

At the end of the evening, as we approached our house, I could see specks of glass sparkling in the moonlight on our front lawn. "Paul," I said, "look."

We squinted to get a closer look. "The RC Cola bottles that we've been saving," Paul suggested.

We could hear Dad's angry voice booming inside the house. *Next year's horror stories will be about our house,* I thought.

In the next instant a nightstand came flying through the window, landing with a thump in the middle of the lawn, adding even more broken glass to the scene. We silently exchanged looks and then gathered the courage to walk through the front door.

As we tentatively entered the living room, Dad turned to us with a beaming smile. His voice transformed from the raging tone we'd heard from outside to a cheerful and giddy, "Show me what you've got in your bags!"

We tried our best to adjust to the shift in mood, stunned by the spectacle we'd observed outside moments earlier.

"Wow, look at that!" Dad smiled proudly like a little child as he happily upturned our candy-filled pillowcases onto the carpet and began to sort through the night's harvest. His favorite treats were soon separated out from among the treasures and stacked neatly on the table where he began crunching through them.

"Well, the Milky Ways and Snickers will keep me happy for now," he giggled, "but you guys had better start working on your treats, or I'll eat them next."

We enjoyed Dad's celebrative mood for the rest of the evening, never learning exactly what had been going on before we walked through the door.

In my earlier childhood Dad was usually good at keeping up appearances. Our house was brand new and always tidy. We had expensive new cars: a Cobra and a Ford Galaxy, and a groomed front lawn and a garden to prove that we were well off and respectable. Dad was captain, and everything had to be kept shipshape, so whether it was out of fear or good discipline, we kids never missed our chores. We knew better than to leave our toys scattered around or our beds unmade. The cans in the kitchen cupboard had to be lined up neatly, sorted by size and type, with labels facing front. No matter how dire and chaotic Dad's circumstances would become later in life, his place of residence was always meticulously organized and clean. Even up to his last days, he never failed to keep his shirts hung neatly in his closet, sorted according to color and shade.

But even if things looked good on the outside, on the inside, things were starting to fall apart at the seams. Dad had always been a heavy drinker, but now he was popping Valium to boot. Dad and Uncle Ralph made frequent trips down to

Tijuana, coming back with jars of amphetamines, also called *Bennies* or *Speed*.

"Does it make you go real fast?" I asked.

"Yup, it helps me get my work done," Dad explained. He and Ralph had opened a machine shop, and I guessed that Dad needed the pills to help him work the long hours.

His scary, unpredictable behavior had been escalating alongside the substance abuse for some time. Family members constantly tiptoed around him, never knowing when the ice would crack.

Then there was the paranoia. Over a year had passed and Dad had become increasingly suspicious that he was being watched. He was late on payments for both new cars, and was afraid that they would be repossessed. So, Dad started to accuse Mom of failing to make the car payments and spending the money instead.

My brother and I, along with my step-sisters had strict instructions not to open the door to anyone. At night, when I would get up to use the bathroom, I would see Dad standing in the living room, stark naked and glaring through the curtains. Day and night, Dad maintained surveillance by constantly staring out the front window.

To deter repossession, he rigged booby traps on the garage doors, wired the door handles, and even took the engine out of one of the cars. In spite of his efforts, we came home one day to find the garage door open with both of our fancy cars, and the engine, gone. We still had Dad's old Rambler station wagon, which, though unimpressive, served us well.

Perhaps the worst manifestation of Dad's increasing paranoia was his obsessive insistence that our step-mom was having an affair.

One quiet evening, while we were all sitting down at the dining room table for dinner, she told us that Dad was in the garage working on something he wanted to finish. Little did we know that he was actually shimmying across the beams through the attic—headed toward their bedroom to tap into the phone line with a cassette recorder. All of a sudden he slipped and fell, crashing through the ceiling. He landed in a heap right next to the table where we had all been sharing our meal.

Everyone stared at him in silence, no one daring to make a sound. Debris from the ceiling was scattered all over the dining table and floor. Dad got up, left his tools and tape recorder among the bits of popcorn ceiling, and stomped to the bedroom. A couple minutes later he slammed the door to the bedroom, walked back through the dining room, and marched out the front door. We sat, still in silence, listening to the garage door open, the engine to Dad's old Rambler start, and the car pull out of the driveway. The moment we all felt the tension of Dad's presence dissolve everyone burst into roaring laughter.

As funny as that scene might have been, Dad's delusions and anger over Mom's supposed affair was no laughing matter. Sometime between Thanksgiving and Christmas things began to heat up even more.

***

On a typical evening in our house, all five of us kids would hang out in the living room while Mom and Dad took drinks in their bedroom. The TV was always on in the background and we were engrossed in an assortment of games such as Lincoln Logs or Chinese checkers, using a wooden board that Grandpa had made for us. But our main entertainment came when Dad would pound on the wall that separated their bedroom from the living room. This signal would send us all on a mad dash down the hall into their room. The first one there would grab the empty whiskey glasses, race to the kitchen to refill the drinks, and deliver them back to the bedroom.

On this night, as usual, Paul got there first, but as soon as he had grabbed Dad's glass, Linda, the oldest step-sister, stepped in. "Let me do it, Paul. I mix a better drink than you!" she boasted.

I really wanted my turn, but the two of them always beat me to it.

"Dad, it's not fair," I whined. Becky and Micky didn't seem to care much; they just jumped on the bed, giggling.

"Alright kids, let Mike have a chance." It felt good to have Dad stick up for me. Beaming, I grabbed the glasses and zoomed down the hall to the kitchen. Dad's drink of choice was Wild Turkey whiskey. Sometimes they just wanted it on ice, sometimes mixed with Coke. I didn't know much about the drink, but I liked the picture of the turkey on the bottle.

When I got back I joined in the hysteria of rolling around, wrestling, and jumping on the bed while our parents tickled anyone who came near. When the fun and laughter died down, we returned to the living room to await our next summons.

The next time Dad banged on the wall I let Paul (older than me by two years) and Linda fight over the task of refilling the drinks, and joined Becky and Micky, who were trying to tickle Mom's feet. I didn't even notice who ended up running to get the drinks, but we were all back in the bedroom the moment Dad smashed his glass into the wall. It was as if someone had flipped a switch.

"Get the fuck out of here now. And I mean now!" he shrieked, grabbing Paul by the shirt and throwing him across the room.

I couldn't understand if we had done something wrong, or what had angered him, but we all ran for our lives.

From the living room we could hear them fighting.

"What'd you have to go and do that for?" Mom screamed at him. "You could have hurt Paul."

"It's my fucking business what I do with my own son," Dad answered.

"Well, you scared my girls to death, too. They were having a good time, and you just burst out like that!"

"Don't start screaming at me now," Dad yelled. "I know you've been screwing around—you worthless cunt." I didn't really know what *that* word meant at the time, but I knew it was some-thing terribly mean.

"Now you're changing the subject."

"So you're not even going to deny it! Dammit Geri, you whore."

"I have not been sleeping around," Mom insisted. "Where are you getting this idea from?"

"Dave told me he saw you pouring drinks and smiling at that bastard, Howard, who used to come around to the shop."

"I'm a cocktail waitress, Paul. Pouring drinks and smiling is what I do for a living. If you don't like it, I can quit my job." She knew Dad didn't want her to quit; he was too happy with the income she was bringing in to help him make ends meet.

"I'm not telling you to quit your job. I'm just telling you to quit fucking around!" Dad howled.

The fighting continued for some time that night. There was plenty more banging on the walls, but not the kind we kids had been eagerly anticipating moments earlier.

The next morning, life was back to normal. We kids were all sitting in the living room watching Saturday morning cartoons and eating breakfast.

"Okay, who's got the *TV Guide*?" asked Linda. I tried to hide the book behind my back, but she had already seen it.

Paul grinned. "What do you need it for, Linda? There's plenty of toilet paper in the bathroom, I just checked."

"Don't be a dumbass, Paul." Linda's hand was outstretched in my direction, "Alright, hand it over."

Defeated, I focused my attention on my bowl of Frosted Flakes. I had just poured the milk as fast as possible because I didn't want my cereal to get soggy.

"Are there any Christmas movies on tonight?" asked Micky, trying to peek over her sister Linda's shoulder.

"I've already checked," said Becky coolly. "*The Grinch Who Stole Christmas* is on tonight at 7:00." I think we all cheered. It was one of our favorite movies, and it made the anticipation of Christmas more palatable.

Dad sauntered into the living room. "Alright kids, go get dressed; we're going for a ride."

When Dad said that, nothing else mattered anymore. I immediately left my half-eaten cereal and ran to my room to get ready. Within minutes we all piled into the station wagon. We never talked about Dad's most recent outbursts, but it was always as if he was trying to make it up to us.

"Where are we going?" I asked.

"We're going to see a man about a horse." It was the same reply every time, or a variation, with either the man or the horse being dead. I always wanted an explanation as to why he died, which Dad would oblige. This would raise more questions, and the word game would continue.

On this particular day, Dad was in a good mood, so we were too. We were literally bouncing off the seats of Dad's old heap. After a quick stop at McDonald's where Dad and Mom treated us all to breakfast, we arrived at our destination: the Christmas tree lot.

All of us kids poured out of the car squealing, and screeching in every direction, looking for the perfect tree. Dad stood by the car and watched us run around until we had taken a little too long.

"Pick the damn tree already...and let's go."

Mom had the final say. The tree was loaded on top of the car and we headed home. There was always a certain point with Dad where enough was enough and we knew not to push things any further. His mood didn't squelch our joy, but it certainly limited our expression of it. The ride home was pleasant, all of us smiling, but much quieter than during the morning ride there.

By the time we had finished lunch, Dad had the tree set up and he had pulled out Mom's cherished and neatly packed boxes of Christmas decorations from the garage into the living room. He went out to do his yardwork and left us with Mom to decorate the tree.

Mom put on her favorite Christmas music and soon we were dancing and singing along to Burl Ives' "Have a Holly Jolly Christmas" and Johnny Mathis' "Winter Wonderland". Paul and I strung on our awesome bubble lights. Then we all took turns putting our favorite decorations on the tree under Mom's careful direction, ending with the old-fashioned tinsel. As the tree reached Mom's standard of perfection, and we kids began to get bored, the heavy strands of stiff, shiny aluminum tinsel were wadded up into balls and the living room turned into a battle zone. This was the closest we could get to a snowball fight in Southern California. But the finishing touch was always left to Dad. The moment he entered the room, the fighting stopped, and we all stared wide-eyed as Dad climbed up on a chair to place the angel on top of the tree.

Once again, Christmas had officially begun. The smell of the pine tree in the living room soon mixed with Grandma's first batch of freshly baked Christmas cookies and the home-made eggnog she brought over that afternoon.

That evening, it wouldn't have mattered whether we were eating Mom's awful mushy eggplant parmesan or our favorite goulash; we finished our dinner as fast as we could so we'd be dismissed in time to watch *How the Grinch Stole Christmas*. (Often, if Dad found us pushing the food around and lingering to finish our plates, he'd dump his change jar all over the living room floor. Whoever finished his plate could go get it. This would get us all racing to show Dad our empty plates and running to scramble up as much change as possible.)

This particular Christmas season, Dad had already been drinking for much of the afternoon, so it wasn't long after the movie started that we began to hear the yelling coming from their bedroom, but we were used to that. This time, things took a turn for the worse when we heard the sound of the bedroom door being kicked from its hinges, snapping us all to attention. Stone cold and horrified, we all watched while Mom was dragged, crying, into the living room in her bra and under-wear. Dad, as was common for him, wasn't wearing anything. He had a handful of her hair in one hand, a rifle in the other, and was obviously aroused.

"Tell them you're cheating on me," he demanded, while placing the barrel of the gun between her legs, aiming toward her vagina.

I sat frozen with fear, wishing I had the courage to tell him to stop. Mom was curled up in a fetal position crying, which only fueled his rage. The more he insisted, the more she denied his accusations. Dad had total control. There was power running through his veins. He had taken on the body of the devil on his bicep. *He's going to kill her*, I thought.

With the kind of captive audience that every villain craves, Dad was willing and able to take it to the next level. He instructed her not to move as he walked out of the living room and returned with an armload of clothing that he had ripped from the closet. He opened the sliding glass doors leading to the backyard and dumped her clothes on the lawn, returning several more times to make sure he got everything. He then began carrying out her dresser drawers and emptying the contents on the pile while we all sat there stunned.

I don't recall if he ever gave her another chance to confess before he doused the pile with lighter fluid and lit mom's things on fire. After taking a moment to warm his hands at the fire and admire his handiwork, he turned in for that evening with a banal "goodnight". The atmosphere was as if nothing had happened.

The next morning after Dad left for work we watched Mom dig through the scorched remains, hoping to salvage something. No such luck. All of her belongings were ashes.

Later on in life as a man, instead of a boy, I learned why the next day only brought us more of the same. In fact, life would give me experiences that showed me both why Mom would react the way she did—and it became clearer what was causing Dad to be the alcoholic tyrant. Addiction had most certainly grabbed our family on all levels—all of us paying the price.

Chapter Three
Reeled In

The walk to school every morning was about a half-mile, and I always took this time to reflect. The kids at school seemed to live fairly *normal* lives. Ours was anything but normal, but no one could tell on the outside, anyway. We were all good at keeping secrets, and the carnage stayed within the family. At age nine I was already being catapulted into losing the ability to be a normal child.

At morning recess I could air my thoughts again. As much as I felt fearful and hopeless, my dad's voice was in my head reminding me to "suck it up". This was one of the more useful sayings I'd learned from my dad when he would put on his Confucius hat and pass along his wisdom. I discovered this phrase early on as a sort of coping mechanism, but most of what he taught us was worthless. *What a lot of bull!* I thought to myself. *Look where his philosophies have gotten him.*

The rhythm of the swing set was my momentary escape. I didn't imagine I'd be brought back to reality by the voice of my mom. "Come on Mike, we're going." Her eyes were red and puffed up from crying, but her voice was strong with resolve.

Before I had the chance to protest, she grabbed my arm and steered me toward the parking lot. Paul was already with her, and the girls were waiting by the car. "It's just not safe anymore," Mom explained. *I'm not sure it ever was.* "We're going to go away, and no one can know."

I was quite sure that 'no one' included my dad's parents, and I was not okay with that. *Sure, Dad's an idiot,* I thought, *but what did they ever do to deserve this?* Grandpa and Grandma Casey were the main reason I never ran away; it would break their hearts to lose Paul and me. The last thing on earth I wanted was for them to worry.

We all climbed into the car and Mom explained that we wouldn't be going back to the house. She had taken some of each of our things that morning over to a friend's house around the corner from us. Her plan was that we would be spending the night there and were to leave in the morning. As she drove away from the school, poor Mom was bombarded with all our questions and concerns.

"What about our stuff?"

"I took what I could."

"What about my bike?"

"I'll buy you a new one."

"Did you get Grandpa's Chinese checkers?"

"I brought what I could."

"We have to say goodbye to Grandpa and Grandma Casey."

"No, Mike, I'm sorry, but we can't tell them we're leaving."

I don't think, at that moment, that I grasped the gravity of what was happening, but things at home had reached a boiling point. Mom was in fear for her life, as well as ours; this I understood. There were so many times that I was convinced he would kill her. There is nothing normal about watching your dad stick the barrel of a rifle in your mom's vagina.

Mom parked the car behind a fence, fearful that Dad might notice it and find us. As much as I knew that finding us would mean terror, I still secretly hoped he would.

***

The next morning we loaded what we could into the car and headed out, driving north from Los Angeles. Linda, Becky, Micky, Paul and myself sat quietly for the entire journey with Mom. There was no laughing, no playing, no fighting. I had time to come to terms with what was happening. Mom was only doing what she thought was best for all of us. Really she didn't have to bring Paul and me along. We were not biolog-ically, or even legally, her kids. But she treated my brother and

I the same as if we were and she feared for our lives as much as she did for her own and those of her daughters, Linda, Becky and Micky.

***

Pacific Grove, which was six hours away from Norwalk was a totally different experience from Norwalk. In the beginning I wasn't happy with the foggy and dreary weather, and I longed for the sunshine of Los Angeles, but after a while I started to admire the cool summers with the woods, stray deer, harbor seals and old canneries. It was almost magical. We arrived when I was a little more than halfway through the third grade. It was toward the end of butterfly season, which started in mid-October and stretched until Valentine's Day, when the only department store in town, Holman's, would remove the red hearts from its storefront.

The Butterfly Grove was just a few feet behind my new school, and I found myself wandering there on the third day. It was enchanting to watch the masses of giant bright yellow, orange and black monarchs chasing each other around the trees in their playful, yet violent, breeding game. The male monarchs would swoop down on the females, tackling them to the ground to get a strong grip, and then he'd fly them up to the branches to mate. I was captivated. *Maybe it's not so bad to be away from home,* I thought.

The six of us were crammed into a tiny apartment in a place called 17-Mile Drive Village. Although 17-Mile Drive is famous for its beauty, our new place was a total dive. It was cold and damp, and everything smelled musty. I had never known what it was like to be poor until now. All of a sudden we were living on welfare and food stamps and shopping for school clothes at the local Goodwill.

Mom was doing the best that she could to provide for us. She would cook us tuna casserole or goulash; it was never very exciting, but better than nothing. The cooking stopped when Mom got a new job transporting cars for a car dealer; with her long hours spent away from home, we were left to fend for ourselves. The five of us kids often found ourselves at Holman's department store, scouting out the free samples. They had a Swiss Colony meat and cheese counter, I think it was on the third floor, and we would take the elevator. It was an adventure for us to be as fast and sneaky as we could, grabbing samples of beef log and all kinds of cheeses and crackers. More often than not we'd return again for seconds. Part of the fun was trying not to get caught by the lady working the counter.

We kids also discovered ways to take advantage of our food stamps. If we bought things from the Top Hat Market, they would give us change that we could use to get treats from the Scotch Bakery. Occasionally we would save up enough change to go to the movies.

In spite of our economic situation, life had become fun and carefree. For the first time in my memory, I was going to bed at night without pulling the covers up over my head in fear of—not the boogieman—but my dad. Still, Dad was always there in my mind. While on the one hand it was kind of nice not to hear any yelling and screaming, or things breaking, I still missed him. It felt so awful that he didn't even know where we were. I worried that Dad would be worried about us, and wondered if he missed me as much as I missed him. Often I entertained the idea that this whole ordeal would soon be over and we would all live together again, but Mom kept talking about "making a new life" and "starting over". Her words scared me and shattered my dreams of ever seeing my father again. It was a strange feeling, but though the idea of seeing him again terrified me, the idea of not seeing him again was equally terrifying to me.

One evening, when it was my turn to wash the dishes, I let the hot water run over my hands long after the suds had disappeared, lost in daydreams about Dad. Mom came into the kitchen, tired and mellow, and sunk into the barstool beside me. She probably noticed the sad and distant look on my face. "A penny for your thoughts," she nudged.

"Do you think Dad will ever find us?" I asked.

"I certainly hope not," Mom answered, "I don't believe he would ever think of Pacific Grove," she added with a smirk.

"I miss him sometimes. I wish he could come visit."

"Me, too, Mike," she said softly, gesturing for me to come sit beside her. "Listen sweetheart, I know that your dad misses you very much. He loves you dearly, and if he knew where you were he would be here in a heartbeat. I wish things were different, but you know as well as I do that we're better off here without him."

"But it hurts so much," I sobbed. "Why does he have to be so mean?"

"He loves you, Mike. It's just when he's drinking, your dad becomes a different person, and he doesn't know how to stop his being mean. I never wanted to separate you from him, but I also know that you're safer here with me."

"I guess you're right," I nodded.

She offered me her arms, and I cried on her shoulder.

As often as we spoke of my dad during those two years in Pacific Grove, Mom never badmouthed him, but instead her kind words helped cultivate the fondness that remained in my heart.

***

We left 17-Mile Drive Village and moved to a small place on Union Street, just up the street from the Monterey Bay coast and the local landmark, Lovers Point. It was much colder in Pacific Grove than it had been in L.A., but it was great fun having a beach so close to the house. The cold certainly wasn't going to keep me from getting in the water.

One day I was jumping off the pier at Lovers Point and swimming through the kelp. It was kind of scary since I was getting all tangled up in it.

"Hey kid!" I heard a voice calling to me from the pier. "Get out of there!" he yelled. As I scrambled to the shore I was met by a bearded man in his mid-thirties with a rough face and ragged clothes. I was jolted by his appearance, but gratefully accepted the hand he offered to help me climb up over the rocks.

"Dude, that is totally dangerous, what you're doing," he scolded. "If you want your mom to ever see you again, I suggest you stop swimming in the kelp. You could get tangled up and drown... I don't care how good a swimmer you think you are."

I could tell this guy knew what he was talking about, so I took his advice.

"I'm Mike, by the way." He stretched out his hand.

"Hey, me too!" I exclaimed. "I'm also Mike."

"That's rad, man," he said, shaking my hand. "It's the best name."

I laughed. *This homeless guy seems alright.*

"You take care of yourself," he called after me as I trudged home.

***

Besides swimming, there were so many other adventures to be had. I think I must have had the heart of an explorer. One of my favorite things to do was to take long walks along the railroad tracks, which ran north toward the city of Monterey, alongside the ocean. There were an endless number of things to do along the way. We would usually end up either sneaking into the old canneries, watching the boats on the dock or fishing on the wharf. Eventually, I might end up at El Estero Lake in Monterey, where I used to dream of taking the paddle boat to the island and discovering a whole lost civilization living in the trees *Swiss Family Robinson* style. My only worry was being home in time for dinner.

The abandoned sardine factories on Cannery Row made for a great playground. As Paul and I ventured into the ghost-town canneries, I was astonished that we could still walk next to the old canning production lines. Paul found an old can with the words "Portola Brand Sardines" printed on it. I wanted to find some cans for myself, so I began to search over and under the remains of the long steel conveyor belts. It took me a few minutes of looking and I still couldn't find any cans. All of a sudden I noticed that Paul was no longer with me "Hey, Paul!" I started yelling. "Paul, where are you?" I could only hear the echo of my calls coming back at me.

I went out to the street and then back into the dark building and couldn't find my brother anywhere. After twenty minutes of searching, I started to worry.

Suddenly, a familiar voice spoke from a dark corridor. "Hey Mike! What are you looking for?"

I turned quickly to see the source of that voice. It was the homeless guy I'd met on the pier.

"Mike!" I exclaimed, relieved to see a familiar face. "I can't find my brother," I explained. "He was here a moment ago."

"I'll help you," he offered. "I know every inch of these canneries. Don't worry, it is like my second home," and murmuring to himself, "actually my first home, really."

"Do you live here?"

"Mostly, but I camp out in some other places, too." He pointed to the left, "we should turn here. This corridor ain't gonna take you anywhere."

After a short search with Mike for my brother, we heard the loud noise of shattering glass coming from behind us. We turned around.

"Man, is that your brother?" asked Mike.

"Probably," I laughed, recognizing the familiar sound of rocks being tossed at the old factory windows.

"You kids are vandalizing the place, eh?" he groaned.

"Paul, I'm here. We're here. Paul, Paul!" I yelled until we caught up with the sound.

"Mike, where'd you go?" Paul scolded.

"Where did *you* go?" I replied. Noticing the inquisitive look on his face, I quickly introduced my newfound companion. "This is Mike. He lives here in the cannery."

"Oh, hi, Mike."

"Hi, Paul, I believe…" Mike put out his hand. "Hey man, did you know that there are people who live here? Those windows, so long as they are intact, are the only thing that keep us from freezing at night." Mike said it with a friendly smile.

"Oh," Paul replied. "We thought that it was an abandoned place."

"Well, they obviously stopped canning here years ago, but it is not completely vacant. I live here, and there are others. Where do you guys live?"

"Up in Pacific Grove," Paul replied. Quickly and happily we moved past the broken windows.

"Hey, I can show you two around if you like. Do you want to see where I work?" he offered, as we began our tour of the squatters gathering at the end of Cannery Row.

It was a perfect hippie settlement. All the people seemed as rough as Mike, but some had longer hair or more colorful outfits. They sold varieties of knick-knacks, including candles, plastic accessories, tie-dyed shirts and surfboards. The place was loud and friendly.

Mike made surfboards for a living, a fact that turned him from being a random vagrant into an interesting one. We spent a few hours with our new friend and the other squatters. He told us all about the surfboards he was making, his fishing experiences, and his childhood when the wharf was full of Asian fishermen that brought the sardines up to the canning factories. We started to picture the wharf back in the forties and fifties when it was lively with the bustle of fishermen and factory workers canning fish for the entire country.

I returned home thinking about Mike's childhood fishing trips and the sardine extinction. It was the first time I heard that it was possible to 'overfish' the ocean.

Before I knew it, third grade had turned into fourth and the memories of Los Angeles, oddly enough, became distant. In six months we had completely adjusted to the new city. I guess Pacific Grove was going to be home. I found a schoolmate to walk to school with: Craig, who lived next door. At school I met Tim and Jeff, who would sometimes join us on our weekend adventures. Most evenings after school I would stay at Craig's and watch TV or listen to the Beatles on the stereo.

I grew closer to my stepsisters during this time, especially Micky, who was only a year older than me. She and I would often hang out together or go fishing on the wharf, sometimes with Paul, sometimes with Mike, or with my friends from school.

One particular day when we were out fishing, one of my friends began to bully me. Micky responded by pulling one of the cod from the bucket and clobbering him with it. She laughed and exclaimed, "No one messes with my brother." We had been through so much together, and in spite of no blood connection, our bond was tight.

By now, Mike had become a fast friend. He made me a surfboard and taught me how to use it. He took me fishing and exploring, and taught me all kinds of things about the area and the ocean. Before long I was inviting him over to our home to shower and eat dinner with us. Mom was a bit suspicious at first, but Mike was courteous and won her over. Pretty soon she was as fascinated by his stories as were the rest of us, and the two of them stayed up talking long after we had gone to bed. The next morning I found Mike making coffee in the kitchen.

After that, Mike was a regular at our place, and we all knew he wasn't sleeping on the couch, either. I kept my mouth shut until I found the right moment to insert my knife. "So, Mom, do you want us to bring you more homeless men, eh?" But of course, this all stayed within the immediate family— and within the house.

Even if life was fairly peaceful in Pacific Grove, there were still plenty of family secrets to keep. It was not long after we arrived that we found out the reason Mom had chosen this town. She had discovered, as an adult, that her mother had been concealing a secret. The man I knew as my step-grandfather and who was the man who had molested me when I was six didn't end up being my mom's real father. Mom was careful not to give it away. But her real father was in Pacific Grove. His name was Russell Sands, a local well-known businessman, and as far as I could see he would be a wonderful grandfather to have. He helped us settle in and adjust to our new life, and eventually made arrangements for us to move into a big two-story house on Park Street. He would visit us and bring us gifts and treats. A grandfather like that is one that you want to brag to your friends about—but we couldn't. Mr. Sands had his own family, and we also had to help him keep his secret.

***

In fourth grade, when our school took a trip to his local business to learn about agriculture, Grandpa Russ was the one to give us a tour and show us all how important the farm equipment was.

I was beaming from ear to ear in pride to have such an important man as *my grandfather.* I was bubbling up inside, dying to tell Tim, Jeff and Craig, but not even they could know. Grandpa Russ made eye contact with me and smiled, but he made sure not to show me special treatment.

We were always taught to be honest, and this seemed like a contradiction to me. My brother and the girls and I were supposed to tell the truth, but at the same time there were all these lies—so-called "secrets"—we were supposed to keep.

"Other people wouldn't understand," was Mom's reply to my objections.

The other nagging feeling that would never leave me was guilt. It was a feeling that would come over me like a wave. I felt guilty that we had left Grandpa and Grandma, and Uncle Ralph, and even Dad, without a word. I felt guilty for causing them pain. I felt guilty for enjoying life while they were worried sick. I didn't want to go back to L.A. anymore, but I still wanted so much for Dad to find us so that they could all be relieved from their worries.

My answer came with a knock on the door. Mom called up to Paul and me to come down. "You have visitors!" she exclaimed. It was Grandpa and Grandma. Paul and I were thrilled to see them again. We couldn't wait to show them all our discoveries in Pacific Grove. They took us to the beach and to restaurants. It was so much fun for Paul and me, but Mom knew it was the beginning of the end.

After my grandparents left, Mom kept sending us on trips to her lawyer's office to deliver manila envelopes. She had never told anyone that Paul and I weren't really her children, and I think she was scrambling to try to make things legal, if she could. It seemed she couldn't. She knew she had been defeated only a month or two later when Dad showed up at our door.

***

"Here," he said, handing Mom an envelope, without so much as a greeting.

"The boys need to be on the plane first thing in the morning." And with that Dad turned and entered a cab, which was waiting for him. We watched as he drove away.

The envelope we were left holding contained our plane tickets, and the next morning Paul and I were on our way back to Los Angeles, to start all over again. We stood there just staring at one another—we knew deep down what was in store for us.

Chapter Four
Home Is Where the Heart Is

As the wheels made contact with the runway, my eyes filled with tears and I could feel the lump in my throat getting bigger. This feeling was becoming all too familiar.

Paul, who was twelve at the time, and I didn't talk much during the flight. We knew it was time to suck it up once again. *Did I just leave home or am I coming home?* I asked myself, without knowing the answer. At age ten it was very hard to know the answers.

The drive from the airport, with Grandpa and Grandma Casey and Dad, was quiet and awkward. I sat staring out the window, daydreaming about Pacific Grove and remembering our drive there two years earlier. It felt like *déjà vu*. I hadn't wanted to leave Norwalk at that time any more than I actually wanted to leave Pacific Grove now. This time the experience was bittersweet; it was really great to be with Grandpa and Grandma again. They always gave me that warm feeling of security that I longed for as a child.

Grandma was doing her best to break the silence. "You boys will see your Uncle Ralph soon," she promised.

She must have known how much I loved my uncle, because hearing his name was a sure way to put a smile on my face. He always had a million stories to tell, and was sure to make me laugh.

I wasn't so sure how I felt about seeing Dad, though. It made me feel kind of sick to my stomach. If it weren't for the fact that I was scared out of my wits, I might have screamed at him, "Where the hell have you been these last two years? If you really wanted us back, why did it take so long?"

He's got some nerve to show up like this, without so much as a word, and drag us back to L.A. What gives him the right? I thought. *Does he even care that we like Pacific Grove, or that we have friends there—that we were happy there without him?*

As much as I had dreamt about living with Dad again, the reality now felt disastrous. My love for him was always mixed with fear. I never felt completely safe around Dad, but I still always missed him when he wasn't around, no matter what.

As we turned a corner, I realized then that Grandpa and Grandma were taking us to their house. I felt a sense of relief that we would all be living with them, and not on our own with Dad.

Our peaceful life with Geri and our sisters was over, but living with Grandpa and Grandma gave our family life some degree of normality. It was the weekends that I dreaded, when Paul and I would be forced to leave the safety and security of Grandma's house to go out and about with Dad, where anything could happen. Grandma always told Dad that it was important for him to spend time with his boys on the weekend, so he would just take us along wherever he was going. The first stop was usually George's Liquors to pick up a six-pack of Mickey's Big Mouth. This had become his beer of choice, not so much because he liked the taste, but because the larger opening made the bottles easier to pee into while he was driving. I'm not sure if he simply enjoyed being weird, or if he was just plain lazy, but he had taken up this quirky habit since we had been gone. Dad's first goal of the day was usually to get drunk, after which he would find a place where he could score some Bennies. Then he'd head over to Lakewood Club, his favorite topless bar, where he would leave us waiting in the car for hours. It seemed we were just along for the ride, and he treated us more like his property than his sons. Thank goodness my step-sisters were back in Pacific Grove with Geri and didn't have to be subjected to our current living situation.

On Monday morning, the smell of homemade biscuits wafted into the room where Paul and I were still half-asleep, accompanied by the smell of coffee, and my brother and I knew we were safe. These smells will always remind me of mornings at Grandma's house.

"Wake up boys; breakfast is ready." Grandma's voice was strong and firm, yet kind.

Paul and I got up and put on the new shirts that Grandma had made for us. On our way down the hall, an additional smell emerged: fried tomatoes and bacon. The dining table was always loaded with food, made and served by Grandma. Like the breakfast and our shirts, her apron was handmade and filled with colorful flowers.

Before heading off to school we had to do our morning chores, which included emptying the pee-and-cigarette-butt-filled bottles Dad had lined up next to his bed. As nasty as they smelled, Paul and I did the job dutifully. If we didn't, it would be left to Grandma, who would yell at Dad and he would in turn yell at us for leaving the job to her and getting him in trouble with his mom.

We thought it was odd that Dad asked us to empty the bottles into an old fire extinguisher that he kept in the garage. Then one Saturday, on a typical weekend outing with Dad, he brought the fire extinguisher along, and we learned the reason for this strange practice. After a quick stop at the gas station to charge it up with air, the drive-by sprayings began.

"Ha, ha, did you see that?" Dad laughed as a man on a bike was shot down from the pressure of the pee-hose. Dad got a real kick out it, but I was horrified.

"Oh, don't give me that look," he said as I began to show discomfort with what he was doing. "'Sympathy' is just a word in the dictionary located between 'Shit' and 'Syphilis'."

How can he care so little for someone else? I kept my thoughts to myself.

There were plenty of other incidents in which Dad demonstrated his lack of concern for other people. He was always scouting for mischief. Without even looking behind his back to see if someone was coming, Dad could torch a car in perfect calmness. I was always surprised by how much Dad would get away with, but every once in a while he would land himself in jail and we wouldn't see him for a week or a month until he got out. Other times he would disappear from our lives and attempt to get clean at a rehab, but his sobriety never lasted long.

Dad's worst stunts came after someone had the bright idea of buying him a police scanner for Christmas. Most people use these devices to alert them when police are in the area so they can slow down and avoid a speeding ticket. For my dad, it opened up a whole new realm of possibilities. The real excitement, for him, was to test the police force's response time by causing chaos and waiting around just long enough to hear the sirens. He'd take Paul and me with him in the car. Next, Dad backed into the shoe store window across the street from the transmission shop. With a terrifying excitement in his eyes he pulled into the shop parking lot to listen to the police scanner work its magic. This quickly became his new hobby.

Every morning, Paul and I crossed the lawn to the house next door and knocked on the door to pick up our schoolmates Jim and Dennis Rock, who had become our new best friends since moving back to Norwalk. In a few minutes, Paul and Jim would be leading the way in front of Dennis and me. We would watch the older two disappear down the road as we stopped for a rock-throwing competition in the church parking lot at the end of our street.

"Dad's gone again," I told Dennis, throwing the last rock out of six.

"I wish my dad would go away. I had to stay in my room for an hour last night," replied Dennis in an angry voice.

"See, I told you we have to go soon," I said. "I checked the bottles yesterday, I have twenty four. How about you?"

"I have twenty in the garage. Maybe we should look for some on the way back," he said as we started down the road again.

I looked back, grinning, "We're halfway, Dennis!" Our secret plan was to sell the bottles and use the money to run away.

At the end of the day, the four of us would head back together in the same pattern we came. We would stop at the same spot to throw rocks and we would try to remember to collect more bottles. Often, Jim and Dennis would return home with us after school and stay for a home-cooked dinner, since their parents both worked until 6:00 p.m.

The Rock boys also got us involved with the Boy Scouts, where we made friends with another set of brothers our age, John and David. Boy Scout meetings provided a great opportunity to get away from everything and have fun doing something normal kids got to do. All my friends thought it was cool that we got to watch dirty movies, drink beer and smoke pot, but I didn't see anything cool about it. Interacting with other kids and their fathers in Boy Scouts made me wish that our family was a little more normal.

The Boy Scout camping trips and mountain hikes were a great escape from day-to-day life. Learning wilderness survival skills satisfied my adventurous spirit and took me a step closer to the Swiss Family Robinson Island fantasies I had back in Monterey. I was actually cooking my own food out-doors, carving my own sticks, fishing, and lighting my own campfire.

Our first camping trip was to Angeles National Forest for two days. I was especially thrilled with my new Boy Scout pocketknife, which I would get to use for the first time. I held it in my hand for most of the ride to camp. When we arrived, we all gathered around our troop leader, Ed, who showed us how to start a campfire. Then he announced, "Alright guys, now we're going to look for our hiking sticks." We separated into five groups to start our search. Afterward we gathered together and carved the sticks.

Our backpacking trips would vary between five, seven, twelve, and sometimes as many as twenty miles long, all in preparation for the sixty-mile hike in Yosemite National Park that would mark the end of the summer season. On each of these short weekend trips, we mastered the various camping skills we would need for our two-week trek. I learned how to cook dehydrated food, including spaghetti, and our most common camping dish, mac and cheese with chili. It was refreshing to get far away from home and the city, breathe fresh air and drink water straight from a stream.

Paul's favorite thing was fishing. He seemed to have a magic touch, and quickly became the chief fisherman in the troop. He always carried salmon eggs, and fancy neon-colored power bait, and if that didn't work he would hunt for grubs or worms. It was Bill Rock, Jim and Dennis' dad, who introduced us to grasshoppers and crickets as alternative fish bait. It was an additional amusement to look for these during our scouting trips. It was my first summer as a scout, and I had already earned a handful of badges for setting up tents, hiking, camping, fishing and first aid. I added firefighting and fingerprinting before the following summer season.

On these camps I got to know Chris, who was just one year older than me, but under his red scout beret he was bald. "It's 'cause of the radiation treatments," he told me. I learned he had leukemia.

I liked Chris; he was smart, soft-spoken, and intellectual. Also, I admired the different merit badges he had earned for his knowledge of knots, plants, wildlife, and other skills he had picked up from Boy Scouts. His sash was definitely more crowded and colorful than mine. On hikes he would name and categorize all the plants and wildflowers. Because of his sickness Chris was often unable to participate in our activities, but what impressed me the most was that he was always smiling and happy. I couldn't understand why he wasn't scared of what was happening to him, especially when I found out that two of his siblings had already died from the same disease. I was always scared, and I didn't have to face the possibility of dying like Chris had.

Dad was fine with us getting involved with the Boy Scouts, but when the Rocks invited us to their church, it was a whole different story. Every time I asked he would get angry, as if it was a threat to his authority.

One evening Paul and I were out with Jim and Dennis playing in the field down the street. We had just finished mapping out the combat zone with scrap-lumber forts, bush barricades and G.I. Joes lined up for battle.

"Jim, Dennis, it's time for youth group," their dad called from the corner across the street.

"Sorry, Mike, gotta go," shrugged Dennis as he stood up from behind the bush where the two of us were hiding.

"It's too bad you guys can't come along," said Jim. "See ya in the morning."

I crouched back behind the bush to prepare myself for the one-on-one war, but Paul wasn't having it. "It's no fun when it's just us," he complained. "There's no strategy involved."

"Well, what are we supposed to do then?" I grumbled.

"Let's go with them," Paul suggested.

"Dad says no."

"I know that, stupid. It's not like we're gonna tell him."

The room was crowded full of kids having a good time. We played a couple games and then sang some songs. As the youth leader got up to speak, the room grew silent, and everyone heard the door open in the back of the room. We turned our heads to find Dad looming in the doorway. He didn't need to say a word; Paul and I were out that door as quick as a lick.

"What do you think you're doing in church, you fucking pussies?" And then just for good measure he smacked us on the backs of our heads. Paul just shrugged it off, but not me. I burst out crying, which was cause for a couple more hard smacks to the head. "You're gonna cry, huh? I'll give you a reason to cry!" he yelled.

That weekend Dad brought up the subject again in the car. "I can't believe you boys would embarrass me like that, showing up at some old youth group. Sons of mine ought to know better than that." He pulled up to a stoplight and turned to look at me. "Mike, what were you thinking?"

"I don't know," I muttered, knowing he wouldn't like my answer.

"Don't piss me off, Mike," he glared. Immediately he pulled out a box of ammo from the glove compartment and dumped some of the bullets into a can of sterno, then opened the car door and placed it on the road. Just as the light turned green, he lit the can and drove off, leaving the burning can in the road.

"Won't they go off?" I asked.

"Yes," he snapped back.

"If anyone gets killed it's your fault," he told me.

***

The day finally came for our long expected Boy Scout trip to Yosemite. Dad dropped us off at the church parking lot early in the morning and we carpooled with the Rocks. After a six-hour drive, which passed quickly while we kids chatted excitedly in the back of the van, we arrived at the gates of Yosemite National Park. Soon we would be setting up our tents and rest-ing in the shade after the long car ride under the California summer sunshine.

I shared my tent with Chris and was happy for the chance to get to know him better on this trip. He was already getting weak and needed a lot of help. I did most of the work setting up the tent while he held the ropes and tied the knots.

Afternoons would usually contain a couple of free hours directly after lunch. On the afternoon of our fifth day of back-packing, we looked up and saw a waterfall on the mountain range on the other shore of a nearby lake, near our campsite.

"Guys, wouldn't it be fun to cross over to that waterfall?" Paul asked Jim and Dennis.

"My dad said we're gonna hike up there in the coming days," Jim replied.

"But we can cross the lake and go there now," Paul said in a confident tone. Intrigued, Dennis, John and I joined in the conversation.

"You think we could swim across?" ventured Dennis.

"We could make a raft," David suggested.

"I have an even better idea," said the initiator of this adventure. "We can make canoes from tree logs and paddle there."

In only minutes the four of us had devised a plan for crossing the lake, confident in our ability to make it all the way to the waterfall. We worked together as a team, searching for large driftwood logs. We used our axes to cut away the excess branches and chop out an area where we could sit, then we fashioned oars out of tree branches and wrapped a rope around the top of the logs to function as handles. Finally, we had completed our makeshift canoes and were ready to go.

Our team plunged the canoes into the water and began to row across the lake. Dennis and I shared a double canoe, while the other four each had their own. They were not exactly sea-worthy. All of us kept flipping and rolling into the water, but we still managed to paddle our way across, and had plenty of laughs in the process. It took us a long time to arrive onto the other side of the lake, as it was a lot farther than it seemed. As we got closer, the waterfall became more and more powerful and it was harder and harder for us to stay afloat. We made a game out of it and started to compete for who could stay on their log the longest.

By the time we rowed back to the other side of the lake, the sun was starting to sink behind the mountains. It was around dinnertime when we arrived ashore. As we approached, we saw someone walking from the camp down toward the lake, looking for us.

"Oh no, it's Dad!" Dennis shrieked to Jim, and they both held their breath while their dad walked up.

The closer he came, the clearer the cry that was echoing out across the meadow by the lake. "You stupid idiots, what on earth do you think you're doing?" A question that neither Dennis nor Tim, nor any one of us, would answer.

"You've had us all worried sick! You could have drowned out there! You could have hurt yourselves! Tell me how we would have found medical help out here in the middle of nowhere." Bill continued his rant until we arrived at the camp.

That night during dinner, our troop leader, Ed, sat down with our adventure team. Before touching his food he looked us directly in the eyes, and with kindness in his voice said, "What you did today was not responsible. I expect more from you guys. The least you could have done would have been to ask your leaders so that we would know where you went." He never again mentioned a word about this incident.

Unlike our scoutmaster, I couldn't stop talking about our canoeing adventure. The first version of the story came that night, lying in my sleeping bag next to Chris.

"The waterfalls were hitting the lake so hard that it flipped us over and over. Even the double-log canoes turned up in the air and cracked apart."

"Wow," Chris replied, "that sounds scary!"

"It was a lot of fun," I said, "I wish you could have been with us."

"It's okay. I enjoyed walking around the forest."

"Chris," I asked, "do you ever get scared when you're sick?"

"No, I'm okay," he answered, quickly and directly.

"Are you not afraid to die?" I asked, just as quickly and directly.

"I know that when I die I'll be going to a better place," he said calmly. "Don't you worry about me."

His response freaked me out. I knew that he had been getting worse since I had first met him in earlier camps. I couldn't grasp how he could not care that his life was coming to an end. I thought he was way cooler than anyone in his situation should be.

It was not long after our trip to Yosemite that the leukemia got the best of Chris. This would be my first funeral, my first brush with death. I was thinking about him under the shower that morning. I put on my full scout uniform and then went over to the Rocks' to catch a ride with them to the funeral home.

"I've never known anyone that died before," I admitted to Dennis.

"Oh, you're lucky. My grandpa died when I was eight."

"Did you go to his funeral?" I asked

"Oh yeah. It's so weird; they leave the casket open so you can look at the body. It's all cold and stiff," he added, sending chills up my spine.

We arrived at the Norwalk Funeral Home. Mr. Rock stopped his car and the five of us walked in, joined by other scouts from Troop 132. We took turns walking by the casket. It was just as Dennis had described. There Chris was in his Boy Scout's uniform with his hands folded across his chest, cold and stiff. This image stayed with me for a long time. It was Chris sleeping there, just as I had known him—except that his eyes were closed and there was no life in him. We all sat down across from the casket. It was an intense feeling, accompanied by silence. The smell of the place was intense too. I wasn't sure if that's what caused the pain in my stomach, or whether it was just the feeling that I'd never see him again.

I was doing my best to listen while everyone talked about Chris. They talked about how he "fought the good fight" and "how brave he was". I thought back on Chris' last days and how he was able to do less and less. I realized that he had never complained about being sick.

It was his parents' reaction that annoyed me during the funeral. "Chris was so sick that it is a blessing he is not suffering anymore," his dad said calmly. "He has joined his brothers with their heavenly father at the great celebration in heaven."

Holy cow, I thought, *how can they be so fine with it?*

I was relieved when the gathering ended, and glad that the burial was "exclusively for family members". The event was already dragging on far too long.

During the weeks and months that followed, thoughts of Chris' death would come back to bother me. It made me wonder what would happen after death. Sometimes, after school, I would be sitting watching cartoons when the thought would hit me: *Someday I'm going to die, just like Chris.* Invariably this would take me down an even more troubling thought path: *Eventually no one will even know that I ever existed.*

I would think about it until I felt a deep hollow inside me and would have to jump out of my seat and run out of the house. I would run and run until I couldn't run anymore, and then, exhausted, I would console myself thinking, *I probably won't die for a long time anyway.* The thought would calm me down enough to trudge home, where I would seek out Grandma to talk about God.

Faith wasn't something I clearly understood. I knew that Grandma went to church and read her Bible. Also, I knew that she was always praying for people and about people. Before dinner at Grandma's house, we always, without fail, prayed. We had all memorized the prayer that Grandma taught us, so we could recite it at a moment's notice if we were called upon to do so. Grandma usually added a bunch of stuff at the end. At Chris' funeral there was lots of talk about God and heaven, so I thought Grandma might know something about it. To me, death just simply seemed like the end, like a vanishing.

"It doesn't have to be like that," Grandma tried her best to explain to me. "If you trust in God, after you die He'll take you to be with Him in His heaven." It made me feel a little better to hear Grandma talk about heaven, even if the idea still seemed so elusive.

But Dad abruptly ended the conversation. "Stop brainwashing my son," he interjected. He didn't like having Grandma talk to me about God any more than he approved of me going to the youth group with Jim and Dennis. The only time I was allowed to go to Grandma's church was when I'd been asked to be the candle bearer in a wedding. The groom gave me a special Bible with my name engraved on it, which I kept next to my bed, along with the one I'd won at Sunday school.

Not long after Chris' death, our scout troop was forced to face another loss. This time it was our beloved scoutmaster, Ed, who also died of cancer. Ed had been a great role model for me. I have a picture of him on the top of a mountain with his arm wrapped around the base of a sign: "Sawtooth Pass, 11,600 elevation." It's as if he was hanging on to savor every last minute, his face vibrant and full of life; Ed taught me what it means to finish strong. I couldn't understand why death had to take the good and kind people that I knew, while someone like my dad could get away with anything and seemed invincible.

My third visit to the funeral home was to pay respects to our neighbor, Frank. He was Dad and Grandpa's drinking buddy who, incidentally, later in life died from alcoholism. Dad stood there, looking in at the open casket and then, all of a sudden, he lit up.

"There's something I want to do for Frank," he said. "Come with me."

What could he possibly want to do for a man who's already dead? I thought as we pulled up in front of George's Liquor Store. Dad ran in and came out with a pint of Peppermint Schnapps.

When we returned to the funeral home, the casket was already closed, but Dad wasn't bothered. He lifted the lid and, much to his own amusement and my horror, carefully placed the bottle inside, tucking it under Frank's lifeless arm.

Dad's lack of respect for Frank's lifeless body troubled me. In fact, Dad's fascination with death always bothered me. His fascination with Charles Manson and the Tate-LaBianca murders in Los Angeles bothered me. He often told me how they cut the fetus from Sharon Tate's body and how gruesome that must've been. Dad also spoke a lot of Truman Capote's *In Cold Blood*, the story of a Kansas family that was brutally murdered. He used to say, "I wonder what they were thinking just before they were shot." It always troubled me that Dad talked about murders and death. He seemed to place so little value on life. I wondered if he wouldn't hesitate to kill me.

Chapter Five

Overexposure

Grandma always used to say, "Out of the frying pan and into the fire."

When Dad, Paul and I moved into our own apartment together on Bellshire Avenue, only a couple blocks from where we used to live with Geri and the girls, I understood what Grandma meant. It was a typical furnished apartment, the kind I would get used to in the years to come. You know the kind— one with green shag carpet, green couches, end tables, gold lamps and a small dinette set.

Dad went through a string of relationships while we were living in the Bellshire Apartments. He met most of his girl-friends through a video dating service, the kind where you would go to the office to fill out a profile and record a video describing yourself, then return again to sit and watch the videos of women who matched the profile. Every time he met a new woman, Paul and I would brace ourselves for another rollercoaster ride. At first, Dad would be a real gentleman, with all his attention focused on his new love. He would clean up and try his best to behave, winning her over with his charm and good manners. There would be less drinking for a while, but Paul and I never got our hopes up; this was a slow approach toward an undoubtedly destructive end. His rela-tionships tended to end quickly. When the breakup was finalized he would often feign suicide, overdose on Valium, and have to be sent to the emergency room to have his stomach pumped.

Dad was a chameleon when it came to relationships; he was willing to try anything in exchange for a 'piece of ass'. His motto was, "If you can't eat it, drink it, smoke it, or fuck it, it isn't worth having," but at the same time he always seemed to be searching for something deeper, or what Dad called "the truth".

One of his many dating-service girlfriends, Laurie, introduced him to what he thought, for a little while, was the holy grail of truths. This self-reprogramming, self-enlighten-ment program was called the Earhart Seminar Training move-ment, or EST for short. Laurie was really into it, and before long Dad was too. Jumping in with both feet, he paid $5,000 just to attend a weekend boot camp to learn how to achieve inner peace. The whole thing seemed like a scam to me, but at the same time, Paul and I were seeing some positive changes in Dad. I crossed my fingers, hoping it wouldn't end, but the whole thing crumbled alongside the relationship and pretty soon we were again at ground zero. Dad was onto the next thing without ever having achieved Nirvana.

The apartment wasn't too far away from Grandma and Grandpa's, and Paul and I tried to maintain some degree of normality by spending as much time as possible at their house. We would leave home for school early so we could swing by on our bikes to grab breakfast, then we'd stop by after school and stay as long as we could. My grandparents' presence in my life was the one thing that kept me from fulfilling my longing to run away; I knew that Grandma and Grandpa would be worried sick, and I loved them too much to put them through that.

***

Uncle Ralph, who married shortly after we moved, looked out for Paul and me whenever Dad was at the hospital or in rehab—both of which occurred quite frequently and were more or less kept secret from Grandma, who preferred to pull the wool over her eyes. Uncle Ralph and his new wife, Margie, acted like our godparents. Margie never had any kids of her own and Uncle Ralph's kids lived far away with their mother, so I guess we sort of filled that gap. My aunt and uncle would bring us food or pick us up and take us out to do normal things that I could actually share with friends. Paul often preferred to spend time with his friends, but Uncle Ralph and I would go to the pet store to pick out saltwater fish for his aquarium, and Aunt Margie would sit and talk to me like a mom. Both would do their best to explain things, unlike Grandpa, who just pretended it wasn't happening.

Boy Scouts was my other refuge. Without a scoutmaster, there had been some talk of ending the troop, but John and David's stepdad, Steve, stepped up to the plate. I had always envied the guys whose dads were involved with Boy Scouts; it seemed like such a nice activity for families to do together. But with the father we had been issued, truth be told, it was a relief that he hadn't yet shown any interest in taking part. I knew that Dad's involvement would mean nothing but trouble, and boy was I right.

One summer, Dad's interest in our troop started at the fireworks stand where we raised money for our trips. The stand, which we ran each year for ten consecutive days leading up to July 4th, was conveniently located on the McDonald's parking lot across from Dad's favorite booze stop, George's Liquor Store. Our new scoutmaster's wife, Sally Apple, was overseeing the fireworks stand when Dad first took notice. With clear intentionality, he made a straight line from the liquor store to check it out. All of a sudden he was a real fireworks enthusiast. Paul and I both knew that he never dropped a dime in the fundraiser tins, yet somehow when we returned home Dad had a number of pyrotechnics he just couldn't wait to try out.

The following year Dad signed up as a volunteer. It soon became clear that he had other motives besides possibly stealing money from the tins and getting 'free' fireworks; he wouldn't take his eyes off of Sally. I was no idiot, and I knew my dad well enough to know that this couldn't end well. It was the look in his eyes, the smile, the joking, and the laughter that led to a conversation; he was zeroing in on his target. Apparently, she was amused, and unfortunately, my dad hit it off with her husband too, so before I knew it they had all become friends.

Dad started showing up to every meeting and coming on every trip—not for us, but for Sally. Every time we went over to hang out with John and David at their house, Dad came along. Steve didn't seem to care.

How can he not notice? I thought.

Dad's focus on Sally became more and more bold with every meeting. It was not long before he was sitting around the Boy Scout campfire calling her "Sally Juicy Apple" and other flirtatious names. It felt uncomfortable to me, but no one said anything about it.

One Wednesday afternoon, I returned home right after school. I sat down in the living room, waiting the full two minutes it used to take for the television to warm up back in the early 70s. I used to calculate such details. During these relatively quiet moments, I could hear the moans and groans of sex coming out of Dad's bedroom—not an uncommon occurrence. Just as the TV show began, Sally Apple strutted out of the bedroom, followed by my dad. I sat, silent, too cowardly to speak, but obviously not skilled enough to disguise the naïve astonishment that was frozen on my face.

"It's okay," she responded immediately, obliged by my look. "Steve knows I'm here," she added, striding unabashedly out the front door.

It wasn't *okay* for me, not at all. I could hardly wipe the defeated expression off my face, and even after I was able to relax my muscles, I couldn't calm my thoughts. The scene seemed wrong no matter how I reflected on it.

It seemed that my concern was taken seriously—at least enough to be addressed by both Steve and Sally. Steve found an occasion to bring up the issue about two weeks later at their house when everyone else was occupied.

"It's okay," he said, using the same words as his wife. His words didn't change the way I felt one bit. "Actually, Mike, your dad is helping us with something that I've been having some trouble with lately." I guess this was code for "'erectile dysfunction". I felt sick to my stomach. "I hope you can understand," he said.

Then, as if to make everything normal again, he switched topics. "Do you want to come shopping with me? I want to buy something for your dad's birthday." He ended the one-sided conversation without getting a reaction. With that, Steve and I went out to buy my dad a present.

Like every relationship of Dad's, this one had to have a dramatic ending. I remember him storming out of their house late one night, calling us to follow. Sally came running out after us, but Dad drove away, so she followed behind us in her car. When the car was stopped at an intersection with Sally behind us, Dad took off his shoe, jumped out of the car, and began to beat the driver's side window of her car until the glass came crashing in on her. Dad quickly jumped back into our car and drove off, swearing at his shoe for its inability to withstand the heavy blows unscathed. I can only guess the reason for the blow-up, but it was months before I dared to visit David again.

Nightly trips by their house for the sole purpose of intimidation included dumping salt and weed killer on the lawn, and writing "bitch" on the front wall of the house with orange spray-paint, Dad's favorite color.

The affair between Dad and Sally was no secret, and the Boy Scout troop was shut down because of it. All my friends sneered at me, "If your dad hadn't been boning Steve's wife, this would never have happened."

Before the Boy Scout troop was closed, I had started to bring along a neighbor from our apartment complex, Tommy. His dad, Doug, was a postman, and our dads had become friends while lounging around the pool talking about their favorite porn flicks. Doug had a subscription to a rental service that would send him 8mm films in the mail, and he let Dad borrow them. These short films had to be threaded through a projector and wound manually. It was an awful lot of work for a few minutes of cheap entertainment.

Tommy was the only child of a single dad, and the atmosphere in his home was no more uplifting than it was in mine. I could tell that he needed a friend badly, and in that way I felt some responsibility to engage him. Looking back, I can say that I was probably every bit as needy as he was for friendship.

One day I was hanging out at Tommy's place a couple hours before his Boy Scout meeting. It was always dark and creepy over at their apartment, and it seemed to me that his dad did nothing but watch dirty movies.

"Hey, Mike, come over here," Doug suggested, lounging back in his armchair as the latest film came to a close. "Can I touch you?"

"No."

"How 'bout if Tommy stays home from Boy Scouts today?"

"I'm okay with that," I said, though really I wasn't.

The horny postal worker stared at me, let out a sigh, and then called his son over to fulfill the perverse desires I had denied him. It was clear that Tommy was used to the abuse, and I was powerless to do anything about their interactions.

I went alone to Boy Scouts that night.

As much as Doug had creeped me out, my compassion for Tommy brought me back to their apartment. This time, when I refused his dad's advances, the creep tried a different tactic; he threatened to hit Tommy if I wouldn't comply.

"No," I said, and then was forced to watch Tommy get a slap across the face, feeling that I was the one who had caused this abuse to my friend.

The third time, I caved in to save Tommy from the consequences of my refusal. I felt queasy. This sexual abuse and manipulation continued for weeks until I finally was fed up enough to tell my dad. *He's going to think I'm gay,* I thought. But he didn't, and this time he believed me.

"Follow me," he said, grabbing a carton of eggs before heading out the door. He stood in the parking lot, chucking eggs at Doug's car.

"Take that, you fucking perverted bastard!"

Tommy's dad stuck his head out the window of their apartment. "What the hell are you doing?" he screamed, and quickly shuffled outside with his keys, running to his car. He backed out under the onslaught of eggs, and drove his car to the other side of the parking lot, where he took the hose and started cleaning it off.

That was the extent of Dad's vendetta on my behalf. Having sacrificed a whole carton of Grade-A eggs, he apparently considered the score settled and justice served. I was used to seeing my dad torch cars and bash windows with a baseball bat, so it seemed like an understatement. He and Doug stopped exchanging films, Tommy stopped coming to Boy Scouts, and I never went back to their house again. Instead, Tommy and I would hang out in the parking lot until his dad got home, and then we'd split ways before we were seen.

Some of our other neighbors, Nelly and her daughter Debbie, introduced Dad to Marian. This new relationship led to what turned out to be our very own *National Lampoon's dumb-ass drunken vacation* to the Colorado River. Nelly and Debbie came along with a couple of other friends, Ryan and Amy, Marian's kids, plus Paul and me.

***

We made it to Arizona alive after an insane passing-beers-between-cars highway marathon, but the beer was just the beginning. Before long, Dad had us using road signs for target practice as we drove past them. When the fun wore off, he switched his focus to herds of innocent cows.

If only the highway patrol would stop him, I thought. It seemed that Dad could do pretty much anything he wanted and get away with it.

Over the next three days, we kids fetched cold beers from the riverbank, occasionally stealing one to share, as the grown-ups continued imbibing. An increase in beer consumption usually equals a substantial decrease in common sense, and so it was inevitable that Dad, with an inebriated IQ, would come up with the idea for us all to jump off the bridge into the Colorado River, some forty feet below. He said he needed just a few more beers and then he'd be ready for action.

We found that we could jump off the bridge and then let the current of the river take us back under the bridge, where we could swim to shore and climb back up for another go. On about the third round, after Ryan and Amy plunged in ahead of us, Dad stood on the other side of the railing and leaned forward, his arms extended behind him, barely hanging on to the rail.

"I should try a dive from here. Wouldn't that be awesome?"

Paul and I immediately tried to talk him out of his insanity. Jumping from this height was already risky enough. I don't know if Dad meant to let go, or if he merely slipped, but before we knew it he was sailing down, chest first, toward the river, landing in the most epic belly flop in history. *If the belly flop were an Olympic sport he would have gotten tens across the board for this performance.* The humor was only broken by the fact that he hadn't resurfaced as we scanned the river. Paul and I called down to Ryan and Amy, who were making their way back up the hill, and then we jumped in after Dad.

Ryan jumped in after us and reemerged downstream, dragging Dad's limp body to shore. He had been knocked out from the fall and was in bad shape. His chest was flaming red and starting to bruise. Once Dad had been revived, he chose, naturally, to remedy his pain with more beer, his answer to everything.

This wasn't quite the fun that Marian had in mind, so she ended the relationship. For my dad, beer and a breakup were an even worse combination than beer and a relationship. But mix my dumped, dejected, and drunken dad with driving, and it's needless to mention that the trip home was terrifyingly miserable.

Dad's chest wasn't getting any better and he missed several days of work, which was not like him. Normally, no matter how much he drank, he would always manage to get to work. The impact of the belly flop was causing some fibroid tumors to grow, which for us looked a lot like "Dad's growing boobs!" It made him angry, so we weren't able to get much comedic mileage out of the situation.

Because of the bruising, torn tissues, and fibroid tumors, it was suggested he needed a double mastectomy. I visited him at the hospital that Saturday, after the surgery, and was very surprised to find that he was in a better mood than I'd seen him in years. I was just beginning to wonder what had gotten into Dad when his nurse, Janice, came in to check on him.

It didn't take much to figure out that Dad's speedy recovery was largely due to Nurse Janice and her extra-curricular services. Dad's lips curled into that charming smile as his eyes just about drilled through her uniform. She smiled back. *Oh no, I thought, not another relationship. Does he not remember getting dumped by Marian?*

***

Janice and Dad spent a great deal of time in the bedroom and Dad had a renewed interest in breaking out the projector to show us his 8mm porno films. Apparently, he and Janice decided that this was not enough of a sex education for us and we needed something a little bit more concrete. One evening as Paul and I were watching television, Dad marched out of his bedroom, naked, and grabbed two bar stools from the small nook in the kitchen. He returned to his room and came out again, sweeping up the bowl of popcorn Paul and I had been sharing, "Follow me," he ordered. We were both puzzled, but whenever Dad said jump, we did.

Dad had placed the bar stools at the foot of the bed. Janice was lying on top of the bed naked with her legs spread apart. I was embarrassed, though she said not to be. With the patience of a school teacher, Janice began pointing out all of her body parts, describing them in graphic detail. Soon she was joined by my dad where they performed, with full explanations, every sexual position imaginable. *If I could just go back and watch television*, I thought. The demo was on, and continued for what seemed like hours, leaving no stone unturned and nothing left to the imagination.

This self-described nymphomaniac would often roam around our living room, thinly covered and indiscriminately flirtatious. Her advances were even more awkward and confusing to me than those of Grandpa Murphy and Doug. For one, I was paralyzed by utter terror that Dad would see her making a pass and blame me, but also, as a prepubescent twelve-year-old, I wasn't ready to discover my own sexuality. The expectations for performance I had gained from watching pornographic films seemed out of reach, and I had no idea how to cope with the feelings in my body. Some men scoff at the idea of female sex-offenders, but it can be every bit as traumatizing as other forms of abuse. Janice's presence in our house, and her open sexuality, made me deeply uncomfortable.

Eventually, even my dad wasn't able to satiate her sexual demands, and he came up with the bright idea of sticking her on my older brother, with whom I shared a room.

"Your dad sent me," Janice announced as she entered the room in the middle of the night and climbed into Paul's bed. I pretended to be asleep, but within a couple minutes, I'd had enough. I went to the living room to wait it out. Dad, always an opportunist, was already there, digging through Janice's purse for her keys.

"Let's go," he said.

I stayed in the car while he went up to her apartment and came out with a couple items of jewelry, some coins, and whatever else he could get his hands on that might be worth pawning. After that, these raids on Janice's apartment became a regular event. Eventually, Paul picked up on the idea of break-ins, and started to sneak into a neighbor's apartment when he knew they were away. Stealing became just another game in our family.

Dad's fatefully abnormal relationship with the nurse he had met in the hospital had the same typical ending: a drug overdose landing him back in the hospital. The suicide note read: "I have nothing left to live for." *I guess Paul and I didn't count.*

***

My thirteenth birthday seemed like a big deal to my dad, and he had a plan. A trip to Tijuana was always his idea of adventure—a bit scary, but fun, with dirty, crowded, smelly streets, street vendors, and bright, colorful shops.

"You want to try some good dog meat?" Dad joked, handing me a taco.

After we had polished off the last bite, he ran across the street to make a deal with a taxi driver for some Bennies. The deal only took a few moments to make, but we waited in the car for another half an hour before the pills were delivered.

"What the fuck?" Dad screamed. "These pills are made from pressed soap!"

"Well, you can use it for laundry," I giggled. Dad didn't think it was funny. *We're in Mexico,* I thought, *what can we do about it?*

Dad was pissed. "We've got business to take care of, Mike."

The business he was referring to would take place at a local strip bar. As we crossed the street toward the bar, a boy who was selling Chiclets followed behind us.

I asked, "Dad, can I have some money?"

Dad just frowned when he noticed my cause. The kid's mom is probably a whore, and I bet she makes more money than I do," Dad snapped.

As we zig-zagged through the streets, stopping every so often, to look through the shop windows, I was amazed and intrigued by all of the sights and sounds. Everything was so colorful.

I noticed that the young boy selling gum was still following close behind us. There was something about him that was tugging at my heart. Maybe it was because we were both doing things we did not want to do. At our ages, we should have been out playing with friends.

Dad could tell that I was feeling sorry for the boy and it was beginning to annoy him. I was following Dad and the young boy was following us.

"Hey," Dad snapped, pointing to the other side of the street. A blanket had caught his eye and he ran across the street. I followed.

All of a sudden I was startled by the sound of skidding tires, followed by a loud thud. Turning to look for the source of the noise, I was horrified to see the young boy lying in the street motionless. My heart sank as I watched people begin to gather.

"Come on," Dad grunted. *How could he be so cold*, I wondered. As I turned to take one last look, someone had thrown a blanket over the little boy.

Was he dead I wondered. *Was an ambulance coming?* I would never know the answer.

Dad strutted proudly into the strip bar. I followed behind him.

The place was dark and smelled so nasty I wanted to split right there, but I was bound by invisible chains to my father. The large women pole dancing in the center of the room could have easily been mistaken for men had they not been topless. Dad gestured toward another group of women sitting across the room on the bar. Just behind them, the wall was lined with small curtained rooms containing soiled mattresses.

"Pick one," he snapped. "Time to become a man."

By this point in my life, I knew pretty well what was expected to take place behind those curtains. Performance anxiety was definitely a factor in my hesitance, but what it boiled down to was that I didn't want to do it, especially not in this dive, and not with any of the strange women lounging in front of me.

"Why don't you pick the one with hemorrhoids," Dad laughed. That's when I made the biggest mistake I could possibly have made at that moment—I started to cry.

At thirteen, I had failed the test of manliness, and the shame was laid on thick. "Your mom must have slept with your Uncle Ralph," he told me. "You're no son of mine—you big pussy." The truth was, I wouldn't have minded having Uncle Ralph as my dad.

Dad didn't think it was worth wasting any more time on my rite of passage, so we spent the next couple of hours tracking down pills and fireworks that he could sell back home. My secret maniacal wish was that it would all be discovered at the border. No such luck. Instead we crossed the border smoothly, only to break down moments later. We were forced to spend the night in the car before hitchhiking home the following day. After several rides from kind strangers, we were close enough for Dad to call Grandpa to come pick us up.

"I hope you had a great birthday, Mike," Grandpa said.

"Yeah," I shrugged, wishing I could go home with him.

Dad had picked up a ceramic piggy bank while in Tijuana, an upgrade from the classic glass jar he always kept. Soon after returning from my birthday trip, Dad started accusing Paul of stealing money from it. It's true that Paul had recently taken up the art of breaking into our neighbor's apartment, but I highly doubted he had actually stolen any money from the piggy bank. Dad was convinced enough to attack Paul with the television set, swinging the tv by the antennas in his face before hurling the whole thing at him, followed by the piggy bank, which shattered into pieces. Paul, who was thirteen at the time, ran for his life and moved in with the family of his girlfriend, Jill, leaving me alone with Dad.

***

After he got over the incident, Paul started to come over on the weekends. It was on one of these Fridays, after picking up Paul from Jill's house that a strange incident happened. We all went into the local Sav-on on our way home so Dad could pick up his prescription. On our way out, as Dad paid the cashier, I saw him exchange a couple words with the lady behind him.

"That was her!" Paul exclaimed as we got back into the car.

"Yeah," Dad answered abruptly.

"So why didn't you let us talk to her?"

"Don't worry, we agreed that she will see you tomorrow night."

Back in the car, I learned from Paul that the woman had been our mother Kathleen. I tried hard to contain my excitement, but, though it was only one evening, I could hardly wait for the time to pass. That night I tossed and turned in my sleep, drifting in and out of dreams and imaginings about the mother I had always wanted to know. The short moment I had seen her in that aisle replayed itself over and over in my mind all throughout the night and the following day. Finally, after all these years, I would get to sit down with her. *Maybe, if we get along, she'll invite me to come live with her so I can get out of this hellhole.* I was scared to even dream it, but the hope was always there.

***

It was a bright summer evening when we arrived at the address Dad had written down on the back of his Sav-on receipt. We mounted the stairs of the apartment unit and knocked on a door on the second floor. No one replied. We waited for what felt like forever in front of that door, each taking turns knocking, but nothing happened.

"She's not here. I'm sorry guys, but I knew she would do this," Dad said.

"Are you sure she lives here?" I asked.

"Well, this is the address she gave me," Dad said as we spotted a guy entering the building below. "Hang on a sec, let me ask him," he said, running down the stairs.

They chatted for a moment and then Dad turned to us and shrugged. "Come on guys, let's get going."

"That man knows them," he told us in the car. "He said they just moved out last night, suddenly, without telling anyone."

Why would she do that? I asked myself as we drove home. *I guess if she had wanted to see us, she would have shown up years ago.* That was the best conclusion I could come up with that night.

So now, without a doubt, moving in with my biological mom definitely wasn't an option, but salvation came to me from another direction. Grandpa had been having some health problems and while working one day he suffered a collapsed lung and was rushed to a nearby hospital. He would recover, but the doctor recommended a drier climate because of his respiratory problems. The thought of them moving was more than I could bear. They were looking to go some twelve hours north—it might as well have been China.

My grandparents bought a house in Red Bluff and began to pack for the move. Grandma was cleaning the carpets, preparing to leave the house in Norwalk, when she fell and shattered her knee in ten places. The surgeon said this would take a great deal of time to heal. Grandpa wasn't in the best of health either, and their move was already in progress. It was clear that they would need an extra hand.

"What do you think about Mike moving with us?" I overheard Grandpa asking Dad at the hospital. Dad's love and devotion to his parents apparently won over his desire to control my life since, much to my relief, he agreed.

As we walked out of the hospital, Grandpa put his arm around my neck and gave me a reassuring squeeze. "This is going to be a new life," he vowed.

Chapter Six
Hogsback Road

The farther north my Grandpa and I got, the better I felt. We had been driving at least two hours on Interstate 5 when I realized I was still sitting on the edge of the seat with my backpack clenched tightly in my arms, as if I was on a public bus and anxious not to miss my stop. Grandpa had told me the drive would be about twelve hours. I consciously relaxed my grip, placed the pack by my legs, and sunk into the seat, letting out a slow breath. It was exciting to be sitting next to Grandpa in a big moving truck, high above the other cars with a panoramic view of the California roads. I didn't mind that the drive was long. Not at all. In fact, it was comforting to think we'd be moving so far away from Norwalk, and from Dad.

We had left Grandma in the hospital, with her knee in a cast. *If only she had listened to Grandpa and not tried to clean the carpet, she wouldn't have fallen and shattered her knee.* She had to stay in the hospital for another week or so, and then Grandpa and I would return to fetch her.

Just east of the San Francisco Bay, Grandpa and I took a detour to Livermore to stop on our way at Uncle Bob's. I'd only seen my Uncle Bob, Dad and Ralph's older brother, a couple of times. I was excited to spend some time with my cousins, so I begged Grandpa to let us stay the night. He not only agreed, but also assured me that we would stop again to visit them on our way back.

Grandpa is so cool, I thought. My dad never cared about what I wanted.

"Grandpa, where exactly is Red Bluff?"

"We're actually technically going to be in a place called Gerber, just south of the town of Red Bluff in northern California," he told me, laughing.

"Gerber?" I repeated.

"Yup."

It was strange to be able to ask so many questions without getting into trouble. "Sounds like baby food."

Grandpa laughed again. I sat bright-eyed, staring out the window, and wondered what Gerber would be like.

The anticipation grew as we pulled off the interstate onto Highway 99 West. We passed through mile after mile of farmland and olive orchards; a sign read "Olive City".

"That would be Corning," said Grandpa, "Almost there." We were in the middle of absolutely nowhere.

We were pulling up past a small store on the side of the road called Shady Rest at the Junction, and the truck began to slow.

"We're here!" announced Grandpa as we turned down a dirt driveway. The house sat on about half an acre of land. There was a creek that ran behind the property.

This place is incredible, I thought; *I cannot wait to go exploring.*

***

The next morning some of the neighbors came over to help unload the truck. A kid named Jimmy, who was about my age, was one of our helpers. He lived just two houses down. Jimmy told me all about the area and the school that I would be attending.

When the moving was done, we backed Grandpa's truck down off the trailer and headed out again for our journey south in the empty U-Haul. Just as promised, we stopped in Livermore for a couple of days with the cousins on the way back. We couldn't stay longer than that, because Grandma would be out of the hospital soon with no home to return to and nobody wanted to keep her waiting.

We switched out the U-Haul for Grandma's car, picked her up from the hospital, said our goodbyes to Uncle Ralph and Dad, and made our way back north to Gerber. Grandpa and I were becoming experts at the road trip, but for Grandma it was much more difficult. We had to make lots of stops so that she could get out and stretch.

***

When we arrived in Gerber, summer was just beginning and yet it was already unbelievably hot. This new place was different in so many ways. Here we got to burn our trash, for one. The pyromaniac in me just loved that.

Grandma was anxious to start a garden, so Grandpa and I got busy tilling the ground. They went back and forth over the size for a while, and Grandma finally won; it was going to be huge.

"We're not feeding the whole county, Mom," Grandpa grumbled.

"I know, I know," she responded.

Still, having grown up during the Great Depression, she always wanted to be sure we had enough. This principle also applied to household goods and supplies. We all teased her about the amount of junk she collected. Grandma would never just buy one of anything when she could buy ten.

While we were moving, Grandpa would grumble over her hoarding habits. "I don't know why we have to move the whole country," he would say. "They do have stores in Red Bluff, you know."

The garden ended up being massive. We were growing everything: tomatoes, green peas, onions, and carrots, to name a few. Next came the chicken coop, soon to be filled with chickens laying eggs. Grandpa taught me how to gig frogs from the creek behind the house and soon we were enjoying frog legs alongside our breakfast spread. I also learned how to hunt for rabbits, quails and doves. This was country living at its finest.

If we needed anything from the store, we had to take a trip into Red Bluff. There wasn't a whole lot there: a JC Penny's, Zukwiler's department store, and a small grocery store. Everyone was a friend; it didn't take long for the lady at the liquor store to know Grandpa by name. For me, it felt like we had gone back in time to a quieter and more slow-paced way of life.

Only a few days after arriving in Gerber, I was sitting on the front porch, lost in thought. I was thinking about Dad, and how ironic it was that I missed him deeply. I had been so eager to get away from the chaos, and it was such a relief but still the longing wouldn't go away.

Grandpa could tell something was troubling me, "Let's go for a ride."

It was the first time for me to experience the stunning beauty of Hogsback Road, an old dirt road that climbs up the peak to a Sierra Mountain lookout point. Grandpa and I sat in his truck, overlooking the whitewater creek at the bottom of the canyon, laughing and talking about my frustrations with my dad.

"You're going to be staying with us now, Mike. This is a new beginning."

Grandpa opened the glove compartment and pulled out the bottle of Ten High Whiskey that he always kept stashed away from Grandma's view. There was another one in the garage wrapped in a red shop rag.

"This will help," he told me.

It wasn't the first time Grandpa had given me whiskey. I was familiar with the sensation the nasty-tasting liquid left as it burned a trail down the back of my throat into my tummy.

"Congratulations boy," Grandpa used to say. "This will help you grow hair on your balls!"

Dad must have a lot hair on his balls, I remember thinking.

We were strictly warned not to let Grandma know. "It's our little secret." Still, she found out once; she must have smelled it on our breath. "We don't need any more drinkers in this house, do we?" she asked Grandpa.

After that day, Hogsback became my favorite spot. Grandpa took me there often just to get away, or to go shooting or hunting, and later in life I went by myself to clear my head.

In Gerber, I enjoyed making friends, learning to ride motorcycles, and playing the guitar. I often thought of my brother Paul and wondered how he might be doing back in Los Angeles.

My neighbor Jimmy was really good at everything that he did. I helped one of the neighbors cut and bale hay to make some money for the county fair, which sounded really exciting. Red Bluff also boasted "the largest two-day rodeo in the world," according to the posters. Maybe that was the reason there were so many cowboys, or cowboy wannabes.

Grandma taught me how to cook, make jelly and biscuits, how to sew, and butcher chickens. We spent countless hours planting and tending the garden together. "It's important to learn how to look after yourself," she said. Grandma was raised on a farm and was the strongest woman I've ever known, tough as nails.

***

I didn't want summer to end. I was having the time of my life and was ready to live like this forever. Unfortunately, summer was winding down and school would be starting soon. Grandma took me into town to register for school. While in town she and I went shopping. I was thrilled when she let me pick out some new shirts. In the past Grandma had always made my shirts; that was okay when I was in grade school, but wearing a homemade shirt in high school was a different story.

Jimmy came by the next morning and we walked to our bus stop by the Shady Rest alongside a couple of other kids that lived nearby. The school bus seemed to wind down every back road all the way from Gerber to Red Bluff. The high school in Red Bluff was distinctly lacking in diversity; the entire student body seemed to be divided into two cliques: cowboys and hippies. Since I wasn't a cowboy, my long hair qualified me as a hippy.

After school, I spent my afternoons doing homework, helping in the garden, or exploring the fields near our house. I loved to walk along the creek, daydreaming about *The Adventures of Tom Sawyer* and plotting how I might build a raft to sail away, wherever it would take me. The thought of worrying Grandma and Grandpa paralyzed any realization of such schemes. But it made me miss Paul, even though we were still in touch by mail with an occasional phone call. He would probably not have thought twice about building a raft and attempting an escapade.

I was still having trouble in school; it was hard for me to focus and concentrate. I was constantly in trouble for talking, horseplay, and not completing my homework. As hard as I tried, I still found myself bringing notes home from my teacher for Grandma to sign. At least with Grandma there was no yelling, no screaming, no smacks to the back of the head, no being called stupid. Grandma used encouraging words and tried to help me focus on my schoolwork.

***

One rainy day, Jimmy and I decided to go out on his motor-cycle after school in the fields behind his house. The rain was pouring and we were soaking wet and cold, but we didn't care. We were having so much fun that we stayed out until our stomachs reminded us of supper. From a distance I could see Grandpa standing by the fence. I knew then that I was late. Freezing and drenched, I wanted badly to take a shower, but Grandma said that I had to wait until after we had eaten.

"That will teach you not to be late for dinner," she scolded.

I hurried through my meal and then ran a hot bath. It felt so good.

The phone rang, but all I could hear was Grandpa talking. It sounded like he was arguing with someone. Grandma also got on the phone; I could tell she was mad. "Damn you," I heard her say. My heart froze and I began to shake. I didn't want to get out of the bathtub. I knew who must have been on the phone, and what they were arguing about. I added some more hot water and tried to forget the world.

After about an hour, Grandma hollered, "Mike, you're going to turn into a prune! What are you doing in there?"

I finally got out, dried off, and dressed. My head hung low as I slunk into the living room.

Grandpa looked at me as if he was fighting back tears. "I'm sorry, Mike. Your dad wants you back home."

Looking at Grandpa I sadly said, "But you promised."

"I know I did," he said, "and I'm sorry. Damn him."

I walked over and sat down next to Grandma, laid my head on her shoulder, and began to cry. Grandma never knew quite what to do when I cried. I think it made her uncomfortable. She turned back to her romance novel, awkwardly patting my arm.

"Why?" I asked. There was no response.

***

Dad called back the next day while I was in school to arrange my bus trip back to Los Angeles. At least I would still have another week. Grandma tried her best to convince me that the reason Dad wanted me home was because he really loved me and missed me, but I wasn't buying it.

Dad wants someone to control, I realized. I felt like one of the cows I had seen being led to the butcher's shed. My fate was already determined. Every time I started to relax and enjoy life without him, he felt compelled to drag me back into his messed-up world. *Misery loves company,* I thought, *and he wants me to be his.*

As we headed to the Greyhound bus depot in Corning, my heart ached like never before. I looked out the window from the bus and watched Grandma and Grandpa standing there. As we pulled away, I jumped out of my seat and ran to the back of the bus to catch one last look at them. I knew that it was as hard on them as it was on me, and I wondered when, if ever, I would see them again.

Chapter Seven
C-Rations

As the bus pulled away from the station, I did my best to take in every last bit of the scenery. Every smell, the aroma of the rice fields burning, would be something that I would certainly miss. This place had seemed so foreign when I arrived the previous summer, but now it had become home, and I was going to miss everything about it.

The twelve-hour ride seemed to drag on endlessly. Every second felt like a minute, and every minute felt like an hour. Each time the bus stopped, I considered grabbing my stuff and bolting. *But where would I go?* So, as usual, I played the role of the good son and did exactly what I was told to do. At least I had plenty of time to reflect and prepare myself for what was ahead. *I'll just do my best not to piss him off,* I told myself.

As the bus rolled in, so did all my old fears. Dad was standing on the sidewalk chatting up a girl with long blond hair, short shorts and a tube top. *She must be waiting for someone on the bus*, I thought; *I wish he'd just leave her alone. For God's sake, she can't be much older than me.* I walked toward Dad, but instead of parting ways, this young girl grabbed his hand.

"Mike, I want you to meet Jenny," Dad said as he gave me a big hug. "She's been staying with me while you were at your grandparents."

On my way back, my fears were verified. Jenny didn't seem at all shy in front of me. She was all over him—kissing his neck, unzipping his pants, and sticking her hand inside. I was disgusted. He was laughing and telling her what he wanted to do in graphic details. *What a way to greet your son who's been away.*

Dad and Jenny rushed straight into the bedroom and stayed there for hours while I sat on the rundown green couch with even more time to ponder what fate had dished up for me this time. When the blissful couple finally emerged, Dad whipped up a batch of his favorite 'hamburger helper', and we all sat down together.

Quite the welcome party, I thought to myself, keeping my mouth shut as I chewed down my portion.

The following day, Dad and Jenny took me clothes shopping for school and I had the chance to get to know her better. She was nice, but it was pretty hard to ignore the fact that she was only fifteen—just one year my senior—and sleeping with my dad. We picked up a couple more of her friends at the mall and headed over to Transmission King where Uncle Ralph worked. I was eager to see him.

Uncle Ralph was waiting for us outside. "You're late," he told Dad. "Oh, hey there Mike, great to see you!" He gave me a big rewarding smile and a pat on the back as the girls swarmed around him.

"I've already got some boys waiting across the street," he told them. "Let's get going. Jenny, you've got Joe in room 103. Be gentle, he's an old man. Sharon, Jared asked for you by name; he's in 108. Lori, you can come help me out in the office while we wait for more customers." He led her by the hand and nodded for me to follow.

I sat down on a folding chair across the room from my uncle while he took his seat at the desk, tugging Lori along. She knelt down and got to work unzipping his pants while I squirmed in my seat, wondering if I should leave.

"Relax Mike; it's good to see you. Tell me, how are the old folks doing up there in Red Bluff?" Uncle Ralph asked, leaning back in his chair with a smirk on his face. He seemed to get a kick out of this. I tried to just ignore what was going on behind the desk, and told him all about my adventures.

"Sounds like a totally different world," Uncle Ralph commented as Lori stood up, wiping her mouth. He winked at me, "You want one?"

"I'll give him a freebie," laughed Lori. My face turned tomato red as I sheepishly declined.

After that, as much as I loved my Uncle Ralph, I stayed away from the shop whenever possible. Paul was still living with his girlfriend Jill; he and Dad were at odds, so I barely saw him except occasionally at school. I tried reconnecting with Billy, but he seemed to have found himself a new group of friends, and we just didn't hit it off anymore. Mark and I still got along, though, and with Dad outside the picture, it was more comfortable to hang out with him than it had been before. I would go over to his place after school and then head over to the shop to catch a ride home with Dad and Jenny and, at times, with some of her friends.

Sometimes in the evenings we would play board games together, but more often, I had to put up with all the men who drifted in and out of Dad's apartment to take advantage of the girls' services. Annoyed, I chose a passive-aggressive method of protest, choosing the most strategic moments to do noisy chores.

Jenny came running down the stairs, clearly bare-breasted under her loosely tied robe. "Shut the damn vacuum off; can't you see I'm working here!?" she growled in an angry whisper.

"Sorry, but I have to get my chores done or my dad will be pissed," I said coolly.

"Well, I'm working here too, and you're really spoiling the mood," she snapped. "Stop being such a dick. Yesterday it was the radio, and today it's the vacuum. Why don't you just beat it?"

***

The big bicentennial celebration for the American Revolution and the signing of the Declaration of Independence was coming up, so Mark and I decided to build a rocket for the festivities. We picked a large two-stage Estes Rocket and Uncle Ralph gave me some gunpowder to fill it so it would explode. When the Fourth of July arrived, I spent most of the day at Mark's, eagerly anticipating the evening fireworks and the chance to launch our rocket. All of a sudden, to everyone's surprise, Dad showed up. "I want to see this rocket," he said. No one was brave enough to ask him to leave. At midnight our rocket roared across the night sky, over 1,500 feet in the air, and the bicentennial celebration went out with a bang.

I rode home with Dad. He had behaved himself that evening, and it was actually cool hanging out with him. *If only things could always be like this.*

My wishful thinking didn't last long; things were back to normal the very next day. Dad complained that I hadn't been nice to Jenny. Things weren't going so well between them, and he was blaming me for getting in the way. What's worse, it seemed that the Bicentennial celebration had fanned an old flame: Dad and Sally Apple were at it again. My safe-zone had been invaded once more, and as Dad started spending more and more time at Mark's, I started spending less and less time there.

***

I began to find an escape by going out for runs to clear my head. That was when I started to really develop a love for running and began to run track. As school started up again, I joined the cross-country team and discovered that I was 'a natural', and I loved the accolades.

On the day the shit finally hit the fan, my cross-country coach dropped me off at home after practice.

"She's gone," Dad said as he grabbed me by the throat, pinning me against the wall. "She left because of you."

I kept my mouth shut. I'd been down this road before and I knew where it would take me. I tried my best to suck it up and take the beating.

"I should kill you, you worthless piece of shit." The empty gaze in his eyes was at least as scary as the physical abuse. *It's as if he has no soul.* By the time he stopped I was covered in bruises and blood.

Is this why you wanted me to come back from Red Bluff? I wanted to ask him, *So I could be your punching bag?* Wisdom got the best of me so I stayed silent.

Dad was furious with me, but he was also furious with Jenny for leaving him. He started devising a plan to exact revenge on her. I got an earful of it the following evening, and it scared me. "I'll get that gun out from under your bed," he raged, "tie her up, stick the barrel in her snatch, and blow the top of her head off." I had seen the whole gun-in-the-snatch thing before, and I had no doubt that he could do it again. So, the following day when Dad went to work, I removed the barrel from the rifle under my bed and took it over to Uncle Ralph and Aunt Margie's house.

That evening Dad was drinking more than usual. "I'm going to kill that bitch," he kept repeating. I fell asleep to the sound of his rambling, and awoke to the sound of him digging under my bed. Terrified, I waited for that moment when he would discover the barrel of the rifle itself was missing, imagining what my punishment would be. Not unlike what I had envisioned, he began beating me with the wooden stock of the rifle, swinging wildly.

He's actually going to beat me to death, I realized, bolting out of the bedroom and down the stairs. I tripped down the third step and barely managed to throw open the front door, running as fast as I possibly could toward Uncle Ralph's. As I raced down the street, I realized two things: first, that I had been wearing nothing but underwear, and second—that I didn't care. Thanks to my cross-country training, I arrived well ahead of Dad, and Margie had time to throw some clothes on me before Dad caught up with her.

We were sitting down, waiting, when the stock of the gun came crashing through the front window. Uncle Ralph quickly called a family friend, Dr. Kenny Franklyn, who came as quickly as he could to speak with Dad. By the time Kenny showed up, Dad had slashed the tires of Uncle Ralph's camper and scratched up his truck. Out of fear and a warped sense of loyalty Ralph never proceeded with having Dad arrested. Kenny managed to calm Dad down and the two of them left together. After a short time, Kenny returned to talk to me. "We need to get you out of town for a few days until he cools off," he said. "I'm leaving tomorrow for the Mojave Desert; why don't you come along?"

I spent that night with Uncle Ralph. The next morning I snuck home after Dad had left for work to grab some of my things, and then headed out with Kenny to spend a few days in the desert.

Unlike many addicts, my father was able to partake as much as he'd like with his liquor consumption and/or drugs and he'd still be able to go to work.

***

Kenny had a house out there in the Mojave, and he was working on restoring an old plane from World War I. He put me to work helping him stretch the fabric onto the wings and paint it with lacquer.

After about five days, we returned to the city and Kenny came with me to have a talk with Dad.

"You're on your own. I don't care what you do anymore," Dad said.

"Can I go back to Grandpa and Grandma's?"

"If you go there, I will come over and kill you all!" He said, "How many times do I have to tell you? If you fuck with the bull you get the horn."

"So where...?"

"I don't really care where you go, just not back there."

I grabbed as many of my clothes as I could, and Kenny dropped me off at a friend's house. I left my bag on the porch and headed directly to school. Ron, who I had met running track and cross-country at school, was my closest friend at the time. I ended up staying with his family for about a month. His dad wanted to have me there legally, so he contacted Social Services to begin the process. When Social Services contacted Dad, he reported me as a "runaway".

The next day, a social worker showed up at school to inform me that I could no longer stay with Ron. They were developing a plan for me; I would be placed in a foster home. *Great.*

The social worker picked me up at five that evening to drive me to the foster home, which was in the city of Cerritos, just a few miles away.

"Why do I have to stay in a foster home?" I asked her on the way, "Why can't you find my real mom?"

"I'm not sure," she said.

Immediately I recognized the man who was to become my guardian, *Colonel Balder from school.* Colonel Chuck Balder, who was short, stalky and physically fit, taught Military Science, Health and Drivers Ed. He was not the most popular teacher either. He and his wife lived in a nice, two-story house where the cul-de-sac bled onto the other street with two younger foster kids, and their own biological princess, Amber, who was in my class at school.

The first thing the Colonel did was to sit me down and explain the long list of house rules. "Church is mandatory, twice a week, and sometimes youth group," he said. *That won't be so bad,* I thought. It seemed ironic that now I was being forced to go to church when I had been trying for so long to convince my dad to let me go.

The next morning Colonel Balder drove me to school.

"So you run cross-country, is that right?"

It's nice of him to ask me about something I care about. I smiled, "Yes."

"Why don't you play football?" he suggested. "Running is for pussies, don't you think?"

"No," I replied.

"Football," he continued, "now that's a man's game. I'll go ahead and let the coach know that you'll be quitting track and joining the football team. You can start tomorrow."

A group of friends were gathered on the lawn as I got out of the car. I looked around for a way I might be able to sneak past them, but it was impossible.

"What's up, Mike?" they called, as I went over to join them. As soon as my new foster parent was out of sight they started smirking. "Living with the Colonel, huh?" they mocked, saluting me.

On the way home from school, the Colonel informed me that we would be stopping for a haircut.

"Thanks, but I don't want one. I like my hair long."

"Oh, it'll just be a trim," he assured me, "before you start football practice."

I reluctantly allowed the barber to tie the cloth around my neck and surrendered to his chair.

"Cut it all off," Chuck instructed the barber, giving me the death glare. "Don't move," he snapped.

Strapped relentlessly to a straightjacket-like chair, I sat helpless as the barber quickly shaved my head, watching my hair fall to the floor in disbelief. I remembered the grief I'd already received from my friends earlier that morning. *What are they going to say when they see me tomorrow?*

The other two foster kids, Roger and Tom, gave me that sympathetic look when we got home. *They've been through the same thing*, I realized.

Smells of baked bread and roast beef were wafting from the kitchen and my stomach began to growl. "Alright Mike, it's almost time for dinner," said Chuck, "and you've still got to learn the ropes."

He led me into the garage, where he showed me boxes labeled 'Individual Combat Meal', and stacks of plain, bronze-colored cans. This, and not the baked bread and roast beef I had smelled in the house, would be my dinner. As a member of the National Guard, Chuck was stealing C-rations from the armory, and who better to enjoy their contents than us foster kids?

Roger and Tom lifted a piece of plywood onto the pool table and demonstrated how to boil cans of 'Beef and Vegetable Stew' or 'Chicken with Noodles'" on top of a camp stove. The hard part was opening the cans.

"You'll get used to it," Roger told me.

I soon learned that one could earn a spot at the family's dining table by snitching on someone else. Chuck must have learned that from the military, too. I wasn't about ready to become an informant, so I resigned myself to the army rations. *At least the pound cake isn't so bad*, I told myself.

***

The following day, I lined up for my first football practice in full gear. *What am I doing here?* "Hut. Hut, HIKE," the play was in motion. Before I had the chance to figure out what I was supposed to be doing, I found myself clobbered by a much larger lineman than myself.

My head was pounding and my brain was scrambled. By the next morning things were no better, so Chuck took me to the hospital where I was admitted with a severe concussion. Chuck's face reeked of disdain as he came to the realization that I was simply not football material. After returning home, I waited a couple of days before broaching the subject. "Do you think I could just run cross-country?" reluctantly, he agreed.

***

That weekend, Chuck had us all dress up in our 'Sunday best' for church. The local Baptist church felt totally different from the one Tim and Billy attended. It was stiff and cold, and full of prying eyes. The man at the door handing out programs and hymnals was no exception. "Another foster kid?" he asked.

"Yep," said Chuck.

We all sat together in the second row from the front. As the sermon was winding up, the pastor invited those who had an invitation for people who had been spiritually moved to respond by making a commitment. One young man raised his hand and went forward. Chuck stretched out his hand and placed it on my right leg. At first I thought he was making a kind gesture—*maybe deep down he really cares*—but then he began to pinch my inner thigh. "See that guy?" he whispered between his teeth.

"What guy?"

His grip tightened. "The guy that went forward."

"Yes."

"That's what you're going to do next week. Are we clear?"

"Yes," I replied as he loosened his grip. I didn't really know what going forward meant, but that didn't seem to matter.

The following Sunday I did what was expected of me. There was still a big bruise on my thigh to remind me not to think twice. I was given a Bible and told that I would be baptized the following week. Never mind that I had a bazillion unanswered questions. "It's just something you do," was the best answer I ever got.

As we left church, Chuck got lots of smiles and pats on the back. "It's a good thing you're doing for these kids," someone told him.

"Thanks be to God," he answered.

In the week that followed, Chuck invited me to come sit at the dining table with the family for the first time. "No thanks," I said, but he insisted. The other kids glared at me as I grudgingly followed him inside. He knew well enough that they would think I was telling on them, and he did it on purpose. "Just be thankful," he said.

If I had something to be thankful for, it was running Cross-Country. I wasn't allowed to run at night anymore, which was something I really missed, but at least I could practice with the team. I began to focus on an upcoming cross-country event where I would have the chance to compete. I woke up that Saturday morning excited about the race and the bus ride up, which was one of my favorite times to connect with the guys on the team.

"You're riding with me," Chuck barked. *What a dick,* I thought. *This guy's trying to be annoying.*

I didn't say a word the whole ride up, but Chuck thought it would be a good time to give me a pep talk. First there was a win-at-all-costs speech, followed by a make-me-proud speech, and ending with a don't-embarrass-me speech. The icing on the cake was the offer of money, depending on how well I did.

When we arrived, I spent some time stretching and warming up. This was supposed to be a fun run, lots of trails and hills. I was looking forward to having another award to add to my collection, but Chuck's encouragements made me feel like I would rather be a boxer or a wrestler. *I'd really like to tear something apart right now.*

As I stood on the starting line, Chuck called out to me one more time, "Make me proud!"

Make YOU proud? Who do you think you are, anyway? This is not about you, I wanted to scream. The nerve of him, taking all the fun out of something that really mattered to me.

My thoughts were interrupted by the sound of the starting pistol. We were off. I quickly began to pass runners at a steady pace up the first hill and around the first bend. The farther ahead I got, the angrier I became. *If I win this thing, he'll think it's all for him, and it's not.* I just wasn't going to let him have that pleasure, so I threw myself off the edge of the road and tumbled down to the bottom of the hill. When my body stopped rolling I looked up, the taste of blood in my mouth, and watched the other runners passing by. *How's that, Chuck? Does that make you proud?*

My legs and arms were scrapped up pretty badly. As I dragged myself back, I wondered if I was bleeding enough for Chuck to approve of me not finishing the race.

There was disappointment on his face, but even worse was my own disappointment with myself. *Why did I let him get to me? Why did I let him ruin that race for me? I should have stood up to him. I could have won that.*

One afternoon Roger, Tom, and I were given the extra job of weeding the backyard, in exchange for a chance to go to the movies. Roger hollered, "Hey Mike, throw me the shovel."

Just as I tossed it, Tom stood up and got smacked in the head.

"Screw you, Mike," he screamed.

"Sorry, it was an accident." Tom, who had a permanent chip on his shoulder and always seemed mad at the world, stomped back into the house in a fit of rage.

Roger and I turned back to our work. A moment later I was startled by the sound of screaming. I turned to find Tom running at me, full speed, with a butcher's knife raised over his head.

I jumped up and ran toward the sliding glass door. The glass door was open from inside, but the screen was latched shut. I picked up a small wooden stool to block the first blow from the knife, and then retreated to the side yard with Tom in pursuit. I managed to get enough headway to loop back to the sliding door, where I had to smash the stool into the screen twice before it tore enough for me to squeeze through. I ran to the front door and out into the street. The Colonel was able to restrain Tom, who was later arrested.

***

Following the incident with Tom, I requested a visit with my social worker and asked that Uncle Ralph be there with me. In the meeting, I expressed my fear over Tom returning to the home, and told her about the dinner situation. The social worker showed me a list of the things that Chuck had supposedly purchased for me, not one of which I had ever seen. I was told my case would be reviewed, and they would get back to me soon about finding another placement.

In the meantime, I was scared to death when Tom came back to the house, even after he apologized and told me that he was working on his anger.

***

A couple of days later I got a phone call from one of Amber's friends, who seemed to like me. She was trying to convince me to sneak out after bedtime and meet her at Dairy Queen. As I hung up, Roger warned me that it was a set up. Chuck wanted to have something negative to report to my social worker.

"Why should I believe you?" I asked. Just to prove it, Roger pulled out a stack of condoms that he had been instructed to hide under my mattress.

Immediately, I called Uncle Ralph to come and pick me up. As I was waiting, Chuck challenged me about making plans to sneak out, and said he wanted to search my room. Roger avoided eye contact. It was no surprise at all when Chuck pulled out the condoms from under my mattress and began yelling at me.

From the window, I saw Uncle Ralph and Aunt Margie pull up in front of the house. I ran down the stairs and toward the door as if my life depended on it (and it likely could have).

As a result of the recent events, and the inability to care for the foster kids properly, the Balders lost their foster license and I stayed with Uncle Ralph while he and the social worker discussed my future.

I tried several times to bring up the topic of my own biological mom. "Why can't I stay with her?" I asked, receiving only vague replies.

"No one knows where she's at," Uncle Ralph told me.

Because Uncle Ralph lived in apartments that didn't allow children it was not considered to be a good home for us. Through family and social worker discussions it was deter-mined that since my mother was unavailable, they thought the best place for me would be with my Uncle Bob, in Livermore.

Chapter Eight
Emancipation

On my next of my many moves, I strolled out of the terminal at Oakland International Airport to meet Uncle Bob, Aunt Sandy, and their three girls. When we arrived at the house in Livermore, I was introduced to its other resident, a blind man called Rick. Uncle Bob, who was also legally blind, had met Rick at the Orientation School for the Blind, and had been assigned by the court as his legal caretaker.

"Doesn't he have relatives or anyone else who could take care of him?" I asked my uncle.

"Do you have any idea how much money I'm getting for him?" was his response.

Uncle Bob had stopped working and driving several years earlier due to his severe visual impairment. Now he relied on money from the government alongside his wife's salary. He was receiving social security disability benefits for himself and for each of his three daughters, in addition to the money he got for taking care of Rick, and now for being my guardian.

For me, everything was new: new clothes, new shoes, as well as a new high school. I felt safe, at least in the beginning; Dad was far away and didn't really know where I was. The school year was already almost over by the time I arrived, but I quickly made friends with another runner, Duane.

By the time summer rolled around, Duane and I had become inseparable. Together, we spent most of our summer days being lazy bums, apart from a couple of trips we took with the Youth Recreation Department up to the Santa Cruz Beach Boardwalk.

From Santa Cruz, I could stare across the Monterey Bay and make out the foggy silhouette of Pacific Grove and

Monterey, where I had spent so many adventuresome days exploring the old canneries, fishing, and stealing samples from Holman's Department Store. I sat on the beach, soaking up the Santa Cruz sun—which, on the north side of the bay, was in sharp contrast to the Pacific Grove haze down south—and thinking about my stepmom, Geri, and the girls. *I wonder what they're doing now,* I thought.

"What are you daydreaming about?" interrupted Duane.

"I used to live over there," I told him. "Those were some of the happiest days of my life."

"Why did you leave?"

"Well, I didn't want to—" I started. "Actually, I didn't even want to go there in the first place, but then I never wanted to leave."

I told Duane everything. I told him about Geri, and how she snatched us from the playground that day and drove us away from Dad; about the beauty of the new city and the adventure, and how for the first time I really felt free to be myself; and finally about how Dad suddenly returned one day to take us back.

"And your mom didn't fight to keep you?"

"Actually, she was our stepmom, so it was a risk for her to take us with her in the first place."

"Have you seen her since?"

"Nope, but I wish I could."

Duane jumped up and started running toward the water. "Come on, let's go!" he shouted.

"Where are you going?" I called after him.

"We're gonna swim to Pacific Grove!" he shouted, and then dove into the water. I quickly dove in after him, and the two of us swam until we were exhausted. We stopped, laughing at the silliness of our attempt, and then headed back to the beach together. It was the first time I was able to confide in a friend, and it felt good to know that Duane would listen to—and try to understand—some of what I'd been through. Duane's parents had divorced when he was young, and he had some similar issues with his dad.

With the summer ending, Duane and I began to run together to prepare for the coming cross-country season. Now I was running because I loved it, rather than to escape from life.

***

About a week before school started, I got a call from my brother Paul, who I hadn't seen in about six months. He had broken up with his girlfriend and was looking for a place to live and finish up his last year of high school. Paul arrived in Livermore just a few days before school started. It was good to see him. We had lots of catching up to do.

Things seemed to be going well, though I could see what Bob had going on: he was getting financial benefits from the government for housing Rick, Paul, and me. It wasn't as bad as the foster home; we weren't eating rations in the garage, but he was still doing it for the money.

***

With a negligent father and an agenda-driven uncle, the need to belong sent me on a search for my biological mother. Throughout the years I had never stopped thinking about her. Somehow I always had a glint of hope that she might welcome me into her life. But at least, if only I could catch her before she could run away, I might be able to find out the truth. I started to frequent the library to look through phone books and write down numbers. At home I called 411 and made long distance calls even after Uncle Bob started complaining, "Give it up, man. You're wasting your time and racking up my phone bills."

A couple months after Paul moved in, Uncle Bob angrily approached us, "Shit, man, it's expensive having you guys here." We nodded, but I knew he was still full of crap about other things.

"Rick gets more meds than he needs. Maybe you guys could sell some to your friends at school?" I was totally bummed. *He's just like Dad.*

"Bring me back twenty dollars, both of you," he said, while handing us each a small bag containing reds (Seconal sodium) capsules.

"Okay," I replied. We took our pills and left.

The following day, after school, he came to collect. "Got my money?"

"No," I replied. "None of my friends wanted them."

"Well then, find new friends," he barked.

***

The next day, I managed to find a couple of guys at school who would buy the pills. This got Bob out of my hair for a while. I was worried about getting caught selling drugs; I didn't want to get kicked off the cross-country team.

Eventually, I landed a part-time job at a fast food restaurant, which gained me a bit of independence, and Paul managed to get himself a car, which also helped me since I could rely on him for rides.

One evening, Paul picked me up from work. "Guess what?" he smiled.

"What?"

"I found Geri."

"What? Are you kidding? Where is she?"

"They're in Monterey."

***

The following Saturday we both got up early and headed down to Monterey, with address in hand and memories on our minds. The anticipation grew as we got closer to being able to see Geri and my step-sisters. I found myself almost fearful, wondering whether they would be happy that we found them; it had been nearly six years. I could hear my own heart beating as we approached the house. The door swung open, and the look on Geri's face melted all my uncertainties. Through hugs, kisses, and tears we greeted Becky and Mickey, and then drove over to surprise Linda at the Warehouse, a pizza joint down near Cannery Row where she was working. Linda did a double take and almost dropped a pizza as we walked through the doors.

During dinner we reminisced about the good and the bad, laughing and crying until it hurt. In spite of all the years that had passed, the girls still felt like family, and Paul and I didn't want to leave. Eventually, we had to tear ourselves away and make our journey back to Uncle Bob's in Livermore.

"This sucks," Paul complained on the way home from Pacific Grove. "I didn't move to Livermore to be pimped out as a drug dealer. I'm so over it."

I agreed, but there was not much I could do to change things, so as usual, I just tried my best to *suck it up* and keep the peace. Paul wasn't so good at that. He and Bob were bumping heads constantly.

"You just have to hang in there 'til the end of the year," I told him. Paul would be graduating from high school in the spring, and had already been accepted into Riverside University to study medicine. For me, the future was less certain. I'd still have two more years of high school after Paul left.

Uncle Bob was only my temporary guardian, so I had to make a decision: either to make his guardianship legal, or to become emancipated. My social worker told me that filing the emancipation papers would force Dad to decide whether or not he was willing to give up his parental rights. *This way*, I thought, *I'd at least get a chance to face Dad in court at the good old age of sixteen.*

***

Usually I was able to make certain that Uncle Bob didn't know the slightest thing about what I was up to—until I blew it one day after school.

"Buddy, where's the money for the pills?" Uncle Bob nagged me, as he often did. This time, I had sold them to a friend's friend, but he said they were no good and wanted his money back.

"I had to return the money," I explained.

Bob was mad. "I thought you said you sold them."

"You know, you might want to consider finding someone else to sell your pills. I'll be emancipated in a couple weeks!"

"What do you mean, emancipated? When did that happen?"

"I've arranged it all with my social worker, and Dad will be informed within a day or two!"

Mentioning Dad certainly didn't help to give me any sense of protection, but at least I hoped that this new situation would keep Uncle Bob out of my hair for the time being. I was wrong; Bob became consumed with the fact that, alongside my emancipation, his checks would stop.

"Do you know how much it costs to keep you here? Who do you think is going to cover the expenses after you get this emancipation?" He was blatantly annoyed.

I was trying to get out the door. "We'll see. Let's talk about it later."

"What the heck? Discuss it later? I'm telling you I can't afford to have you staying here, and you're going to walk out on me?" He followed me out of the house. "Where are you going anyway?"

"I'm meeting up with some friends," I told him, "I promise we can discuss it later."

"If you didn't spend so much time hanging out with your faggot girlfriend Duane, you might actually get some pills sold!" he said, slamming me against the garage door.

"He's not a faggot!" I yelled back, "and I'm fed up with selling your stupid pills. You can't make me do anything I don't want to do; you're not my guardian for much longer!"

"Well then, you'd better start paying rent."

"I'm not paying rent, I'm moving out!" I ran back into the house and gathered my most treasured possessions: some family photos, a couple mementos of my birth mother, newspaper clippings of the Apollo space mission, and my medals and trophies from track. Stuffing these and what clothes I could fit into my backpack, I grabbed my letter jacket, and left for Duane's, slamming the door behind me.

Duane's mom said it would be fine if I stayed with them. I emptied my backpack and then went back to Uncle Bob's to gather the rest of my things. Upon my arrival, I saw that everything else I owned had been thrown out with the trash on the sidewalk, waiting for pickup.

Bob is no different from Dad, I thought. *What's wrong with this family?*

My things were all mixed up with the banana peels and eggshells; it was too gross for me to bother sorting out what was mine.

To my surprise, Dad didn't even show up on my court date. He simply notified the court that he wanted to go ahead and terminate his parental rights. I was devastated. I had won my emancipation—but still I felt unwanted. I walked out of court feeling like I had just won the battle, but lost the war.

Chapter Nine
Apollo 13

I pinned the last of my Apollo pictures on the wall, and plopped down on my new bed at Duane's house. Now I could feel at home. The wall was covered from floor to ceiling with newspaper clippings and cutouts of anything Apollo, just as it had been at Uncle Bob's. I stared at the centrally placed picture of Neil Armstrong's first step on the moon. I would never forget that day when, sitting with my grandparents, all eyes were glued to the television as we watched the historic moment take place. Ever since then I have been a die-hard Apollo fan. *Someday that'll be me starting up the engine of the Apollo Saturn V rocket soaring through space, walking on the moon.*

At school, I was disappointed and frustrated to find the results of my aptitude tests were not up to par for reaching my dream. The school counselor suggested that, based on the strengths I had shown on the aptitude test, I'd make a good social worker. *No way,* I thought, *I'll be an astronaut.*

For now, my best career option was in the fast-food industry. And after a fight with my boss, I was finally a free person, at least on paper, but this also meant that I was responsible for supporting myself financially. The thrill of being able to write my own sick notes wore off quickly; it was lonelier than anything.

Although my dad hadn't even shown up in court for my emancipation, I was far from free of his influence. It was probably a result of the kind of family values instilled in me by my grandmother—"Family comes first," she had said—but I always felt obliged to call him to check in and keep him informed about my movements. Dad's values were completely different from Grandma's though, and the two voices often played out a conflicting dialogue in my head, each one telling me to do "the right thing".

One particular day, I was telling my dad how frustrated I was at work. "I'm pretty sure they're stiffing me on my paycheck," I told him.

"So what are you going to do about it?" he asked.

Later that day, I spoke to him again. He had taken the liberty of doing some 'research' by talking to a cashier friend of his who worked at a local market. Dad explained to me how I could get a little extra money from the cash register by faking over-rings.

The next day at work, Dad's maxim was ringing in my head, "Don't get mad, get even," easily overpowering Grandma's persistent, yet softer voice telling me, "Let it go, Mike."

I put one of the larger customer receipts aside, and at the end of the day brought it to my boss, Cathy. "These people cancelled their order after I rung them up. It was really crowded at the time, so I just saved the bill, but they never paid for it." The money was already in my pocket.

The next morning I reported my success to Dad. "I'm proud of you," he said. My first reaction was to feel happy that I made my dad proud, but something didn't sit right. *How come I have to do something shady for him to notice me?*

My boss, Cathy, may well have known what I was up to, but she let it slide easily enough. Initially, Cathy had taken me under her wing and shown me her maternal instinct: rubbing my shoulders and clucking "you poor thing" to this motherless teen. It didn't take long for that motherly affection to turn into something more. She started giving me special preference in exchange for certain favors that took place in the office or supply room, after hours, in the car, or wherever the opportunity presented itself. I knew she was married with kids, but I didn't feel I had much of a choice—and I probably enjoyed the attention.

***

That summer Duane bought a used convertible Fiat Spider, and the two of us dreamed of being Starsky and Hutch. We drove around with the top down, beers in hand, pretending to chase bad guys—which was a good excuse for us to race around as fast as we could. One afternoon, in full pursuit of two dangerous bank robbers, we slid around a corner and landed right into a tree. The only damage was to the car and our pride—and, yes, the bank robbers got away. A couple of days later Duane got the news that two of his good friends had been killed while driving drunk on Mines Road. The news was numbing.

"That could have been us," Duane said. We had driven the same road drunk dozens of times. "Rich and Terry were good people. They never did anything to hurt anyone. Why did they have to die?"

This brush with death had a profound effect on my friend; he had always believed in all things mystical, as well as karmic, but now he was starting to doubt this philosophy. "It just doesn't seem fair," he told me. Duane stopped playing guitar, stopped drawing, stopped meditating and practicing yoga, and instead became more and more consumed with drinking.

"My grandma goes to church," I suggested sheepishly, trying to provide him with a possible alternative and maybe start a dialogue. Duane just scowled. I couldn't blame him. My experiences with Christians weren't so hopeful either.

When Duane got his new car, I inherited his old one, a 1966 Fiat with no front floorboard, which meant that I could put my feet on the ground when stopped at a signal, Fred Flintstone-style. It was also necessary to park the car on a hill so I could start it by rolling downhill and then popping the clutch. My girlfriend at the time, Connie, occasionally had to help me push the car so the engine would start. As much as all this frustrated me, she thought it was hilarious.

One afternoon when we were on our way out to dinner, all dressed up, I noticed the creek was still flooded from the rain a couple days earlier.

Unfortunately, I was just driving too fast and it was too late to stop. With no floorboard, to protect us from the water, my girlfriend and I were doomed; the car filled up to the bottom of the seats with muddy water. I looked at Connie, who was covered with mud, as was I, and we both started to crack up laughing. We went back to her grandmother's house to shower, and then walked to get something to eat close by.

I was over the Fiat, but it was all I had. One day I called my dad to ask for some advice on how to change the starter. "You need to look into getting another car," he advised. Later that evening he called me with an idea, "Would you be interested in a 1967 Nova? It would cost you about $700."

I agreed and waited to hear back from him. "It was harder than I thought to get," he paused, "but I got it for you." The car belonged to his neighbor and he had offered to buy it for a couple hundred dollars, but it turns out she didn't want to sell. "I just dumped some Karo syrup in her oil, and the next day she called to say the car was dead and asked if I still wanted to buy it. I swapped out the motor and it runs great. It's all yours; come and get it."

Right away I flew down to L.A. and managed to get all the way back home with the Nova. My new car was better than the Fiat, but it came with the high price of a nagging guilt that I couldn't seem to shake, no matter how much I told myself it wasn't my fault.

***

My brother Paul was living with a friend over the summer, and my boss, Cathy, gave him a job at the same restaurant where I was working. One day, as I was leaving work, Cathy's sister, Lizzie, called after me, "Your brother left his jacket. Tell him if he wants it back, he'll have to fuck me."

Paul seemed to appreciate the challenge. "Oh, cool!" he said eagerly. I had expected him to laugh.

"Really?" I teased Lizzie, knowing she wasn't really my type, "I didn't know you would be excited."

"Why not?" he jabbed back, "You're screwing her sister."

"Well, I guess you do have a reputation to uphold," I laughed. The standing joke among our coworkers was that Paul would screw a snake if he could hold it still. Once, a customer walked in holding a small boa and one of the cashiers called back, "Hey, where's Paul?" The whole crew laughed about it for weeks.

"Well at least I'm not as bad as Dad," Paul said. The two of us were always swapping stories about Dad. At one point we made a pact to stop telling other people our stories, because no one ever believed us. It made the conversations between us seem even more valuable; no one else could possibly understand what we had lived through.

"Man, remember how he wouldn't even let me buy a new mess kit for Boy Scouts?" I recalled. "He would just say, 'If you can't eat it, drink it, smoke it, or fuck it, it's not worth having.'"

Paul fired back, "'Eight to eighty, blind, crippled, or crazy, if she can't walk, drag her.'"

We laughed as we shot Dad's favorite sayings back and forth. Most were quite disturbing, to say the least, but Dad thought they were words to live by. The laughter Paul and I shared was usually awkward and uncomfortable.

Not long after he left to go to school in Riverside, Sheri, one of our colleagues, came up to me at work. "I'm pregnant," she blurted. I knew it wasn't mine. "It's Paul's," she said, and started sobbing. "I'll need money for an abortion," she informed me, "unless Paul is going to quit school and take care of this kid."

I arranged to meet her the next morning to give her the money. "Are you sure?" I asked.

"Yes," she nodded, and walked away.

Later that afternoon, I watched her car pull into the parking lot. It was quite a while before she finally came inside. With eyes shot from tears, she marched straight over to me and slapped me across the face so hard it nearly knocked me over. "You son of a bitch, fuck you!" she yelled and broke down, crying.

I gave her a hug and took her outside to get some air. Sheri told me about her experience. She was devastated. I realized that she had been looking for someone to talk her out of the abortion, but all I was trying to do was protect my brother.

When I told Paul about the girl and her situation, he just shrugged it off. "It wasn't mine," he claimed. It wasn't so easy for me to let go. After that, I dated Sheri for a little while in a half-hearted, short-lived attempt to ease her pain and atone for my brother's sin.

***

As the summer was winding down, Duane and I got serious about running once again. I cherished our long runs together and deep conversations about life. When school started, we began hanging around with some new friends.

Duane and I met Angelo in Mrs. Van Steinberg's English 38, a film studies class that I took as an elective during my entire time at high school in Livermore, and together, we dreamt of being stunt men. All the short films we made for our English 38 class projects were centered on our crazy feats. Our final project, 'Death at Bodine Creek', told the story of a drug deal gone wrong. We all thought it would be cool to make use of a parachute found at the Army Surplus Store, and tried our best to work it into the script with little luck. Nevertheless, we spent hours honing our stunt skills at the rodeo grounds. One of us would run behind the car, wearing the parachute and clinging to an old pair of bicycle handlebars that were tied to the car. As the car gained momentum and the parachute rose into the sky, we would simultaneously lose our grip and our nerve, falling clumsily back to earth.

Duane fell in love with Toni, a girl in our class. Toni was 'normal', we were both attracted to that; her parents were married, she had two brothers and a sister, and a great house with a pool. Duane and I often found ourselves hanging out at the DiMercurio home, using the pool, and even occasionally going to church with the family.

After church one afternoon, I stayed around after Toni and Duane left and spent several hours talking to Toni's mom. She was a great listener and showed genuine concern for me and for everything I was going through at the time. After that day, she always took the time to check up on me and I often found myself sharing my struggles and thoughts. Her responses were attentive and meaningful, and always made me think deeply.

Toni's dad was also thoughtful and supportive. One day he came to me with an offer I couldn't refuse. "If we were to build a room for you in our garage, would you come and live with us?"

They were so genuinely nice and generous; it was hard not to cry. They immediately began construction and within a week I had hung up my Apollo clippings in my new room. It was bittersweet to be leaving Duane and his mom, but it felt so good to be part of a real family, and one that had no agenda but kindness.

My dad was not convinced. "No one lets you live with them rent-free," he insisted.

Not everyone's like you, I thought—something I didn't dare say.

As much as I wanted to connect with my dad, I was terrified of becoming like him. This feeling hit me hard right after Cathy, my boss, lent me her car to go to the junior prom. Everything was fine until I had to return the car the next morning and it wouldn't start. Cathy told me over the phone from work that her husband, Bill, would come over to check it out. I had always known she was married, but this would be my first time meeting him.

I waited on the front lawn until Bill pulled up in his pickup.

"You Mike?" he asked cheerfully. "I've heard all about you," he said, shaking my hand. It was clear that he was totally unsuspecting of any sort of lewd behavior between his wife and me. "Alright, so let's check this thing out."

After determining the problem we both jumped in his pickup and went down to the auto supply store to get a new starter. I helped him install the starter and jumpstart the car.

"We need to keep the battery running for a bit," he said. "Let's go for a spin," and then, "What the heck, let's grab lunch." The man was generous and kind, and it made me feel like a total dirt bag for banging his wife.

"What's your problem?" Cathy wanted to know when I didn't show up for our next illicit appointment. "I lent you my car—don't I deserve a little something in return?"

"I met your husband," I told her. "He's a nice guy; I just can't do it anymore." She was less than thrilled to see that my conscience had gotten the best of me, and was prepared to fight dirty. My name was crossed off the schedule and I was assigned only a few hours for the following week.

Mrs. DiMercurio sensed my anxiety and started to probe for answers. I tried to dodge the subject.

"My boss just hates me."

"But why?" she asked. "There must be some reason."

Finally, I gave in and told her the whole story. She was infuriated. Nothing I could say was going to stop her; she grabbed her keys and headed, like a bulldozer, straight back to work to confront Cathy. I was too embarrassed to go along, but I heard later from my coworkers—who were all well aware of the affair—that Mrs. DiMercurio ripped right into her, accusing her of sexual harassment, child abuse, and who knows what else.

Going back to work was awkward, but it felt good to have someone sticking up for me. Needless to say, Cathy left me alone after that. I stuck around work for a while longer until a dramatic incident the following summer caused me to throw in the towel.

Paul joined the crew as a cook again for the summer, and got right back into his previous role. This time it was Lizzie who announced her pregnancy. Out of frustration Paul dumped a fifty-gallon barrel of waste oil in the parking lot. The next morning, I was the one called on to clean up the mess under the threat of Paul's termination at the restaurant should I refuse. I did the job and then promptly quit.

Not long after that, I spent a night over at Angelo's. My fellow stuntman and I stayed out late that evening, and before we knew it, had passed his curfew.

"Oh crap, I'm in so much trouble!" Angelo blurted, as he looked at his watch.

The front door was locked when we got home, so we went around back to the sliding door, carefully slid it open and crept in as quietly as possible.

The lights flipped on, revealing Angelo's dad, Frank Sposetto—a large Italian man who looked to me like a mobster of *The Godfather* variety, sitting in the living room. "You're grounded!" he shouted in his deep, booming voice with a finger pointed at Angelo.

Angelo froze up like a deer caught in the headlights. I smirked. The finger quickly found a new target. "What are you grinning at? You're grounded too!"

"I don't even live here," I laughed.

"Well you do now, and you're grounded," he said, shaking his finger at me.

I didn't know what to think; he looked pretty serious. "I can't be grounded, I have to find a job," I replied.

"Not anymore you don't; you work for me now."

Is this guy for real or what? I was almost afraid to speak for a moment. I felt responsible, like I had with Tommy. Angelo was in trouble and it was my fault.

The silence was broken by the sound of Frank's booming laughter. He was quite amused by what he had just done.

"So I work for you now?"

"Yep," he replied. "You're going to work at my carwash. Be ready at 5:00 a.m. Monday morning. As for the rest of the weekend, you're both grounded; you'll be pulling weeds."

I didn't even think of opposing him. Monday morning I was up early and ready to go to work at Rainbow Carwash in downtown Oakland. We arrived just in time for the morning meeting. The crew was a rough-looking bunch; most of the guys had been in and out of jail. I was sympathetic with them, as they had similar stories of poor parenting and abuse, and I could see they were doing the best they could to provide for their families. It seemed that I was always drawn to the guys who were struggling the most, trying to encourage them.

One day at work, Frank came by the carwash and called to me from across the parking lot, "Meet me at the car dealership down the street at noon. Don't be late."

When I arrived, Frank was there waiting. "Pick one," he said, pointing to a row of Camaros and Firebirds.

"What do you mean, pick one?" I asked.

"Pick the one you like," he replied. "I'll take care of the down payment, and you'll make the monthly payments after that."

My eyes settled on a 1977 Firebird, "This one is just like the car on *Rockford Files*!" Frank shook his head, laughing. "It's my favorite show," I replied.

"Well, then get that one," said Frank. He hollered at the owner of the lot, "He wants the '77 Firebird!"

I was relieved to get rid of the guilt-ridden Nova my dad had so graciously hustled. As usual, Dad burst my bubble. "No one does anything without expecting something in return."

I quickly stuck up for Frank. "He's just nice like that," I said.

"Don't be surprised if he asks you for a blow job."

I didn't believe that Frank had ulterior motives, but I told myself at the first incident where I saw a hint that he could be anything like my dad, I was out of there.

We had been watching football all afternoon. Frank was really into the game. He had put bets on his favorite team, and had a lot riding on their performance. For me it was just a game. So when Frank jumped out of his seat and started yelling at the screen when his team was down, I found the scene amusing and chuckled at his intensity. Immediately, Frank turned, aiming at me with the same pointer finger he had used a couple months earlier when Angelo and I had been caught sneaking in. "What are you laughing at?" he yelled. "I just lost thousands of dollars on that play. Pack your stuff and get the hell out of here!"

I turned and went straight to my room to pack up. Angelo ran behind me, "He was just kidding, he didn't really mean anything by it."

Later that evening, Frank apologized, "I just got carried away with the game; please don't leave." But I was already having flashbacks to my dad's light-switch temper, and nothing anyone could say would convince me to stick around after that.

Chapter Ten
Shattered Dreams

At the beginning of my senior year in high school, everything seemed to be under control. I was back at the DiMercurio's and enjoying my new job at a local steakhouse, with smells that reminded me of Grandma's kitchen.

At school, what promised to be my best year lay ahead of me. I had a whole heap of good friends and a steady girlfriend, Tracy, whom I'd been seeing since the junior prom. Angelo and I had worked hard all summer filming our feature film, *Death at Bodine Creek*. The film still needed editing, but we were proud of the footage we had shot and anticipated that it would be a great hit at school.

In cross-country and track-and-field, I was a star athlete. With strong performances my junior year, this led into my senior year where I would be the one to beat from Granada High. All hope was on me to come in ahead of my rival, Rob Wentworth from Livermore High.

In spite of all I had going for me, I felt terribly lonely. I was angry with my dad for not taking responsibility and playing an active role in my life, and at the same time, I longed for a relationship with him. The DiMercurio's had welcomed me back with no questions asked, and they were great, but they could never replace my real family. I felt sad to have blown things at the Sposetto's, and I still thought often about Frank, who for a while had been such a positive father figure. I couldn't understand why I wasn't able to forgive him for his outburst. After that I avoided their house, but Angelo and I remained friends.

My relationship with Tracy was constantly on the rocks. Dad had taught me that sex was the answer to everything, but that didn't seem to be working out in this case. I was learning quickly that sex and love were two different things, and I had no idea how to love. Instead I was building walls while trying my best just to stay afloat.

That year I was under a lot of stress. I got tired of giving fake smiles and telling everyone I was fine when I wasn't. At some point, I began drinking to help numb the pain enough to cope with daily life. Occasionally I found comfort in talking to one of Tracy's neighbors, Irene, a single mom with a young son, who was more than willing to offer motherly advice. She could see the pressure I was under and seemed genuinely concerned about my wellbeing. When Irene offered to let me stay with her, the idea of being close to Tracy was more than I could resist, so I packed up and moved in and once again found a new home.

I hadn't stayed with Irene for long before things started getting complicated. One Saturday afternoon, after I returned home from work, Irene let me know that my dad had called. She had taken the liberty of having a discussion with him regarding the level of stress I was under.

"We both think you should slow down a bit," she told me.

"Thanks, but I can't," I replied, trying to censor the sarcasm I felt. "I need the work hours to make my car payments and have enough left over for gas and food."

"You know," Irene said, "you could drop out of school to take some of the stress away. You can always go back and attend night school to earn your diploma after you've saved up a bit."

"Finishing school is kind of important to me," I told her, annoyed, but trying my best to stay calm. "I just need to focus and get it done."

"But Mike, you're under so much pressure. Your dad and I just want you to know that we both think it would be okay if you need to do that. Look at me, I only went as far as the tenth grade, and I'm doing just fine."

"That may have worked out for you but I'm wanting more for my life..."

Wow! I thought. *Typical Dad, running away from his responsibilities, and now he wants me to do the same.* I felt myself fuming. *Instead of offering to help me out so I can finish high school like a normal father, he advises me to just drop out and give up!*

Quitting school was a solution that had never even crossed my mind, and there was no way I was even going to give a second thought to the idea. I tried to politely deflect Irene's comments, but that conversation turned out to be only the beginning of her unsolicited advice about the matter. It started to feel like she was on a mission, and I couldn't grasp why she was so determined to see me drop out of school—that is, until the day she took the initiative to draw out a budget and savings plan for me. Irene had figured that by quitting school, I could work more hours, pay my car loan and expenses, save up a little and have enough left over to—and here's the catch—begin paying rent. *I really thought she had my best interest in mind.* There had never been any discussion about me paying rent. It was a letdown to discover her true motives. *Dad was right,* I thought. *No one helps you for free.*

Meanwhile, my relationship with Tracy had been turning sour. I was miserable at communication and was borderline abusiveness in my behavior toward her. Eventually she had had enough, and called it quits.

***

Since Tracy and I were no longer an item, and Irene had turned out to be a disappointment, I decided to find myself a new place to live. I was tired of living off the kindness of others. The DiMercurio's would probably have taken me back, but I felt guilty about having moved out twice already, after they had made a room especially for me in their garage. I couldn't face asking them again.

Bound and determined to make a change, I began looking in the newspaper to find a roommate. The apartment share I settled on was farther away than I had wanted, but the price was right, and the two other guys, Todd and Josh, seemed nice enough. Todd was tall and lanky, and extremely shy, but seemed to have a great personality. Josh was a short, stocky bodybuilder who was totally in love with himself and his muscles. The jock was rarely home, and when he was, he spent most of his time working out at the gym and posing in front of the mirror, which Todd and I found hilarious.

Having a place of my own was kind of exciting. We had no furniture and began to populate the living room with apple crates and a couple of lamps we picked up at Goodwill. Finally I found an old couch that someone had dumped on the side of the road; it was stained and smelly, but comfortable.

Working at the restaurant was proving to be a lifesaver for me. After school I would work at the steakhouse and grab as many half-eaten steaks, potatoes and veggies I could off the plates that were coming back to get washed. At home I would whip up some of the craziest concoctions imaginable. What the heck, it was food, and I was just trying to survive the best I could. Sometimes, it came down to food or gas; I needed the gas to get to work, so scrounging off plates made perfect sense to me.

By the time track season arrived, my life was purely about maintenance. I was on autopilot: school, work, run, eat and sleep. I didn't want anyone to know how badly I was struggling, so I tried my best to put up a façade. I wasn't quite as good at that as my father, and my friendships were suffering.

With a big race ahead of me, I would be going head-to-head with my cross-town rival, Rob Wentworth. The pressure was on and I was having flashbacks to the time when Colonel Balder drove me to the cross-country meet back in Los Angeles. I could hear his foster-parent voice urging me to win, not so much because he cared, but because he didn't want to be associated with a loser. He was no longer in the picture, but now at Granada High all eyes were on me. Everyone wanted me to win: the coach, the team, my teachers, the whole school. I don't know whether I was more afraid of winning or losing, but still, I froze. That morning I stayed home from school and showed up at the track meet toward the end. From the times that were clocked that day, I could easily have come in first.

Still, I managed to move past the day of the race and was soon back on top of the game. Race by race I continued my winning streak through the Tri-Valley semifinals. With an easy win, I was confident I'd steal an easy win at the finals as well. When the day finally came, I was in the home stretch with no one in sight. The finishing line was just a few yards ahead and I was already celebrating my victory when out of nowhere I was passed in the last few strides.

The local paper sports headlines read, "Lemke Edges Out Casey". The funny thing was that it felt like a relief to me not to be in the limelight. It was easier to deal with the disappointment than to have to bear the praise of everyone around me. I felt anything but praiseworthy.

***

My favorite teacher, Mrs. Van Steinberg from the film studies class, picked up on the fact that I was struggling. One afternoon she called me at work to encourage me to hang in there. It felt good to know that someone cared.

We were getting ready to screen the movie I had been working so hard on, and I didn't care about the grade, I just wanted her to be proud of me. Finally, the day came, and the film was shown in class to rave reviews. Everyone loved it. The event was one I had been anticipating for so long, and it was every bit as successful as I had dreamed, but to my surprise winning didn't make me feel any better. I couldn't understand. *Why do I still feel so empty inside?* I was totally cracking under the stress of trying to support myself.

The next week was spent with a headache, which was just too hard to shake. I didn't even go to work, but called in sick. I didn't want to see or speak to anyone. After about a week, I just snapped. I packed some clothes, tossed them in my car, and headed to Los Angeles, arriving at Dad's house late that afternoon.

"What are you doing?" Dad asked.

"Don't know," I answered. I had no idea what I was doing or why I had run to his house. That was the very place I'd spent so many years trying to run from. After arriving, I completely lost control and broke down crying. I don't think he knew what to do, so he whipped up a batch of Hamburger Helper, which strangely helped.

I spent the next few days just trying to gain control of my emotions. Dad and I had some good laughs, and he seemed to be happy to have me there. I took a job at McDonalds and with one month left in the school year, resigned myself to being a failure and completely gave up on my dream of finishing school and becoming an astronaut.

On what should have been my graduation day, I climbed into my car and headed up to Livermore. Parking outside the school fence and peering in from a distance like an invisible ghost, I watched as each of my friends walked up to receive his or her diplomas. I listened for the spot where my name would have been called, and felt the full force of failure when there was not even a pause reserved for me.

"Life's a bitch and then you die," my dad's voice was ringing in my head.

The shame I felt bore a hole through my gut. In my mind, I was a complete and total failure. I think this was the first time that I had begun to feel completely empty inside. The very next day, with no place to live, I decided to move to the Del Valle campground with my brother Paul.

Chapter Eleven
Same Shit, Different Day

The Del Valle campground was just fourteen dollars a week. The price was right since neither of us had much to spend, and it gave me the opportunity to hide from the familiar faces I might see in town. At fourteen dollars a week, the price was right since neither of us had much to spend, and it gave me the opportunity to hide from the familiar faces I might see in town. I had been well-known at school, and had already run into a couple of people who had, unknowingly, applauded me for graduating. It was as painful to realize that they hadn't noticed I was gone as it was to be reminded of my failure. It was a sore subject I had no desire to confront. At the campground I had control of who knew where I was and who would come for a visit. I did get back in touch with a number of my closest friends that summer, including Duane, Angelo and Todd. After a couple of months, when we had finally outstayed our welcome at the campsite, I moved in with Todd, who had taken up work installing carpets in the East Bay area. He helped me get a job at a carpet store.

Two years later, the carpet store folded, and I was out of work, barely making ends meet when Dad called and invited me to join him in Denver, Colorado. He had already convinced Paul to settle not far from him in the small town of Lafayette. So when Dad contacted me, he didn't need to do a whole lot of convincing.

"Promise me that we'll all go skiing together, like a family."

He promised, and by the end of the phone call, Dad had me writing down the names of the interstates and highways I should take. A couple days after our conversation, I received a large packet in the mail containing AAA maps with detailed instructions telling me which roads to take, where to stop for gas, the motel where I should spend the night, which steak I should order at a restaurant, and where to pull over on the highway and take a picture by the "Welcome to Colorful Colorado" sign. It was the exact same journey he had taken, and I followed it to the letter—it was never an option to question Dad.

My arrival in Denver, Colorado reminded me of a scene from the movie *Apocalypse Now.* My favorite line in the movie is the very first line in the opening scene. Martin Sheen, who played Captain Willard, is in a hotel room. He's awakened by the loud vibrating sound of a passing helicopter. As he goes to the window and lifts the blinds, he peers out onto the chaotic scene outside his window. The reality of where he's at and what he sees hits him. "Saigon... shit!!!," and wonders exactly what he has gotten himself into.

I felt the exact same way driving down Interstate 70. As I crested the hill, I got my first glimpse of the city. I said to myself, *"Denver....shit!!!"* The reality of my decision hit me— *What the heck was I thinking?* I had no idea.

Denver was a big city. It looked just like Los Angeles. I was beginning to get homesick already. It was difficult to leave Todd and Duane.

My first impression of the city was not the mountains, as I had imagined, but rather the same huge buildings and busy downtown that I had left behind in L.A. I had heard Denver was known as the "Mile-High City", and had expected to find a big mountain town nestled in Colorado's famous Rockies, rather than the flat plain-land city with a distant mountain skyline that met me. As I drove down I-70 through Denver and pulled up in front of Dad's Aurora apartment, I was already having second thoughts. Still, I always clung to the hope that things could be different.

Upon my arrival in Colorado, it was easy to see Dad had been sober for a while, and he looked good. I had to laugh as I looked around his apartment. *It seems the same guy who designs furnished apartments in California has also penetrated the Colorado market with the same green shag carpet and green couches.*

The next morning when Dad left for work, I started to feel scared. Every time I was suckered into this whole father/son thing, I was the one on the losing end. "Keep an eye on him," Grandma told me when I stopped in to say goodbye. "Okay," I had told her, chuckling to myself. *Isn't he supposed to be the parent?* Grandma was certainly happy to see me going to Denver. *Am I crazy to think things could be different this time?*

By the time I had hauled my things up to Dad's apartment, he was already itching to go out.

"Time to go, we're burning daylight," he claimed. It was a line straight out of his favorite John Wayne movie, *The Cowboys.*

We picked up Paul in Lafayette and drove to Lookout Mountain where Dad said there was a great steakhouse. It was a long scenic drive, which gave us plenty of time to catch up.

"So how do you like Colorado so far?" Paul asked.

"It's nice, but I guess I just always thought that Denver would be in the mountains."

"Just wait until the snow comes in, and you'll get plenty of mountains," Dad piped in. "Denver's got character—you'll love it. We get three hundred days of sunlight a year here."

"So why's it called the Mile-High city?" I asked.

"It just doesn't feel that high since it's so far inland," he explained, "but just 'cause it's flat, doesn't mean Denver's not high. It is literally 5,280 feet above sea level. If you go to the state capitol building, you can find that it's written on one of the steps that it's exactly one-mile high—but they marked the wrong step, so the right one has a gold dot on it."

I was impressed, "Wow, how'd you know all that?"

"I read about it, it's really interesting. You should see the capitol building, too; it's beautiful. The dome on top is covered in real twenty-four karat gold leaf, because Denver started as a mining town during the gold rush."

"Are you sure you're not moonlighting as a tour guide?" I joked. We all laughed. "What else do you know about this city?"

"Well, it has a heck of a lot of breweries," he smiled. "But don't worry, I'm not going there. I've been sober since I got here." *What a relief,* I thought. I could hardly believe this was my dad talking.

We dropped Paul off and headed home. Dad said that he and I needed to make a stop downtown so he could pick something up. We pulled into an alley behind a big apartment complex. "Wait here, I'll only be a minute." From the looks of the place, I was more than happy to wait in the car.

After about thirty minutes, I started to feel like I had when he used to leave me in the car at the topless bar. Finally, after about an hour, he returned. I was so glad to get out of that place. We stopped at the store to pick up a few things, and then headed home.

As we put away the groceries, I searched quickly through the bags and was again relieved to find that there was no beer. I turned to Dad, smiling, only to find him pulling a big bag of weed out of his pocket. He sat down on the couch and began to roll a joint.

"Same shit, different day," I mumbled under my breath. Dad offered me a hit, but the smell made my stomach turn. He finished the joint on his own and then moved on to a bowl of chocolate ice cream covered in Captain Crunch.

Dad got me a job working with him at the machine shop, where I enjoyed learning to weld. Dad was quite talented, and it was amazing watching him work, but life at home was a different story. Sitting around and watching him get stoned night after night was getting old fast. After a while of working at the machine shop, I began looking for a second job. The plan had always been to get my own place as soon as I was making enough money, and I wanted that to happen sooner rather than later. Before long, I began working for a drugstore stocking shelves.

When I finally saved enough to get my own place, I was so excited. "Dad, I looked at an apartment today," I told him.

"What's wrong with the place upstairs?" he replied.

I wanted to be farther away so that I could have a chance at having my own life, but I didn't want to upset him. Unable to find a good excuse that wouldn't hurt his feelings, I found myself signing on another furnished apartment, exactly like Dad's, in the same building. At the age of nineteen I was hoping to be completely out on my own.

"Let's you and I go get some stuff for your new place," Dad suggested.

The following Saturday morning, Dad came up with what he considered to be a great idea. We drove to some model homes just outside of Aurora.

"Just look around and if you have any questions I'll be in the office," the salesman said as he walked away to speak to other potential clients. I looked around and admired the decor in the model homes.

"Do you like this?" Dad asked holding up a platter.

"I guess," I replied. Dad swiftly dropped the platter down the back of his pants. This was his idea of shopping.

"What about this candle?"

I nodded, and he slipped it into his pocket.

"Be right back," he said. "I'm going to the car to unload."

After the second trip to the car, I was getting nervous. "Come on, Dad, let's go."

"Okay," he replied as he walked back into the house, boldly strutting out a moment later with a large framed painting.

***

Feeling lonely and far from home, I spoke regularly with my friend Todd, who still lived there.

"What would you think about me moving there?" Todd asked.

"Dude—that would be totally awesome!"

Over the next few weeks we began to devise a plan to start our own business, T&M Carpet Installation. I would have to quit the machine shop, and I knew Dad wouldn't relish the idea, so I postponed telling him. Dad and my brother Paul had been arguing, which made things worse. As the time got closer to Todd's arrival, Paul announced that he would be packing up and heading back to California. *I'm surprised he lasted this long,* I thought. I still hadn't told Dad about Todd's imminent arrival, and it was getting even harder to muster up the courage. So I did what I normally did: I waited until the last minute.

Todd would be arriving sometime that afternoon, and we were driving home from work when I finally opened my mouth. "Well, he's just coming here to check things out and—maybe—start a new business if all goes well. You know, with construction booming, there's a lot of work to be done."

In a matter of days, Todd had moved into his own apartment in our building and landed a job as a sub-contractor with Colorado Carpet World, and our new business was up and running. We immediately got to work installing carpet and linoleum at a local condominium project called Hearthstone, which had about sixty units in the first phase.

I quit my job at the drugstore, but continued working at the machine shop, which left me only evenings and weekends to work with Todd. This arrangement was clearly not going to work for long, and I'd have to break the news to Dad eventually.

One Saturday morning, when Dad and I went skiing, as was our weekend tradition, I waited until he was good and stoned before I spoke to him.

Dad could tell I was trying to get up the nerve to say something. "Spit it out," he said.

"Well, I was thinking..."

"Well that's something new—you're thinking?"

"Yes," I replied in a quiet voice—not wanting to get him angry. "Dad, I'm going to go to work for Todd."

"If you want to spend so much time with Todd, why don't you just get married and move in together," was his response.

At first he was pissed, but by the time we had finished skiing, he was over it.

One night after dinner, Dad told me about another one of his so-called "great plans". The owners of the machine shop were Jehovah's Witnesses, and they had tried to convert him. Apparently, they had even implied that he would make more money, so Dad had been playing along. "But when it comes to going to their stupid church, fuck them," he said. "I have a better way to make more money."

We jumped in the car and drove to the shop, which had been closed for several hours. My dad, who was shop foreman at the time, opened the door, punched in the alarm code, and retrieved a list from his shirt pocket and disappeared. He came out of the shop with about eight boxes of transmission parts— mostly clutch plates, and pressure plates, he said. I helped him load up the car, and we went home.

Dad decided that since I was more available during the day, I should go around Denver and visit a few transmission shops to let them know I had parts to sell. He said that the parts in the box were worth about $1,200, and I should offer to sell at about $500. "If anyone asks, tell them you got the parts from a friend in California. And make sure you ask them if there's anything else they need."

My first call was in Lakewood, on the opposite side of Denver. As luck would have it, the first transmission shop I stopped at wanted everything I had and even placed an order for more. I let them know that I would be back in about a week.

Dad was as giddy as a child when he learned of my success. The money was like a drug to him. "Half for me, half for you," he said. I didn't want the money, but it was hard to say 'no' to Dad.

"We probably shouldn't be doing this," I mumbled uncomfortably.

"Cool it, Mike, it's okay; that's why people have insurance."

"If Grandma knew what we were doing...."

"Pussy," he fumed. "You always do half the act, like such a pussy."

After the fourth trip, the orders were getting larger, and I was starting to fear getting caught. I didn't want to go to jail, but Dad didn't seem concerned one bit. By now I was on a first-name basis with Betty and Tim from the transmission shop. Even though I tried to space out my visits to their shop to give me time to have been able to get to California and back, they were getting wise to the fact that I was getting the parts locally.

"I don't give a damn where you're getting them," Tim said, "just as long as they keep coming."

Dad was eager to meet our faithful clients, so I took him along one Saturday. He quickly hit it off with both Betty and Tim.

"Say," said Betty, "I was wondering, do you folks only deal with transmission parts, or is there anything else you can get?"

"What did you have in mind?" my dad schmoozed.

"Well, we're remodeling our house right now, so there's a lot of different things we need," she said. "Just tell us if anything comes up."

Before he opened his mouth, I knew what he was thinking. "Why don't you just make a list of what you need, and I'll see what I can do," he winked.

He waited until we got in the car to ask, "What kind of security do they have at night at Hearthstone?"

Dad had been out to see me numerous times while I was working at Hearthstone. The new units under construction were filled with interesting items: cabinets, vanities, sinks, faucets, and all variety of materials one would need to remodel a house.

The following evening Todd and I found ourselves looting the construction site. My dad was able to do a lot of convincing and conniving small talk and before we knew it, Todd had already been paid off. "Two hundred bucks," he told me. "How much are you guys getting?"

"I have no idea," I answered. "I'm really sorry my dad got you involved with this."

"I wasn't about to turn him down. Dude, your dad terrifies the shit out of me."

"Tell me about it."

My dad was able to do a lot of conniving small talk and before I knew it, Dad and I were keeping the money we were making in safety deposit boxes, since it wasn't safe to deposit it in our bank accounts. Before long I had about $4,000, while Dad had more like $20,000. Obviously not quite the fifty-fifty split I'd been promised, but I didn't care.

Other than stealing, working, and skiing, most of my time in Colorado still consisted of sitting around in Dad's living room watching him and Todd get stoned and eat ice cream. Not exactly my idea of a good time. Pot just wasn't my thing.

After a while I started thinking about an old girlfriend of mine, Tami, who was now living in Texas. I called her up, and we began to chat over the phone. The relationship was reignited, and we began to talk about getting together again.

"Are you talking to that dumb bitch again?" Dad growled. I could tell he was getting mad because I wasn't spending as much time with him.

"Her name is Tami," I replied. "She's not a bitch... and she's coming to visit, so I hope you'll be nice to her." I was trying my best to stand up to him, but I wasn't very good at it.

"How long is the bitch staying?" he demanded.

"I don't know, a couple weeks, maybe." I backed down. As much as I was excited about her visit, Dad seemed to resent the idea, so I played it off like it was no big deal. "Tami needs a vacation," I said, "and she wants to see Denver."

During her visit, Tami offered to cook dinner for all of us over at my dad's. The meal was delicious, and an inviting change from our usual hamburgers. After we had finished eating, Tami ran upstairs to my apartment to take a shower. As soon as she was gone, Dad dug in. "I wouldn't feed that shit to pigs."

"I thought it was great," I said.

"I enjoyed it," agreed Todd.

"Well, next time she decides she wants to poison us, don't invite me!"

Tami came back after her shower, cleared up, and did all the dishes. The next morning Dad informed me that he had stayed up half the night rewashing all the dishes and re-cleaning his kitchen. "Dumb bitch doesn't even know how to wash dishes," he complained.

When Tami and I were alone together, things were great, but in front of my dad, I kept my distance. His disapproving looks constrained me from showing affection or enthusiasm in his presence. It didn't take long for Tami to take notice.

"Your dad doesn't like me, does he?" Tami asked.

"No, that's not true," I tried to tell her.

"Oh, come on, Mike, it couldn't be more obvious," she said. "Look, I really like you, but I don't want to come between you and your dad."

I knew what she really wanted to say was, "Why don't you stick up for me?" So I resolved to confront Dad; I was ready to set some boundaries. I rehearsed my speech and thought through the answers to his potential reactions. When I felt ready to face him, I entered his apartment with clear intention.

Dad spun around and looked me in the eyes. "Got something to say? Spit it out!"

"No," I replied, sheepishly, losing my nerve.

"Well, I guess that bitch will keep you company when I'm gone," he resumed.

"What do you mean, 'when you're gone'?"

"I'm moving back to California," he said, catching me completely off guard. "I'm over the snow and the cold weather, so if your girlfriend wants to stay here, be my guest."

Is this just a threat to get rid of Tami? I wondered. In either case, it was infuriating. *I came out to Colorado just to be with you, Todd followed, we were starting a new life together, and now you're just leaving?*

Well, the next time the subject of Dad came up between Tami and me, I could tell she'd had enough. "Maybe if I wasn't around, your dad would stay. Do you want me to just go?"

My silence was all the answer she needed.

It frustrated me that Dad got his way, but it didn't change his tune. He continued to talk about moving back to California. Other than skiing, I wasn't a big fan of the snow, and with Dad leaving, I didn't see much point in sticking around either. It seemed like a good excuse for me to return to my grandparents in Red Bluff and get away from Dad. I felt bad leaving Todd, but he gradually accepted the idea, and Dad and I made plans to make the journey together.

Just before leaving, Dad got in a dispute with the landlord over the deposit. On the morning of our departure I climbed upstairs for the last time to double-check the apartment before leaving. As I entered, I heard the water running in the bathroom. I tried to turn it off, only to discover that all the faucets had been super-glued. I tried to open the cabinets, but they were also sealed. Even the refrigerator door had been glued shut.

Dad was standing downstairs, laughing. "That'll teach them to screw me with regard to my deposit!"

We headed out in our two-car convoy through Utah and Nevada on the way back to California. After a long day on the road, we stopped at the same hotel in Nevada where Dad had previously told me to stay on my drive to Denver. We checked in, relaxed for a while, and then headed over to the hotel restaurant to order the same steak Dad had recommended to me a year earlier. I thought the steak tasted great, but apparently this time it didn't meet his expectations, and he had it sent back to the kitchen twice before finally settling on a hamburger. He was pissed.

The next morning Dad hollered to me from the shower, "Could you check and see if this hotel has a Bible?"

"What do you want a Bible for?" I knew darn well he wasn't about to read it. *So what's he up to?* I thought as I began opening the dresser drawers. The third drawer I opened, my eyes landed on a giant turd sitting on top of an open Gideon's Bible.

"You're going to go to hell for shitting on a Bible," I told him.

"Well, I guess they shouldn't have messed with my steak," he said, laughing hysterically.

Chapter Twelve
Rescue Me

After Dad decided to return to Los Angeles, I decided to go live with my grandparents in Red Bluff.

Grandpa was sitting back in his rocking chair watching *Jeopardy* with an open can of Budgie beer on the coffee table across from his seat. I was lying on the couch dozing and half-watching. Grandma, who had just hung up the phone, walked in with a serious look on her face.

"Dad—that was Paul. He needs help, now. We'll need to send Mike down there."

"What are you saying?" I jerked, suddenly fully alert.

"Mike, your dad's been using drugs again; now he's addicted to heroin."

"Heroin, are you sure?"

She nodded her head, eyes tearing up.

"How's he doing it?" I asked.

"He's shooting it, whatever that means."

I didn't want to go, but I wasn't really given an option. I was always the one who played the role of caretaker in the family. *Mike will fix it* seemed to be mantra.

We'd only been back in California from Colorado for three months. I was relieved when Dad had moved to Los Angeles, and I was just starting to enjoy a more peaceful existence in Red Bluff. Now, dutifully, I was packing up my things and heading back into the fire. During the drive, I planned out and rehearsed everything I would say to my dad to rescue him. As I arrived, he was just getting home from work; yes, as always, no matter what Dad was doing to cope, he made it to work. The two of us exchanged hugs in the parking lot and I followed him upstairs to his apartment, which had the same green shag carpet and couches as all the other apartments he and I had ever lived in. I unpacked a few of my own things and then geared up for my confrontation with him.

The Nancy Reagan-style "Just Say No!" speech I had prepared was anything but a hit.

Dad stared at me with blank sarcasm. "Shit, Mike; you have no clue, do you?"

"I know that that shit can kill you, or at least totally mess you up. What if you just quit?"

"If I just quit, huh?" He began ranting, "If, if, if!" Then, seeing the look of panic on my face, he toned it down a bit. "If a frog had wings he wouldn't bump his ass every time he hopped, Mike. It's not as easy as it looks. Don't start passing judgment until you've tried it yourself."

I'm not passing judgment, I thought. This wasn't my first time watching this rodeo, and I could see he was taking me for a ride. "So what you're saying is that I have to shoot up first, to understand what you're going through?"

Dad stood up, his face filled with rage and teeth clenched. He tore his blue work shirt off and yelled, "Get the fuck out of here!" The veins in his neck were bulging and the devil on his arm puffed up as his muscles contracted. He threw his shirt on the ground and pointed to the door. "Get the fuck out of here and don't let the door hit you in the ass on the way out!"

I wasn't about to stick around and become a punching bag, so I opened the door and began my determined exit.

***

Driving north on I-5, I began feeling angry and sad. *What will I tell Grandma?* I thought. *She'll be so disappointed.* I'd been driving about an hour and a half and was nearing the Grapevine area, when the seeds of guilt that Dad had carefully planted finally started to take root. *I should have known better,* I thought. *What a juvenile approach. I was treating him like a teenager; no wonder he got mad!*

The Grapevine is the highest point on California's Interstate 5, which runs north to south. For me this had always been the tipping point between the chaos of L.A. and the freedom and sanity of the road to Red Bluff. *I shouldn't have left so quickly,* I reflected. *But I felt defeated. I should have been more patient and understanding; after all, Dad's right, I don't know what he's going through.* I had driven all this way to stand next to him at a moment when he had no one else. There was no way I could return to Red Bluff without having given it my best effort.

Dad was not at all surprised when I knocked on his door again. It seemed like he had expected me to return. Without saying a word he led me directly into the kitchen, and began his ritual with the devotion and precision of a priest preparing an altar. He took a spoon out of the drawer, bent it, and set it on the table. Then he took out an insulin syringe, a cup of water, and tore off a small piece of his cigarette filter. He added some water to a small pinch of powder on the spoon and brought the concoction to a boil over his lighter. The needle passed through the cigarette filter and the mixture was drawn up through the filter into the syringe.

I was scared to death. *What if he gives me too much—what if it kills me? Why don't I finally have the courage to stand up to him and say 'no'? Why am I still willing to risk my life to keep him quiet? Sad that over the years I learned that pain was to be avoided at all cost.*

Now he turned to me to present the sacrament. Reaching back into the drawer once again, Dad pulled out a rubber tie like the ones doctors use when they take blood. He fastened the tie around my arm, causing my veins to bulge. After carefully choosing a vein in my arm, he slid the needle in and pulled back the plunger of the syringe. I watched as my blood entered the chamber, mixing with the heroin in what I later learned is called "the flash". Dad reached up and released the band from around my arm as the very chemical I came to save him from was now rushing through my veins.

This drug rush felt as though I was being propelled through space at a million miles an hour. Immediately I began to sweat. My head was spinning and I could hardly keep my eyes open, but I still managed to fumble my way to the bathroom to vomit. As I washed my face and rinsed out my mouth, Dad appeared in the doorway and tossed me a towel.

"Time to go score!" he said.

I've never seen him in such a good mood, I thought.

***

We drove to Paramount, the city where Dad grew up, to a low-end hotel. The seedy rooms in the little Heinz hotel had no kitchens. Cooking took place on a hotplate, and dishwashing was done in the bathroom. It was there that I became acquainted with Ray and Dallas. Ray was in his late sixties with extra wrinkles on his face and twenty-plus years of addiction that added a decade to his biological age. Ray loved to talk; I had just met him, and he was already telling me about all the things he planned to do when he quit.

"Shut the hell up Ray; don't get started!" Dallas chimed in, then turned to me. "Been hearing it for ten years, it's getting old." Dallas was in his mid-thirties and said he had a daughter in Texas that he had only seen once.

Dad seemed to get a kick out of telling the guys about how I had thrown up right after shooting up the drug for the first time.

"Paul, don't you think that's kinda fucked up, shooting your boy up with dope?" Dallas replied.

Dad silently shot him a glare and as one might imagine, the conversation moved somewhere else.

What a bunch of losers, I thought. It was odd how drugs, in a bizarre way, could unite people who would otherwise have nothing in common. From my vantage point, it was easy for me to judge them. The math seemed simple enough, and it didn't add up. *If this is the cost of addiction, it's so not worth it. Of course I had these thoughts long* before the power of even the first use of heroin was in my veins. Soon I realized that I was falling into the same trap.

A spider begins to weave its web with a single thread. After that, each thread builds on the next, from line to triangle to spiral, forming an intricate trap. It didn't take long for me to get stuck in the deadly web my father was spinning. I had come to help pull him out, but instead he, along with the demon, had dragged me in, and I didn't have the strength or willpower to resist.

Before long I was doing everything that Dad was doing. I began to work at the machine shop downtown, and in the evenings we would head to Long Beach to score, always checking our backs to see if the cops were following us.

Our dealers, Bobbie and Bud, lived off of social security checks, using heroine to numb the pain of their son's death. They sold it to be able to afford some extra luxuries. The couple—both probably in their forties, though they looked more like they were in their sixties—lived in a two-bedroom dive that was always crawling with people from every walk of life. On any given day, you might run into Gloria the hooker, John the lawyer—who was disbarred due to his drug problem—or Lacy, a bare-bottomed, Kool-Aid bottle-clutching nine-month old whose young addict parents couldn't afford to buy diapers. Addiction doesn't discriminate; all are welcome.

As Dad made negotiations with Bud in the kitchen, I sat with Bobbie, watching reruns of "Emergency". I listened to her recount the details of the motorcycle accident that had killed her son.

"I still have the autopsy report," Bobbie told me as she opened a drawer on the coffee table and pulled out a manila envelope.

I tried to be as sympathetic as possible while listening to her read through the painful pages line by line.

"You're such a good kid," she said, wiping away her tears. "He'd have been about your age by now, you know."

She neatly folded and smoothed the report, put it back in the drawer, and turned to me. "You're clean-cut, Mike. What the hell are you doing here?" Her eyes were serious. "Get out while you still can."

***

I knew she was right. *But what about Dad?*

Dad told me we'd need to look for a new dealer since, as he taught me, it isn't safe for an addict to stay in the same place for long. Our new connections, Raymond and Leo, were in Compton, which was only four miles from home and work, so his current plan made a lot of sense. A bunch of us would head over to Raymond's apartment every night after work to hang out. Leo would deliver the dope and then we'd all shoot up. If someone didn't show up, we would directly assume that he had either overdosed or been arrested.

Money was our biggest challenge at the time. Dad was making about $4,000 a month and I was bringing in $1,200 to $1,500 a month, and we needed about $500 a week for dope. My car payment was ninety days past due, and we were late on rent and utilities, as well as everything else. For a while, I found that I could earn a few grams of dope every weekend by trading my Firebird for Leo's MG Midget so that he could drive his girlfriend around with her two little kids. Soon, my Uncle Ralph helped me find a better investment using the very same car. His close friend, Sergeant Broxton from the Downey Police Department, was willing to help me pay off my debts in exchange for using my car for surveillance. Since it was already known around the local drug scene, it wouldn't stand out. They used the car for a short time and then returned it, and soon we fell into debt again.

Naturally, Dad had his own solution for how to pay off our debts. Just as we had done in Colorado, we would sneak into the machine shop where we worked, steel parts, and sell them. It was even easier to find buyers in California; my dad had lived in the area his whole life and knew all sorts of shops that were willing to make a deal.

Still, we soon found it was necessary to develop a line of credit with Leo, which he was more than willing to do for his 'best customers'. Every Friday, we would cash our checks at the liquor store, buy cigarettes, and then head over to Ray's to 'get well': buy dope, cook it up in the kitchen, and shoot up. We would drop the used syringes into a hole that had been knocked into his wall and head out to the closest Mexican restaurant, then go home and nod off while watching *The A-Team*.

Dad knew we were pushing it with our overextended line of credit. "Leo's goanna be pissed," he said on a Saturday morning as we passed the little MG Midget parked on the street in front of Ray's apartment.

As soon as the apartment door swung open, Leo reared and pounced. He whipped out a twenty-five automatic and pushed it into my side.

"Go get the fucking money, Paul. If you don't, I'll shoot him."

"Dude, I almost thought you were serious," I laughed, lifting my arm to pat him on the shoulder.

"I am totally fucking serious! If your dad doesn't get me that fucking money, you'll find out how fucking serious I am." His face didn't flinch. *There's no way my life's going to end in this nasty dope house,* I thought.

Leo put the gun back in his pocket, and I retreated to the couch to watch TV and wait for Dad to come back and pay up. I was dope-sick, but I knew better than to ask for a fix. Instead I just sat there, staring glassy-eyed at the TV as the usual cast of characters drifted in and out, until eventually I dozed off.

When I woke up, it was evening and there was still no sign of Dad. I tried calling the house, but got no answer. My body was shaking from the heroin withdrawal, and I wanted a fix badly.

"Know where he might be?" asked Leo as I got off the phone.

"Nah, but I'm guessing he's out scamming to raise some money," I laughed, but I wanted to cry. "Don't worry, he's pretty good at that!"

As the night wore on I was getting sicker and sicker; the diarrhea and sweats had kicked in. *Come on Dad, I need some dope to get well.*

Leo came and sat beside me on the couch. "You're not looking too good."

"Yup," I said, "I've been sick all day."

"You know what, I'll give you a taste until your dad shows up with the dough," he said, shaking his head sympathetically. "Shit, man, where is he?"

I shrugged. Leo wasn't such a bad guy. In fact, other than this incident, I had always like him.

"Maybe he's been busted for robbing a bank," he joked, trying to lighten the mood. When he laughed, you could see his gold tooth. I smiled to myself, thinking about how Dad and I had often joked about pulling Leo's tooth and selling the gold to buy dope.

I must have dozed off, because I woke up, nauseated and sweating, as the sun was rising. I was still imprisoned on the couch in Ray's apartment, and I still hadn't heard from Dad. Leo took pity on me again and gave me another fix.

"It's not your fault your dad's not here yet," he said, "but he'd better have a damned good explanation for this."

It started to look like Dad wasn't coming, so we decided to go out and find him. We jumped in Leo's MG and drove toward Dad's apartment, stopping at a small taco shop in Compton for a burrito on the way.

Leo smiled and winked at me as he paid the cashier. "I'm still keeping tabs," he said.

I don't know who felt worse: me, for being left behind, or Leo, for not being taken seriously. For when we arrived at the house, Dad was in bed asleep as if nothing had happened.

"What's up?" he grumbled as I woke him up.

"Leo wants his money, and he could have shot me!"

"Tell him I'll get it for him in a couple hours," he said, pulling the covers around him and closing his eyes.

Dad had called his old boss, Jerry, who had agreed to front us some money, but only if we promised to make an appointment at the Methadone clinic.

Within a couple of hours we got the money to pay off Leo and to get just enough dope to get well for that day. We would have to go to the methadone clinic soon.

That night I had a bad dream. I was walking around at the beach and went to explore some tide pools when I saw my Grandpa floating face down in the water. I pulled him out, but there was nothing I could do; he was dead.

The next morning, after sharing the dream with Dad, we decided to call Grandpa to check on him.

"Everything's fine over here," Grandpa said. "How are things going with your dad? Are you making any progress?"

"Sure, yeah," I assured him. "Things are looking a lot better," I assured him. "I should be able to come home soon."

I sat and stared at the wall. It was good to hear Grandpa's voice, *but what was I supposed to tell him? That I was now as ensnared as my father? That I had run out of money and had been held at gunpoint for not being able to pay off my addiction?*

That night Dad and I were watching television after dinner when the phone rang. We were told that Grandpa had been rushed to the hospital, with CPR in progress. He was pronounced dead on arrival.

I directed my anger toward an internal punching bag in the shape of my dad. *I should have been home with Grandpa. THUD. Not here wasting my life away. THUD. All you ever do is drag me down. THUD. I know misery loves company, but why do I have to be yours? THUD, THUD, THUD.*

We had to score before we could leave for Red Bluff, so I put down the boxing gloves, and pulled out my thinking cap. *Leo is out of the question, but...*

"Bobbie and Bud will understand our grief!"

We headed over to Long Beach, where the sympathetic dealers fronted us some dope. Then we drove off toward Red

Bluff, the place I had left nearly a year earlier, but still thought of as home.

***

The funeral was well attended; Grandpa had lots of friends. I wanted so much to stay with Grandma, but I was far too embarrassed. It was no longer possible to hide the fact that my rescue efforts had failed. It was clear as day to Grandma, as well as to everyone else that I had fallen down the same rabbit hole. In any case, it is hard to hide under the veil of being a heroin addict even from those who do not use.

***

Three days later, we were on our way back. It was time to make good on our promise to go to the methadone clinic. We arrived early for our 8:00 a.m. appointment, both in early withdrawal with runny noses and feeling like crap. The long line looked to me like a herd of cattle, just like at the dope house: same people, same stories, same lost hopes and certainly the same shattered dreams.

"First time?" asked the lady in front of us.

"Yes, we're here for the thirty-day detox."

"Wow; that sucks."

"Does it work?"

"Hell no, man. This place is like Hotel California. Hell, me and my old man have done the detox program at least ten times." She went on to explain how she was on maintenance, which meant she would be coming in every day... forever.

I was feeling defeated before we had gotten inside the front door of the clinic. Eventually, we were pushed forward, squeezed through the door and driven into the doctor's office, where we were each given the first daily dose of government-sanctioned dope, which would decrease each day over the next month.

Each day, as our dose got smaller, we felt worse and worse. People standing in line around us were constantly talking about dope and making deals, but somehow we managed to make it through those grueling thirty days without caving. The day we finished, Dad gave me a "high five", "We made it!" he said. "Let's go celebrate!" Dad's idea of a celebration was heading over to a new connection he found, and we were right back where we started. Only this time our connection, Candy, expected me to provide her with sadistic sexual favors in exchange for a good deal on dope.

Candy's idea of a good time was forcing me to pinch her nipples, spank her and slap her face. What scared the hell out of me was that, often times, her boyfriend was nodding out in the living room with the rest of the crowd.

Around that time things began to get a little scary. Dad was always talking about how much he missed Grandpa and that's when he came up with the bright idea: "Hey, let's kill ourselves". A chill ran down my spine because I could tell by the look in his eyes he was serious as a heart attack. He looked like he had it all planned out in his head that we would over-dose together. "What if it didn't work and one of us woke up? He paused and thought, *well, we will just have to make sure that does not happen.*

In the days following, Dad was becoming more and more obsessed with the idea of our deaths. I was afraid to get in the car with him because he would constantly say, "I could steer into the path of that truck head on and boom, it would all be over." He even went as far as to say, "Well if you are going to be a pussy about it, I'll just cut your throat in your sleep and then take care of myself."

This is when I began having trouble sleeping. I was dreaming of what Dad might do to me. I was unhappy with where my life was but I certainly was not ready to throw in the towel. As much as I hated performing for Candy, I still had hope.

"Just give her what she wants and suck it up," Dad ordered. "What's the matter with you? Are you gay?"

I was sick and tired of being pimped and molested—I didn't know which was worse. It was awkward and repulsive, and turned out to be the straw that broke the camel's back.

On Father's Day, I woke up with the same sour taste in my mouth that met me every morning. I wanted badly to be able to call Grandpa, but I couldn't. *I should get something for Dad*, I thought, *but what do you get for a dad that has spent his life screwing up yours?*

We went about our day as usual, trying to get money to score. Dad pulled up to the liquor store for some beer. *Maybe I can find a small gift for him here.* So after he had paid, I lingered behind, but couldn't find anything he wouldn't scoff at.

"Happy Father's Day!" called the clerk as I headed toward the door. *Me?* My dad had already left. *A father?* He may as well have dropped a brick on my head. *At this rate, I'll never be a father,* I realized. *And if I were, would I treat my kids the way Dad treats me?*

As Dad drove us home that evening, I remembered my brief exchange with the clerk and began to think about my future. Dad hadn't seemed to notice that it was Father's Day, and I wasn't about to remind him. I was not exactly in the mood to celebrate his role in my life.

"What would you like for dinner, Mike?" he asked me.

"I don't know," I replied. For a moment, I had managed to forget how much he hated those words. Dad went crazy. His foot jammed down on the gas pedal and he started weaving in and out of traffic.

"I'm going to crash this car and kill us both, dammit!" he yelled at me.

This was not the first time he had pulled something like this, so I frantically grasped at the first answer I could come up with. "Burritos!" I shouted, gripping the sides of my seat. Like a flipped switch, it ended as quickly as it began."

That night I waited for Dad to go to bed, packed up what I could, and left.

***

I went to my brother, Paul's a little more than an hour away, in Riverside. After he gave me what money he could, I headed to Uncle Ralph's house. He gave me a bit more money for gas and food.

"Mike, whatever you do, don't ever come back," Uncle Ralph made me promise.

Feeling as if I had no choice, I drove away slowly, while reflecting on things.

Dad would be looking for me soon. I couldn't stick around for long, so I drove north to Berkley to stay with my best friend from high school, Duane.

Duane had pulled his life together since I'd seen him last. He had stopped drinking, become a vegetarian, and was focusing on physical fitness and exploring his spirituality. He took my addiction seriously and put me through his own rigorous detoxification program, which included exercise, Chinese medicine and music therapy. Although I had always been the better runner, Duane was now running circles around me, while I, red-faced and sweaty, struggled to catch my breath even running just a mile. It was humiliating, but I was determined to submit myself to his entire regimen. Every day he had me drinking brews of ginseng and who-knows-what and taking three to five soaks in herbal concoctions prepared for me based on advice he received at a Chinese herb shop down the street and whatever literature he could get his hands on.

"If John Lennon could do it, you can too," Duane would urge me as he pulled out his guitar and masterfully played Lennon's own addiction-recovery song, 'Cold Turkey'.

For thirty-four days he dealt patiently with my vomiting, cramps, sleepless sweat-soaked nights, and endless tears.

Finally, I was ready to face my grandmother, an urge I had resisted earlier, knowing that she would have wanted me to go back and take care of my dad. There was no way I was going to put myself through that again, and I didn't have the strength to oppose her. Now that my courage was back, I climbed into my car and headed to Red Bluff to resume my abnormal life.

Chapter Thirteen
Free At Last

The always-incredible-no-matter-how-familiar beauty of Mount Shasta was looming on the horizon. Even with the car windows closed, I could smell the wild rice fields burning as farmers prepared to plant the next crop of Northern California's longest-cultivated grain, leaving the fields a burnt brick color and the air around them filled with gray smog. "Burning the old to make room for the new," I murmured. Talking to myself in metaphors, I sounded like some corny emotional Hallmark commercial. With the drugs out of my system, it was like I'd given myself permission to feel real emotions, however syrupy. Thankfully, the rice field smog, unlike the L.A. smog, diffused when it reached the outskirts of the inhabited towns.

Singing along to the radio at the top of my lungs, with tears streaming down my cheeks, I rolled down the window to let in the smells and feel the wind blowing on my face. I was returning to Red Bluff at last, having made it home alive. I could care less if anyone could see me making a fool out of myself. *I'm fucking free! Totally fucking free!* I yelled out the window.

***

Things at my grandparent's new home had changed since the time I had left to pull my dad out from the pit that I wound up in myself. The place was now empty of stories, the kind that my grandpa would tell, like the one about their journey toward the better world, from Bentonville, Arkansas to Los Angeles in a Ford Model A. At the time, Uncle Bob was eight years old, Ralph was six, and my dad just four. They had all sat together in the back seat of the car, lumbering thirty miles per hour through the bumpy roads of the 1930s, when their move took place. Grandpa had decided to settle in L.A. where his brother-in-law, Grandma's brother, had already been living for years.

Grandpa was gone now. *I'm so glad that he never had to learn about my addiction.*

My Firebird bumped excitedly as it reached the gravel driveway of the house where Grandma now lived alone. She peeked from the door with a smile. Even with Grandpa gone, she was still as spirited and feisty as ever.

"I'm clean, Grandma," I told her, even though she never asked.

"I wish we could say the same about your dad."

"I'm so sorry I couldn't help him. I'm sorry I left him, I really didn't want to disappoint you." I knew deep down that leaving Dad was the only chance I had at survival. Still, it didn't make me feel any less guilty when I came face-to-face with my grandma, who had been counting on me to rescue him. If I had called her before leaving Dad, I never would have made it out the door.

"It's okay, Mike," she said, "You did what you could. All we have left to do is pray." *Does that actually work?* I wondered. *Did she pray for me while I was gone?*

"Everything is going to be okay." It felt good to hear her say that and encourage me.

Grandma's garden was still just as large and as well-kept as it had always been, and her kitchen every bit as busy, even without Grandpa around to share in the meals. She was taking barrels of surplus vegetables to the curb for neighbors and passersby, as well as donating some to the church.

With plenty of fried potatoes, pot roast, green beans soaked in gravy, and homemade biscuits, the familiar smells made me feel safe and at home. I could hardly wait to dig in. The previous year had certainly taken a toll on me; I was gaunt and pasty pale, a shadow of my former self.

I used to sleep deeply, when I was a normal human being. Now I was a wreck, with track marks and scars all over my arms, legs and feet, not to mention the ones I carried inside. Still, I was very ready to delve into Red Bluff life headfirst.

The first thing I did was to head up to Hogsback Road to breathe the fresh air, reflect, and spend some time alone. It felt so lonely without Grandpa. "Grandpa!" I yelled out at the top of my lungs where my voice could carry over the mountain-tops and down the canyon without being heard, "I'm free!"

***

While back in town I made contact with old friends, and spent those hot summer nights cruising Main Street, meeting girls, getting drunk, and staying up all hours of the night.

Grandma didn't seem to mind no matter what time I got up in the morning. She babied me with breakfast and even made my bed. Soon enough I had regained my strength and put on a few healthy pounds. Ultimately, the realization hit me that it was time to go out and find a job.

I was way beyond my old dreams of becoming an astro-naut and flying to the moon; now the cook that greeted me upon arrival at Francisco's looked like a much better bet. Francisco's Mexican restaurants were great places to eat in our town; there were two locations, plus a small store of pre-pared food. I just needed to cross the street and talk to Umberto, one of the owners, to set me up for an interview.

Umberto was able to find me a job as a cook at their location on the other side of town. *Closer than working on the moon*, I told myself. A local taqueria, even with all the tips that were dropped in the plastic half-bottle, paid even less than carpet installation.

It was not my first job in a restaurant. However, I had been away from this atmosphere long enough to forget how many people one could meet on an average work day. Making new friends was therapeutic. I also enjoyed working around the owners, who were Mexican immigrants. They were more carefree than I was at the time, and it was fun to talk to them. I found joy in the smallest things, like learning to cook chile rellenos and taquitos. My new job was opening up a whole new world to me.

On a fifteen-minute break during a restaurant lull, I stepped outside to have a smoke with Dale, another cook. I'd had my eye on one of the waitresses at work.

"Man, she's cute, Dale," I commented, "and intriguing."

"Yeah, but she's a Christian," he warned.

"A what?"

"A Christian. You know, she goes to church and all that crap. She even listens to Christian music in her car."

Wow, I've never known a girl like that, I thought. The sharp contrast between Shelly's Christian music and the heavy metal and hard rock I was listening to at the time enticed me all the more.

The other Christian at work, Sherrill, had introduced herself to me early on while I was doing dishes after the lunch rush. She first approached me with, "You look like you got a lot on your mind."

"No, I'm okay," I had replied, but I could tell she was being sincere, so after a while I began to open up and talk to her about my life. I found Sherrill to be a compassionate ear, and we soon became fast friends despite the fact she was several years my senior. She seemed to appreciate my friendship, too; especially that I was never bothered by her obesity— something that sadly seemed to cause others to avoid her company. Whenever we would talk, she would always find a way to bring God into the picture.

"So, I heard you and Dale got wasted last night," she would say.

"No, not too bad, just a few beers." It never bothered me that she asked; it felt kind of nice to have someone who cared.

"You know, I wasted a lot of years drinking and partying," she admitted, "and then God saved me and showed me that he had better plans for me."

Both Sherrill and Shelly had a reputation for being the party-poopers at work. The rest of us would go out drinking and having fun, but everyone knew better than to invite these two 'good girls' who preferred to go to church on the week-ends.

Before going back to work, I stopped to take a look at myself in the restaurant's restroom mirror. No surprise–I looked pale and yellow. *What's wrong with me?* Even the whites of my eyes looked yellow. As I leaned in for a closer look a drop of blood fell on the sink and in an instant my nose started bleeding uncontrollably. I nervously cleaned up the bathroom, and then asked if I could leave a couple of hours earlier to "check on my grandma". When I arrived home, my entire body was aching.

"Mike, are you okay?" Grandma asked. "You don't look well."

"I don't know what it is. I don't feel good."

"What's going on, Mike?"

"Don't look at me like that. I am not using drugs, if that's what you think!"

"Whatever is going on, we need to get you to the hospital; you look terrible."

***

On the way to the nearest hospital I assured her that I would ask the doctor to give me a drug test, just so she could have peace of mind that I wasn't violating the sanctity of her home.

The moment the doctor laid eyes on me he said, "Looks like hepatitis. Are you an IV drug user?"

I hung my head in shame, "Yep, been clean about six weeks though."

The lab work confirmed his observation, and with a clear drug screening I was sent home for six to eight weeks of complete rest—and no more Francisco's.

I was supposed to be at home, lying low, but instead I went out cruising with Bill from across the street. On one night while Bill and I were out, we ran into a couple of girls.

"You take the fat one," Bill told me. *That's not fair.* I wanted the girl he had been talking to.

Suzie was tall and cute, with a bad-girl attitude. *I don't think this one's a Christian,* I thought.

Over the next few weeks, during my recovery, Suzie and I became quite close. The first time she came over to our place, Grandma told her, "I'd like to show you a picture of my late husband, Mike's grandpa." She pulled out a picture, which she had cut out from the *National Geographic* and framed, of a frontally nude and well-endowed tribesman. Suzie laughed so hard she snorted.

At Suzie's place there was a whole gang to hang out with: her brother Cliff and his girlfriend, a cousin and her boyfriend, and Suzie's two little kids, who were a lot of fun to play with. This was a social group that made me feel right at home. We would order takeout and get drunk together.

Suzie wasn't expecting an exclusive relationship, as much as she might have wanted one. With her, it was easy to fool around and have a good time without talking about long-term commitment. The pressure was off, which was a relief since the idea of a ready-made family was a bit intimidating, and also because I couldn't stop thinking about Shelly, that cute Christian waitress at Francisco's.

My health was returning, and I was finally released to return to work. Shelly was as attractive to me as ever. Dale was quick to put in his two cents' worth: "I'll bet you a case of beer that girl wouldn't go out with you."

"You're on," I grinned, and headed over to prove him wrong.

Shelly and I hit it off. Coming from completely opposite roots, we were drawn together like positive and negative energy. When we were together, the space between us was electric.

Shelly really was a good Christian girl, and she really did listen to Christian music in the car. She had been raised by both her parents, who were still together. She didn't smoke or drink. Nor had she ever been exposed to the kind of ugliness I had grown up with. Yet she was a good listener. She seemed to sympathize with me when I told her about my past, and my addiction. I never felt judged when she and I were together.

On working days, I looked forward to seeing Shelly and hanging out together after our shifts ended. On non-working days, I was still seeing Suzie. Each one seemed to fill a different need for me. With Suzie, I could let loose. She was bold, edgy, adventurous and playful. Her world was comfortable and familiar, with no real responsibility. Oddly enough, she knew all about my relationship with Shelly, and let it slide.

With Shelly, I was fascinated by her innocence, stability, and normalcy. Thinking about her made me imagine the possibility of settling down to a nice, peaceful family life, a thought both attractive and terrifying at the same time. Yet Shelly was more demanding, and certainly expected me to be faithful.

***

Grandma got used to seeing me bring both girls home. She pulled the same 'late-husband' trick on Shelly as she had with Suzie. Shelly just laughed uncomfortably and then looked at me to rescue her from the awkward moment.

When Grandma saw me getting ready to go on a date, she'd put down her Bible to ask, "So who is it tonight?"

If I said, "Suzie," she'd just mutter to herself, "Boys will be boys," and then call after me, "You'd better strap a bale of hay to your ass; that way if you fall in, the chickens can scratch you out." And if I said, "Shelly," she'd roll her eyes and another derogatory remark.

Shelly and I were constantly on-again, off-again. The cycle was always romantic bliss, followed by sexual intimacy— which seemed the natural conclusion on my part, but triggered outrageous guilt on hers—leading, therefore, to horrific explosions, profuse apologies, and back to our starry-eyed cloudland.

Grandma could see all the tension and heartache between us. "If Shelly's so damn hard to get along with, why don't you just cut her loose?" she would ask me.

There were plenty of others who knew about my two-timing, especially at work. Most people just minded their own business. Sherrill gave me plenty of "God is watching you" lectures, but never gave away my secret. She had become my closest friend and confidante, and I trusted her enough to share with her whatever was on my mind: my struggles, my attraction to Shelly, as well as details about my relationship with Suzie. Sherrill constantly advised me of the risks of playing the field.

"What if you get one of them pregnant?" she would ask, "or even worse, both of them!"

From time to time, Sherrill even invited me to church, hoping it would rub off on me. Eventually, I accepted her invitation. People there seemed happy and so *normal.* It was attractive to me, but it all seemed so foreign and beyond my grasp. Shelly also invited me to her church, which gave me a similar feeling. Even though I was completely closed-minded to the whole idea of church, somehow there was added hope that it was possible to achieve a degree of normalcy in a world Grandma had always made me imagine: the world of the white-picket fence and Sundays at church alongside the wife and kids.

The whole issue of church was a conflicted sore spot for me, from my dad's refusal to allow me to attend church activities to the hypocrisy and shame I'd felt with my foster family. However, I was used to attending church with Grandma. I'd even brought Suzie along with her short mini-skirt and braless tank top that felt out of place in the Lord's house. Grandma didn't seem to mind, but not all her fellow church-goers had the same attitude, which was made quite clear by their looks and whispers.

"Did you see the looks that people were giving her?" I asked Grandma.

"Damn them to hell if they don't like it; at least you're here," Grandma would say. That was how I understood church was supposed to be, but I had met very few Christians who lived up to the name of the one who had sat with prostitutes and tax collectors.

Suzie seemed just as conflicted. She had grown up in the church and seen nothing but double standards and abuse of power—not exactly the message one would hope to get from those representing God, but one that seemed to both of us to be the norm. With both Shelly and Sherrill, though, there was a whisper of something genuine.

In reality, it was a lot easier for me to bring Shelly into my world than for me to enter hers. I was corrupting her and causing her to compromise her values. Shelly's parents could see that I was leading their daughter astray, and they tried to encourage her to sever the relationship. As a result of this tension, our relationship was extremely volatile. Tempers were flaring at work, and passions were hotter than the chilies used to make the salsa. One moment we'd be slamming plates in the kitchen, and the next we'd be making out in the walk-in refrigerator.

"You and Shelly have got to stop arguing at work," Sherrill would never hesitate to reprimand me.

In spite of her disapproval, whenever I needed an alibi with Shelly, I would solicit help from my friend Sherrill.

"If Shelly asks or comes by, can you tell her that I went home sick? Suzy and I want to go see a movie in Redding."

"No," she replied, abruptly.

That was not the answer I was looking for. "I thought you were my friend."

"I am your friend."

"Well, if you were really my friend, you would help me out." I was trying the guilt trip.

"I don't want to see you hurt Shelly."

"As long as she doesn't know, no one gets hurt."

"Well, she may not know, but I know… and God knows. You'll have to answer to Him in the end."

"Oh, come on. If anything, God wants me to be happy; that's what God wants."

"Are you really happy?"

"Yes."

"Okay, then, whatever makes you happy," she'd say, sarcastically.

"So, you'll cover for me?"

"Fine, just this time, but you better not ask again."

"Okay, I promise. Thanks."

I had learned the art of manipulation from a true master. While I may never have been quite as gifted in this area as my father, I had been taught at a young age how to spot and then exploit someone based on their weaknesses. I managed, in royal jerk fashion, to convince Shelly to continue a relationship with me in spite of her moral conflict, all the while continuing in a relationship with Suzie, and persuading everyone else to join in on my masquerade. With this arrangement, I was doing a decent job of keeping my worlds separate until my brother, Paul, finally tore down my hologram when he came to stay with Grandma and me for a while.

"Two girls! Man, that's not fair," he teased.

"Well, it's working just fine for me, so shut up and stay out of this," I demanded.

Paul thought it would be funny to reveal the magician's secret.

The next day at work I was put through the wringer. "Your brother Paul stopped by yesterday after work." Shelly's eyes were sharp as lasers and penetrating like lasers.

"I didn't know. What happened?"

"Well, for one, he was hitting on me. I kicked him out, just so you know."

"Shelly, I'm sorry. He's an idiot. I'll teach him a lesson," I promised.

She glared. "He also told me that you're still seeing Suzie. You're both so full of crap."

I tried my best to assure her that I really cared about her, and that my brother had been lying. She was inconsolable.

At first, I wasn't able to face up to Paul. When I got home, I tolerated his teasing me about his having hit on Shelly, and about how furious she was when she learned about Suzie.

"It's high time someone puts Paul in his place," Grandma commented.

Up until this point in my life, I had always refused to fight my brother, no matter how badly he provoked me, but after two weeks of putting up with his bullying, I could no longer hold back.

One night, after dinner at Grandma's house, Paul and I were horsing around in the front yard when I finally lashed out at him. Paul, in typical big-brother fashion, had just pinned me down to wrap duct tape around my head when I lost all restraint and started punching his face. He ran toward the front door, but Grandma locked it right in front of him, letting me have at him. Paul had beaten me up plenty of times over the years, but this was the first time I had ever won a fight between us.

***

I managed to patch things up with Shelly, convincing her that things were over with Suzie, though they weren't. Things got even more complicated when the two of them moved into the same apartment complex. If I was at Suzie's, I'd have to look out the bedroom window to see if Shelly's car was parked out front. If her car was there, I would either stay put, waiting for her to leave, maybe even staying the night until she left for work the following morning, or I would sneak out the side window, where I could reach my car without running into her. Sometimes I would leave Shelly's house and drive around the block before returning to Suzie's to hang out with her and the gang.

After playing this juggling game for a little while, the whole situation started getting a little too complex, even for me. Finally, I took Grandma's advice and ended things with Shelly. We had broken up several times before, but it had always been me who had initiated the making-up. This time was different. I made a decision, and I wouldn't go back on it. I was tired of all the drama involved in lying and sneaking around. I was ready for something different—dating no one. Heaven only knew what that might be, though.

Chapter Fourteen
A Family of My Own

Shelly quit her job at Francisco's to avoid seeing me. The breakup felt like the right decision for me anyway. We were ill-matched to begin with—my partying to her piety, my scattered and broken family to her prim-and-proper parents, my crudeness to her softness. I had hoped that some of her qualities and skills would rub off on me. As much as her parents disapproved of me, I still looked up to them and respected them for their Christian faith and good values. I just wasn't cut out for that kind of life, and I couldn't bear the responsibility of having corrupted their precious daughter. When I had met Shelly, she was convinced she was saving herself for her wedding night. After a while it was a bit draining to have to deal with her weeping from guilt every time we had sex. The whole relationship was a train wreck.

A couple weeks after we split up, I felt totally free. I took Sherrill and a couple of waitresses on a business trip to San Francisco. We attended a food convention at the Moscone Center, which promised to offer the newest in the food industry. I went mainly to meet some new vendors, but I managed to find spare time for drinking and sightseeing at a couple of strip bars in the red-light district.

When I got home, Grandma was waiting for me with some news. "Shelly came by on Sunday wanting to talk to you," she said. "She seemed really upset."

Shit, I thought, *the girl's probably pregnant.*

"Damn her," said Grandma, shaking her fist in the air after reading the reaction on my face. Just like it was with my dad, I could never do anything wrong in her eyes. In Grandma's view,

Shelly was trying to trap me into the relationship and deserved no pity.

I needed to clear my head, so I headed up to my favorite spot on Hogsback Road for a breath of fresh air. After that I drove over to the restaurant to find Sherrill.

"So what are you going to do if she *is* pregnant?"

"I've always told myself that if I got a girl pregnant, I'd do the right thing," I told her.

"And that is…"

"Marry her, have the baby… be a man."

"So that means you'll stop seeing Suzie?"

I hesitated. Suzie and I had been getting more serious.

"If you say you're going to do what's right, then you'd better."

Later that evening, I got up the courage to call Shelly. We made plans to meet the next day for lunch.

"I'm looking for a new job," Shelly said, sitting calmly while I drove toward Redding in search of a restaurant where we could have lunch.

"What about your job at the convenience store?"

"I'm going to quit. I can't stand it."

"Yeah, I'm looking for a new job, too."

"Really? I thought you liked Francisco's!"

"I need something more fulfilling."

"That's how I feel."

My mind started to look past my fears. *I'm jumping to conclusions; maybe she just wants closure.*

"How about seafood?" I asked as we arrived in Redding.

"Sure."

I turned down the street toward the part of town with the seafood restaurant.

"I'm pregnant," she blurted.

However prepared I might have been to hear this news, it didn't change the level of shock. I swerved.

"Mike, watch out! It's a one-way street!"

There was a deluge of honking and cussing as the oncoming traffic veered out of my way. I was stunned and really didn't know what to say. I did a U-turn back to the highway. Lunch was dropped, and we began discussing our options. Shelly was not exactly thrilled with the idea of getting married, but abortion was definitely not an option for her.

"Nothing like this has ever happened in my family before," she said.

For Shelly's family, it would shame their whole clan. She was horrified to tell her parents. For my family, it was no big deal. I knew what I needed to do. I had always told myself that if I ever got a girl pregnant I'd do the right thing, and that meant manning up to my responsibilities and starting a family. As daunting as the whole prospect might have been, it also brought back my longing for the peaceful life I'd always dreamt about. *With Shelly, I can have a nice, normal family,* I told myself. *I'll be there for my kids, and if I ever treat them the way Dad treated me, I'll kill myself.*

"We're going to raise this child together, Shelly," I tried my best to assure her. "I'll be different, I promise. I'll quit drinking, I'll be responsible, you'll see." My addiction to heroin must have been a lingering concern also.

I had to borrow Sherrill's credit card to get the ring. She was thrilled that I was planning to settle down with Shelly, but her willingness was conditional, "No more fooling around. That's it. You've made your choice. I will not cover for you or lie for you no matter how much you guilt trip me or threaten our friendship." I knew she was serious, and I agreed.

A couple of days after I got the ring, I stopped by the coin-operated self-service carwash bay outside the mini-mart where Shelly had found a new job. We stepped outside for a short talk. My plan was to ask her out for dinner and then pop the question, but impatience got the better of me. In the least romantic way possible, I pulled the ring from my pocket and proposed right then and there.

Her response was an ecstatic, "Yes!"

Shelly loved the ring. She insisted that we drive around to show it off to our friends, among them Suzie's brother. She wanted to make sure Suzie knew that she had won and that there would be no more fooling around.

Later, I met with Suzie privately—to close the door behind me as gently as possible. This was difficult for me to do because I cared about her so much. Still it needed to be done. "I can't see you anymore. I'll be a married man, and I need to do the right thing."

Shelly found us a small two-bedroom apartment and I began packing up my things at Grandma's in preparation for the marriage. I was loading up my car to take things over to the new place when Grandma let me know that she had talked to my dad.

"Is he still using again?" I asked.

"No," she replied. "He said that he's been clean for a couple of months. He wants to know if he can come up for the wedding."

"Are you kidding me!?" I stopped myself, realizing that the tone I was using on Grandma was really not appropriate. I apologized, and then attempted to reason with her in a calm voice, "He's just going to mess things up."

"He's your dad. He has every right to be there!"

"Okay, Grandma," I said, trying just to keep the peace.

For over a year, I hadn't seen or talked to my dad since leaving on Father's Day. *I hope he's telling the truth about being clean.*

A couple of days before the wedding, I caught sight of Dad coming out of the liquor store around the corner from Grandma's. *Great,* I thought, *I hope he'll just look a bit sober on the wedding day.* Before I had the chance to duck away, Dad saw me and immediately broke down crying.

"Mike, I really appreciate your invitation. I wanted to tell you, I'm so sorry I haven't always been around for you and

Paul. I know I've been a real pain in the ass." He transitioned seamlessly from this profuse apology to making jokes about the times we were strung out together in Los Angeles. "Too bad Leo couldn't be here," he smiled.

I was beginning to feel sick to my stomach just thinking about it. "Yeah," I responded.

"So Leo got arrested a couple of months after you left," Dad laughed as he told me the story. "Raymond ripped him off, so Leo chased him down Long Beach Boulevard shooting at him. Isn't that funny?"

I said "yes," just to appease him, but I saw nothing funny about the situation. *I had been the one held hostage at gunpoint by Leo.*

"All I really want is to move forward," I told him.

With that he gave me a huge hug and stumbled to his car.

Shelly and I were married on November 17, 1983 at the First Church of God in Red Bluff. I wouldn't call it a shotgun wedding, although it was planned and executed rather quickly. We were fighting the clock with a baby on the way, and Shelly definitely wasn't thrilled with the idea of having a bulging belly under her wedding dress.

Dad didn't cause any major problems at our wedding, as I had feared, but I can't say the same when it came to the marriage. Now living close by at Grandma's, he managed to wedge his way back into my daily life. His voice always seemed to be in my ear, dispensing his own brand of 'wisdom'. "You do what you want, Mike; you're the man of the house. Her job is to take care of the kids." Not exactly the most helpful advice for a new husband.

With a baby on the way, I managed to get a job welding and fabricating metal dumpsters at the local waste management company. The pay was way better than Francisco's and it was kind of fun to learn a new trade. After I'd been working there for some time. I had experienced a work-related injury, which sent me to San Francisco for a series of surgeries on my jaw.

The medication I was given to handle the pain was having the same numbing effect on me as the heroin used to, and that scared me. When I told my dad, his response was, "Hell, give them to me." Wheedling me out of my pain meds was just the nudge that sent Dad sliding down a long, slippery slope. Soon I was coerced into calling the doctor for refills, and when that wasn't enough, he began making up reasons to go to the doctor so that he could get his own prescriptions. Dad was inspired. During one of his visits with the doctor, he swiped a prescription pad and began writing them out for himself. Before long I was recruited as his lookout, waiting in the parking lot, on 'watch' for cops.

Next, Dad began his slip-and-fall scam. This entailed spilling liquids on the floor at department stores and then falling. This would get him a free ambulance ride to the hospital, where he would stroll out the front door with meds.

"That's why businesses have insurance," he reminded me whenever I questioned his tactics.

When my brother Paul finally graduated from nursing school and got a job nearby in Chico, he saw this as another opportunity to get some pharmaceuticals. Also coerced by Dad, Paul quickly began a prescription-writing scheme, which resulted in his arrest, trial, and the loss of his nursing license. Paul had been staying with us at the time of his dramatic arrest. Undercover police rushed the house, dragging Paul out of the bath and into the front lawn, naked, handcuffed, and covered in bubbles.

***

Having our son, Ryan, did change me to a certain extent. I learned the true meaning of love the moment I saw that precious little one. Seeing him made it a lot easier for me to swallow the fact that I would need to sell my prize 1977 Firebird to make ends meet. That car—the one Frank Sposetto helped me buy and that had been used by the Downey Police Department for surveillance—had been my pride and joy. It was really hard to watch a stranger drive away in it, but my love for that car couldn't even come close to the love I felt for my son, Ryan.

Still, I wasn't able to change as drastically as I needed to in order to function properly in a marriage. Marrying Shelly and having a baby had seemed to me like a ticket to a normal family life, but Shelly and I had different concepts of what that would look like. The best model I had of 'normal' was my grandparents. Grandpa had always worked hard to support his family, while Grandma kept the home, but I never saw an emotional connection or healthy intimacy between them. Shelly always wanted more from me than I was able to give, and I didn't know how to connect on a deeper, personal level. Neither of us knew how to communicate or compromise.

Shelly's second pregnancy was unplanned, but we were both totally excited. My daughter, Sarah, would end up stealing my heart. With a family to support, I needed a little extra income, so I started to work a couple of side jobs. Dad and I got involved with a friend who was raising and selling pigs. I brought a small wiener piglet home and Shelly just loved it. Our new pet would sleep on our bed and ride around in the car with Shelly and our son, Ryan.

Then Dad had another idea for making some easy money, and this time his idea was totally legit. We would borrow a trailer and hit all the junkyards in the area, purchasing torque converters to resell. Dad had enough connections with machine shops in L.A., so we could easily make a couple thousand bucks. I was *all in*.

We drove down to Los Angeles together and connected with Dad's old boss in Norwalk to sell the converters. After resting a while at our motel in Downey, Dad wanted to go on an errand.

"Where are we going?" I asked, knowing to be cautious of his ideas.

"You'll see."

It wasn't too hard to figure out once we hit the Long Beach Freeway. About twenty minutes later we arrived at Bobby and

Bud's. It felt good to see them; they had aged a great deal in the past couple of years, but other than the lines on their faces, everything else was preserved.

"Paul, you're an asshole bringing Mike here! He's a *father* now!" Bobby yelled.

At first, she was so mad that she refused to sell him anything, but after Dad sweetened the pot with a $100 bill, she was happy to oblige.

"I'm not doing it," I announced.

"The hell you aren't," Dad replied. "I'm not doing it by myself. Don't worry, we will just do it this one time. No one will ever know."

It was going to be a long drive home and I didn't want Dad to have an excuse to go crazy on me, so I caved. The fear of his anger was strangling me more than the fear of relapse.

After that trip, I vowed to myself that I'd spend less time with Dad and more time at home. My new resolution didn't last long, though. Soon, Dad was knocking on my door with a mountain bike in his hands and an irresistible excitement in his eyes.

"Hey, let's go for a ride," he called. "Oh," he added sarcastically, "you don't have a bike? Get one!" As he rode off, he called out after me, "'Bike, Not Booze,' you know!"

I wanted so badly to see my dad stop drinking and start doing something productive with his life. Although he was in his early fifties, this seemed like a good alternative, and I had no option but to support him. Even though my wife and I were on a tight budget, I splurged on a bike and my dad and I began riding together pretty much every day.

The bike rides provided some of those moments of connection with my dad for which I had always longed. It didn't matter to me what we talked about; it was the fact that we talked that counted. On these rides he and I would reminisce. We would talk about memories of picnics and adventures we'd shared while I was growing up. While Dad laughed, inside I cringed, as he recounted maniacal pranks he'd pulled, like setting someone's car on fire or vandalizing their house to set things straight. Once in a while I would get to see a little glimpse of his humanity, such as him showing remorse for some of the decisions he had made. "If I would have kept it together, life could have been so different," Dad would say, recalling how businesses he had helped start were flourishing, but how he'd wasted his money on addictions. And every so often he would reveal little bits of history that I had always wanted to know, but never had the courage to ask. "If I hadn't fooled around with your mom's friend, we might have stayed together," was one of them.

In spite of the nicer moments Dad and I shared, my relationship with him during that time was still as detrimental to myself and my marriage as it had always been. He had a way of consistently placing himself between Shelly and me, just as he had done with Connie when she visited us in Colorado. My dad picked a fight with Shelly whenever he had the chance. Whenever he came over to our place he would constantly undermine whatever she said and complain about whatever she did. "I'm just testing her," he would say, "and she's failing."

"She's my wife, Dad. She's not going anywhere," I told him, but that was about the extent of my standing up to him.

Dad continued to play an active role in my life until the day that he moved with Grandma to Arkansas. When Grandma first told me that she was moving to live near her sisters, I was devastated, but with Dad going with her, my feelings were mixed. I knew that his leaving would be good for me, as it would free me from his influence and manipulation, but I would miss our bike rides and conversations. It would also be less stressful in our marriage and family life with the kids. With Grandma, I felt I was losing a load-bearing pillar, without which the ceiling might cave.

***

The best thing that happened to me during this time in my life, besides becoming a dad three times over with two boys and a girl, was finding that fulfilling job I had dreamed about.

It didn't involve going to the moon, but it felt just as important to be saving lives as a fireman.

It was our new neighbor, Brad, who first gave me the idea of becoming a fireman. He was attending the Butte Fire Academy near Chico, and I loved sitting on the steps at night, listening to all the stories he would tell me about fires and traffic accidents.

"Red Bluff Fire Department is hiring, by the way," Brad told me.

"Would they hire someone like me?"

"Why not? Do you have any felonies on your record?"

"No."

"Then you should go apply."

The next morning I marched into the fire department and filled out an application. A couple weeks later, I was accepted into the Fire Academy in Red Bluff.

I was never a great student in high school, and I can't say the Academy ended up being much easier for me, but Shelly helped me study at home. Soon the other students and I were learning practical skills, working with ladders and hoses, taking the engine out, making connections, and learning how to properly don the breathing apparatus that would be our lifeline in a fire. Finally, after about three months of intense training and hard work, we officially graduated and were each given a pager to respond to calls in our own vehicles.

It felt good to be a hero, carrying a badge and a pager. My son Ryan loved coming with me to the fire department. The joy in his face when he looked up in awe at the fire truck filled me with pride. Some of his first words included "fire truck", which he would repeat over and over.

As a fireman, I would be responding to a variety of calls including grass fires, car fires, and house fires, as well as traffic accidents, homicides, and suicides, of course. I was a natural at starting IVs, though of course I never told anyone of my past experiences with needles. However, I found myself fascinated by the work of the paramedics and the complexity of the human body. As patients were loaded into ambulances, I would stand and watch until the doors slid closed. Whenever I had the chance, I would inquire after the destiny of the victims we were serving. This interest led me to enter the EMT program and work both fire and ambulance crews at a local hospital.

Before I had become an EMT, as a fireman, the first call I ever responded to was to the medical aid of an elderly woman at a local nursing home. I will never forget that call. When I arrived, there was already a flurry of activity. CPR was in progress and the paramedics were working feverishly to revive the woman. I took my turn with the CPR, placing my hands on her chest, quickly checking my landmarks, and beginning chest compressions, counting them out loud. It was so different from doing compressions on the mannequin.

I could overhear the paramedic giving the report over the radio; it sounded pretty hopeless. The radio cracked: "Confirm patient is in asystole. We're done here," the paramedic announced, surrendering the poor woman to the afterlife; she had because she had flatlined.

For all those around me, this seemed so routine, but it affected me deeply. *I don't even know this woman,* I thought, *but I'm sure she has a family somewhere that loves her.* Eventually, I would learn coping mechanisms to help me deal with the numerous tragedies I would witness in this line of work. For now, it was surreal and unsettling to watch life slip through my fingers. As much as I wanted to play the hero, I was powerless to save that woman, just like I couldn't save Dad, and not long after that, my marriage.

***

Shelly and I had managed to stick with it for the births of our first and second child, each new birth bringing us closer together for a while. During the in-between times my wife and I drifted apart, experimenting with times of separation. Probably what was most detrimental to our relationship was the distinct lack of support we received from family and friends around us. It wasn't only my dad. It seemed like everyone, except Sherrill, was against the marriage, and no one believed we would succeed. We had no guidance, counseling, or encouragement to try to make things work. In the end, it was Shelly's parents who hired and paid for the divorce attorney, a decision that felt hypocritical to me in light of their family's Christian values, which I had been hoping would rub off on me. Deep down I understood their desire to protect their daughter. However, I thought Christians were supposed to be supportive of family and against divorce. I knew deep down I was just looking for someone to blame and Shelly's parents seemed to be the likely target.

Shelly and I had both hoped that planning the birth of our third child, Dustin, would bring us back together, which it did, but that was short-lived. I think we both realized that having children was not enough to keep us together. I had no idea how to be a real husband and/or an attentive and active father. By the time Dustin was eight months old, we separated for the last time.

I began working nights at the fire department. I wanted to keep busy and try to take my mind off things, and work would do this. It was a pretty cool gig where I would show up for work at 8:00 p.m. and check out the equipment, watch a little TV and go to bed. I loved working at the fire department; it made me feel good to help others. I just could never figure out why I wasn't able to help myself with my own problems—I could help others but I was a disaster. As I lay in my bunk, struggling to fall asleep, I was drifting in and out. Suddenly, I was snapped back into reality by a loud buzz, "Red Bluff Fire Department, respond to a report of a structure fire." We jumped out of bed into our boots. I snapped my suspenders over my shoulders, grabbed my coat and jumped into the engine grabbing the radio. "Engine One responding."

"Copy Engine One responding," as I pulled out of the bay of the station, we rounded the corner. I could see that familiar glow in the distance, the dream of every fireman.

I announced, "Dispatch, we have flames showing."

"Copy, Engine One flames showing."

My heart began pounding as I smashed my foot down on accelerator. I was running on pure adrenaline and hooked up to the closest fire hydrant. "Dispatch, Engine One is laying in supply line."

"Copy Engine One laying in."

I quickly made my connections and got water flowing with the deck gun. Other engines began to arrive while I handed off my duties to a more experienced engineer. Lines began flying off the engine for the initial interior attack. I grabbed a line and headed in...the flames were dancing around as if in slow motion...we were quickly losing ground. The flames had me mesmerized that was, until the CO_2 canisters from the soda machine began to vent, which quickly snapped me back to reality. I loved fighting fires and helping people on the ambulance. The only problem was no matter how much I helped others I still felt empty inside.

***

Shelly and my divorce was finalized when our third son, Dustin, was ten months old. We moved on and started other relationships. I started seeing a girl named Michele while I was still separated from Shelly and before the divorce was finalized. Shelly eventually remarried, which didn't bother me as long as i was still able to see the kids. The hard part started when she and her new husband, Don, decided to move to the Monterey Bay area to be near his aging parents. I was devastated at the thought of having my kids so far away, and a bit jealous because I had suggested to her many times that we move down to Pacific Grove to get away from our families. She and Don ended up settling near Pacific Grove in Carmel Valley.

Thankfully, Shelly was homeschooling the kids, so their schedule was flexible, and I was able to have them every other weekend. Sherrill, my guardian angel, volunteered to do most of the driving, faithfully taking the five-hour journey there to pick them up, driving five hours back to Red Bluff, and returning them at the end of the weekend. At the time I was working as a firefighter for Red Bluff Fire, and a paramedic at both St. Elizabeth Community Hospital, and Life Flight at Mercy Medical Center. Whether on an ambulance or in a helicopter, zooming in to save lives made me feel important, and I was often on call. Sherrill's schedule was more flexible and it made her feel useful helping me out with the kids, so I let her help me as much as possible.

On one of their weekends at my place, my kids asked me if I would take them to church.

"Hell no!" I said, "Go to church when you're at your mom's!" If their mom wanted to take them to church, there was nothing I could do to stop her, but for some reason the very idea of them going to church angered me. At the same time, I could see they all really wanted to go. *My dad used to have the same reaction.* I stopped for a moment to think about why it bothered me so much. Perhaps because the whole idea of people not measuring up to Christian rhetoric was not something I wanted for my children. Or, on the other hand, was it Dad's hatred for any type of church ideas brought up in our past?

Not on my clock, I thought. *This is my time.*

Chapter Fifteen
A Cry for Help

"Mike, it's your dad, I need your help!" My grandma's voice shrieked in panic on the other end of the phone.

I could hear Dad's voice blaring in the background, spouting expletives about the police and how he'd blow their heads off if they came to get him.

Dad's drinking had escalated. Three months earlier he had rolled his truck while driving drunk. In the wreck he had run into an older couple, who ended up in the hospital with serious injuries. Dad was given a sobriety test and eventually accepted a deal for seven years in prison at his pretrial.

"He's been drinking again, and now he's walking around buck-naked with a pistol loaded and cocked. Who knows what he might do!" I tried my best to calm my grandma's crying over the phone.

"I'm not going to fucking prison!" Dad yelled like a madman in the background.

"Bang!" a gunshot rang out and the line went dead.

He's attempted to commit suicide at least twenty-five times before. Did he succeed this time? Where was that gun aimed when he took his shot?

I redialed as quickly as I could and breathed a sigh of relief when Grandma answered the phone. "He shot a hole in the damn ceiling! He's crazy."

Grandma was forced to call the police, but apparently firing a gun indoors is not against the law in Arkansas. I reassured Grandma that he would soon be taken into custody for the car accident, following his trial. It felt horrible to be wishing for my own dad's imprisonment for the sake of safety and peace for the rest of the family.

Not long after that, the phone rang again. It was Dad, and he was laughing. "Mike, the hospital lost my blood test results; the case was dismissed!" he said in a jubilant voice. *This guy has more lives than a cat,* I thought. *He's like Teflon: nothing sticks.*

Grandma got on the phone and hit me with her best plea, "Mike, I can't take it anymore. You've got to help me. You're the only one who knows how to deal with your dad."

My girlfriend, Michele, was listening to the conversation and I could see those wheels turning. She had that look in her eyes that said, "We should help him."

"No, no way," I said, "don't give me that look."

"Just saying…"

Michele had no idea what Dad was capable of doing because I hadn't told her the extent of his insanity yet. It would be like trying to describe colors to a blind person.

"We should bring him here," she encouraged—'here' meaning the house she and I had been sharing for the last six months.

I had to air my thoughts. "No, wait, Michele, you don't understand. This could really mess me up; it has never been normal around him. He has this evil effect on me that's really depressing. I can't live with the man. It doesn't do me any good."

I was disclosing more about my past than ever before, and Michele wasn't able to reason it out like I was because of my experiences with him.

"Mike, he's your dad. Don't you think that he needs help?" Michele replied naïvely. I didn't want her to think that I wasn't compassionate, but I couldn't find the words to explain to her what Dad was like.

"I don't think anyone can help him."

"So you're just going to leave him for your grandmother to deal with?"

The guilt train was gaining momentum and I finally caved. The decision resulted in Dad coming to stay with us.

***

Michele and I had met just a few months before Shelly and I split up. Things hadn't been going so well at home and in my heart I'd already given up on things.

One day while washing the ambulance behind the hospital, I noticed an attractive girl in the distance. "Who's that?" I asked Melissa, my paramedic sidekick for the day.

"That's trouble," she replied. I didn't know what Melissa meant by it, but I was curious about *Trouble* after that. I soon learned that she was the daughter of our human resources director.

Not long after that, I learned that her name was Michele. She was nineteen and had a young daughter named Lindsey. When Michele learned that I was twenty-nine with three kids, she told me not to talk to her anymore because I was *old*. However, I wasn't easily deterred and I continued to be persistent.

Everything about Michele was so different. She was petite and super stylish, coming out of the Bay area with funky, colorful clothes, complete with spandex, big hair with large bows, and hoop earrings--a stark contrast to the button-up blouses, flannel shirts, and wranglers that most people in rural Red Bluff wore in the late eighties. It was no wonder that she was often a subject of staff gossip and had to endure the complaints from the other, more traditional ladies. To me, Michele was like a breath of fresh air. I loved it that she wasn't afraid to be herself, even though it caused her plenty of problems at the hospital.

I invited her to an EMT class I was teaching. She seemed interested, but a week later she told me that her husband didn't want her to take the class. *I didn't realize she was married.*

Not too long after that, I learned that *Trouble* was filing for divorce. With my own divorce already in motion, I started looking for more opportunities to bump into my new mysterious acquaintance. The last proved to be an easy one, as *Trouble* soon transferred to work on the night shift, like me. She worked in the emergency room registering patients and dispatching 911 calls. At night, there was plenty of lull time to make conversation.

One day, she invited me over for breakfast after a night shift. I was really excited, but she almost immediately burst my bubble. "I am nineteen, you know... I just got out of a relationship. And I am not ready to get back into one!" Michele had married at sixteen and given birth to her daughter, Lindsey, at seventeen.

Although Michele didn't want another quick or serious relationship, we still hung out regularly, often bringing our kids together. I had high hopes, but she played it tough and soon started playing the field. Sometimes she would even drop Lindsey off at my place to play with the kids so she could go out on a date. It bothered me that all the other men she dated didn't seem to want to have anything to do with her daughter, and I think it bothered her, too. When Michele and I would go out, we would take the kids along and make it family time. This, at least, scored me some points in her eyes, but not enough to convince her to be my girlfriend.

The lasagna episode led me to consider moving on, myself. I had learned that Michele loved lasagna, but had no idea how to make it. This seemed the perfect way 'in' for me. I bought lasagna noodles, sauce, a baking dish, and all the other ingredients needed to whip up a batch. That night I lingered by her desk in the emergency room, waiting for the right moment when she would leave her keys unattended. When the moment came, I took her keychain and snuck out to her car. I put the ingredients in the back seat and attached a helium-filled balloon to the driver's door handle. When she left that day, I followed behind her subtly to see her reaction. She simply grabbed the balloon and the ingredients and placed them into the trunk of her car. I was desperate enough to go back home and wait by the phone in case she might call me for a dinner invitation that evening.

The following day Michele courteously thanked me for the lasagna, and said she would have me over to teach her how to cook it soon. She didn't say more, and I was left guessing that she must have had a date the night before.

Someone else had noticed my balloon.

"You're some balloon shopper," Jeanne told me. "Not everybody likes balloons, I guess!" She was the head of one of the hospital departments and knew me well enough to start up a conversation.

"She's probably not settling down anytime soon," I replied.

"Oh yeah? You just need to look for someone who's ready to settle," she added flirtatiously. It became obvious to me that Jeanne was more than just inquisitive.

With my new interest in Jeanne, I approached Michele for a final answer.

"Michele, you know I really don't like to be hanging on like this, so why don't you make a decision?" She nodded her head without a reply, so I added, "It's either yay or nay."

"You know I never promised you anything," she shrugged, "so you're free to do whatever you like."

***

After that conversation with Michele, I tried to remove her from my sphere of hope and start anew with Jeanne. She was nice to my kids and I liked that. She also had a better job, a better car, and a better house, and this time I was the recipient of all sorts of flowers, balloons and gifts.

There was nothing not to like, but I still couldn't get my mind off Michele and her colorful, outgoing spirit. Jeanne seemed to always notice when my mind would drift to Michele, but she was determined to win me over, and would say things like, "I'll make you forget about her."

Christmas was another excuse for Jeanne to get me presents. "You and your kids can come over for a big dinner and open some gifts," she told me.

Just before the holiday, I got a phone call from Michele inviting me over to her mom's for Christmas.

I immediately said, "Yes."

Now I'd have to break the news to Jeanne. "I don't think we'll be able make it on Christmas," I told her.

"What's wrong?" Jeanne asked in surprise.

"I got an invitation from Michele's mom, and I already told the kids about it."

She paused for a moment and then started speaking slowly, "Well, can you at least come long enough to let the kids get their gifts?"

Her gifts were embarrassingly generous. The kids were thrilled; I was mortified. The heartbreak in her face reminded me of the double-timing I had done years earlier with Suzie and Shelly.

As bad as I felt about Jeanne, it didn't ruin the time with Michele and her mom that Christmas. Michele seemed to be happy to have me there, and her mom was even more enthusiastic. *Score.* Over the next several months, Michele, and I continued an on-again, off-again relationship until we finally decided to move in together. The excuse was to save money and give our kids a house.

In truth, Michele knew very little about me when we moved in together. I didn't want her to know how screwed up I was, so I was selective about what I shared from my past. I let her believe that I had it all together, while on the inside I was just barely keeping my head above water. Starting over with a new relationship seemed to me like another chance to turn things around and cure my own brokenness.

From our long conversations, I knew that Michele had been adopted as an infant and didn't know her birth mom. We had that in common, so I shared with her how my only mother figures had been my stepmom, Geri, and my grandma. We often talked about the possibility of meeting our biological moms and what that would be like. But I was careful never to say much about my maniac father. I had even gone to great lengths to shield her from finding out about him the last time he'd been in town.

Dad had come to Red Bluff to meet my youngest son, Dustin. This happened when Michele and I first started talking. Since Shelly and I were separated, I was living in a small apartment, and Dad stayed across the street at a hotel. He ended up perpetually wasted, and his visit extended from the initial week to several months while I tried to get him sober enough to be able to board an airplane. During this time, he was picked up twice by ambulance in different spots around town and brought to a hospital to be treated. He was beginning to become a well-known face in the emergency room; people were starting to figure out that he was my father, and rumors were spreading. I was embarrassed to have my colleagues find out what a loser of a dad I had, but was especially worried that word would get around to Michele. I warned everyone who knew of the situation, not to mention a word to her.

I didn't want Dad to be picked up by the ambulance again in case Michele might see him, so I kept a close eye on him. The next time he went missing, I took Sherrill along and we searched the town up and down, checking all the usual spots at the River Park until we eventually found Dad under a bridge, passed out and covered in vomit and urine. Sherrill and I dragged him back to my apartment and straight into the bathtub; she helped me strip off all his clothes, throw them in the washing machine, and bathe him. I took a quick trip over to the hospital to sneak out some supplies I could use to treat him at home. At the hospital I prepared a 'banana bag' and started an IV, a mixture of thiamine, folic acid, and magnesium sulfate often given to alcoholics. I spent the rest of the day nursing my dad back to health—a scenario that unfortunately would repeat itself several more times.

He promised that he would behave, so I cleared the house of alcohol and let him stay at my apartment that night while I went to work. The next morning, I returned to find him once again passed out on the living room floor, lying on two empty Listerine bottles. This went on for several more weeks before

I was finally able to sober him up enough to put him on a plane and send him back to Arkansas. Six months after he left, Michele and I moved in together. The whole time I had managed to shield Michele from the drama so that she wouldn't be left to wonder what the heck was wrong with me. Now Dad was coming back and she would be finding out firsthand.

***

Before Dad arrived, I tried my best to prepare Michele by filling her in on some of the horror stories from my childhood. She seemed adamant about wanting to help him, but I knew it was more complicated than she could possibly have imagined, and there was nothing I could do to fully prepare her for what was ahead.

There were a million reasons why I didn't want Dad back in my life, but I still loved him and wanted to believe that he could change. I thought back on some of his more endearing moments, like how he used to make model rockets, or take us camping or fishing. *This could be a chance for my three kids, and hopefully Lindsey, to get to know their grandfather,* I thought, *and maybe they could have a better relationship with him than I did.* At the same time, I was afraid of getting my hopes up. *Can he really change? Or am I just setting myself up for disappointment?*

Although I was never fully at peace with Michele's well-intentioned plans for Dad, somehow her optimism had managed to rub off on me. I had begun to gather hope that things could be different. This time I was determined to do everything in my power to help him overcome his addictions. I had lots of ideas for things Dad could do in Red Bluff to stay busy, and ways that I could help him to stay sober.

When I picked Dad up from the airport, his aging face looked gloomier and cruder than ever before. Amazingly, he seemed willing to cooperate with my rehab plan. We had plenty of time to catch up on the drive home from the airport, and as we talked, I felt more and more hopeful about his future.

The night after Dad arrived, I had a vivid dream: *On a hot summer day, Dad and I are heading up to Perris, California. The surroundings are familiar; we've been hunting in the area before. Dad pulls off the main road and turns down a long dirt driveway, parking the car in front a singlewide mobile home.*

Dad reaches behind me and grabs a shotgun. "Let's go," he barks as we get out of the car. Taking the shotgun, he walks up the steps and knocks on the door, then takes a couple of steps back.

I'm standing, wondering what's going on. I hear someone in the house walking toward the door. Dad has a look on his face. I've seen it before and it scares the hell out of me. A man appears in the doorway. He's average height with brown, shaggy hair and a large bushy mustache. He's wearing a red plaid shirt and blue jeans. A blast from the shotgun strikes the man in the center of his chest, throwing him forcefully back onto the trailer's linoleum floor. I stand stunned; warm blood splattered on my face, its metallic taste in my mouth. Dad doesn't waste a second. He immediately walks into the house, grabs a package, and stuffs it down the back of his pants. My ears are still ringing. Dad pushes past me, tosses the package on the front seat, throws the shotgun in the back, and retrieves a shovel. Dad drug the lifeless body by his ankles and loaded him into the back of the station wagon. Then we drove for what seemed like miles when Dad found what he felt was a perfect spot. Dad removed the body from the trunk of the car and quickly dug a hole and dropped the body into it. He hastily covered it, all the while not a word is spoken. In fact, not a word is spoken on the ride home.

I woke up trembling. *Let it go, Mike, it's just a bad dream,* I tried to tell myself, but I just couldn't shake the feeling it left within me. I finally managed to put it out of my mind when I went to work that evening, and had nearly forgotten about it by the time I went to bed. That night I had the exact same dream again. This time it really freaked me out. *Is this a dream, or a memory?* Every detail seemed so real. After having the dream, a third or fourth time, I decided to tell Michele.

"Maybe you need to talk to someone."

"I'm talking to you."

"No, I mean a professional." She looked serious. "I'll call the insurance company and get a referral for a counselor."

My agreement came reluctantly. *He's probably going to think I'm crazy,* I thought. I was not looking forward to bringing the counselor up to speed on all of my dad's crazy antics, either.

Talking to the counselor was difficult for me. He wanted me to journal and write down my memories. This was opening up a whole bunch of old wounds and making me anxious, and that started taking its toll on my relationship with Michele. The dreams were relentless. The counselor said that it was entirely possible that seeing my dad was bringing up repressed memories, and that paralyzed me with fear. *If the dream is true and I contact the authorities, Dad will go to prison.* I thought. *But then I'd feel guilty for telling on him... And how on earth would I explain that to the kids! Having a murderer for a grandpa is not cool.*

At the same time, things were actually going smoothly with Dad. Michele was having a hard time believing the stories I had told her because he seemed to be a totally different person than the one I had described. He was following all of the rules, and the kids loved having him around. Even I enjoyed having him around, though I spent most of the time waiting for the other shoe to drop.

I had wanted to take Michele on a little trip to Lake Tahoe to propose, but I was nervous about leaving Dad alone at our house. After going back-and-forth about what to do, Michele and I decided that things were going well enough to give it a shot and pack our bags.

***

Michele and I had our romantic getaway. In our hotel room, after a lovely dinner, I told her how much I loved her and that I wanted to spend the rest of my life with her. I pulled out the ring, and she just stared at me.

"We're already living together. Why not make it official?" I told her, "Besides, everyone's waiting for an answer."

"What do you mean?"

"Everyone at work knows that we were coming up here so I could propose..."

"Yeah, I guess so," she finally answered, reluctantly.

Even though disappointed, I definitely understood her lack of enthusiasm. Still, we both got past the moment and before long we arrived home and opened the door. The familiar smell of drunkenness hit me in the face like a shovel. Dad was passed out on the couch. If Michele hadn't been there I might have gone mad, but instead I patiently cleaned him up and fed him dinner.

Shelly and I had made a deal that I wouldn't allow Dad around the kids if he was drinking. Neither of us wanted to have the kids exposed to drunkenness, and I certainly didn't want to risk losing joint custody of my children over something like this. So Michele and I checked him into Right Roads, a thirty-day rehab program, and straight from rehab he moved into House of Grace, a Christian transitional housing program run by a nice elderly woman I knew from around town. We kept our fingers crossed.

Dad was doing surprisingly well with his recovery. He was enjoying the new environment, and crazily enough had totally bought into the whole 'church' thing. When I came around to check on him, I discovered that he was enthusiastically attending church, as well as 'morning devotions', which he told me meant reading and discussing the Bible every morning with a local pastor. Pastor Gilbert, a recovered heroin addict himself, took special interest in my dad's recovery and raved about his progress. Apparently Dad's good attitude was having a positive effect on the whole house. Dad had mobilized the other guys to go out biking, hiking and barbequing, and was holding extra Bible studies.

With Dad's blessing—"She's the best thing that's ever happened to you"—Michele and I were able to sneak away for a quiet wedding just a few months after our wedding in February. Dad continued to progress and thrive at the House of Grace until the end of the summer, just a few days before my daughter Sarah's fifth birthday party at our house.

As I arrived at work for the night shift, I was greeted by the off-going crew: "Hey Mike, we picked up your dad earlier today at the city park. He was suffering from an alcoholic seizure. I think he's been treated and released by now. Just thought you should know."

Here we go again. I thought. *So much for Pastor Gilbert's good wishes and the "sober living environment" that was supposed to help keep him clean.*

Immediately I attempted to set firm boundaries. "Dad, you are welcome to come over for Sarah's birthday," I told him, "but you need to be sober at the party. Michele and I will not let the kids see you drunk again!"

As Sarah's birthday celebration began that Labor Day weekend, a taxi pulled up in front of our house; the door opened and out tumbled Dad evidently drunk again. I ran to help him back into the cab, instructing the driver to turn around and take him home.

When he arrived back at the House of Grace, he called us on the phone and threatened to set our house on fire. "I'll wait outside and kill each one of you as you run out screaming!" he added for good measure.

This time I took his words seriously enough to make a police report. I had a good relationship with the police department, having worked with them on various calls through the fire department, and with the ambulance crew. It was embarrassing to have to call them to report my dad, but it was something I felt I needed to do. He was immediately taken into custody and ultimately, released the next day.

That night was only the beginning of the threats, retaliations, police reports, and Dad's drinking spiraling out of control until eventually he ended up on the streets. Over the next several months I would be faced with some of the most significant challenges, as well as some of the most dramatic life events, I had ever experienced.

Chapter Sixteen
The Search is Finally Over

It was during this time, amidst escalating drama around my dad, who was not far away at the House of Grace, that the search for my biological mom intensified.

I had spent years searching for my birth mother, ever since I found myself in foster care and looking for a guardian. In a time without cellphones or Internet, this meant taking countless trips to libraries to pull out phonebooks for all the counties in and around Los Angeles and thumb through them looking for her married name, her maiden name, or the name of a relative who might give me a lead. I had filled notebooks with names and numbers, crossed out and starred. I had made phone call after phone call, going to the bank for more quarters to slot into the pay phone at school or on the street corner. Every open door seemed to slam in my face, every lead seemed a rabbit hole, and every hope had faded.

Michele had not even tried looking for her birth mom. She had thought about it, but had never actually tried. Our conversations opened up that longing in her to discover her roots, and my search inspired her to start searching herself. For Michele it was easy. She simply contacted the adoption agency, and within a month they put her in touch with her biological mom, who had apparently only recently made contact with the agency as well. Michele flew to Seattle to meet her.

I was jealous, but I was also discouraged, and couldn't find the strength in myself to make any more calls, so Michele stepped in to help. The search continued with Michele's determination and perseverance in spite of my foot-dragging.

"We've got to go to L.A. if we're going to find her," Michele concluded after all the names on our list had been crossed out.

The trip was a total bust. Before I left, I had searched quickly for an old magazine picture that I had always dreamt of showing my mom, but I couldn't find it. Michele and I decided to try the hall of records for the city of Los Angeles to look for any information that could help us find her. I managed to locate the marriage license for when my mom had married my dad, as well as their divorce documents. I also found the information about her second marriage, to a man named Bill Crawford, and their divorce. But I had already known about that, and the search brought no new information. We called it a day and went to see Uncle Ralph.

I was excited for Michele to finally get to meet my favorite uncle. After a nice dinner out, we went back to his place for the evening. Aunt Darcie had just gotten home from work, and we had a great time sharing pictures of my kids, laughing and catching up. When it came time to say goodbye, Ralph called me over and put his arm around me. Giving me a tight squeeze, he said, "If you want me to find your mom, all you have to do is ask; you know I have connections!" Uncle Ralph always liked to brag about his connections.

"Would you please...?" I replied weakly.

The drive back was long, and I felt discouraged.

As we entered our house, I could see the steady blinking of the green light on the answering machine from across the room. "Mike, this is Ralph. Grab a pen; I have your mom's address and phone number."

I felt like I had been hit in the gut. This was the moment I had been waiting for my whole life. I called Ralph and thanked him, and he made me promise that I'd stop by and pick him up when we came back to L.A. to see her.

"I want to come along," he said.

It was excruciating to have to go back to work that week and wait until the following weekend to return to Los Angeles. I decided not to call her before going, so she wouldn't have the chance to run away, as she had done when I was younger.

When my dad heard that I discovered a way to possibly meet my mom, he wanted to talk. By this time we had been through hell and back with Dad, and I didn't really want to see him. He'd been homeless for about a month, and Michele had been bringing him a clean change of clothes and food at least once a week. She convinced me to give him an ear.

"I need to tell you something that will probably upset you."

"What?"

"The truth."

I took a deep breath.

"You know how I've always told you guys that your mom walked out on us, and that she never wanted to be reminded of you? Well, that's not totally true."

Not totally true, or totally not true? I thought, maintaining a silent stare.

"There were actually many times that she tried to find you, and I made sure she wouldn't. Your birth mom was afraid to contact you because I threatened to kill her and her new family if she ever tried again."

"What about that time when we were supposed to meet her and she didn't show up?" I asked.

"I went to a different address. I arranged it with a colleague who had an empty apartment in his building."

"That man you talked to...?"

"Yes, that was him."

I replayed the scene in my mind. *Why had I ever believed his story? Why hadn't I seen through it?* I thought.

"Well, she'll probably tell you all about it herself. I just thought you should hear it from me first," and with that he slunk off.

I was too overwhelmed to cry. When I got home, I began a more determined search for that magazine clipping I had been saving since my sophomore year of high school. It was a picture of a family riding a rollercoaster—a mother, a father, and two young children—which I had stumbled upon. The woman in the photograph reminded me of a picture of my mom that I had seen when I was younger. I couldn't help but wonder if this had been my mom with her new family, and if so, what was wrong with me and why did she leave? I cut the picture out of the magazine so that if I ever found her, she would know that I had been looking for her all these years.

As we drove into Los Angeles, I tried to quiet my mixed expectations, but my heart was pounding so hard that I wondered if Michele could hear it. We drove straight past the exit to Uncle Ralph's house. I was so focused I didn't want anything or anyone to delay us. We found the address, looked around the complex, and located the unit. It was empty.

"What's new?" I grumbled, "Let's go home."

But Michele wasn't willing to give up so easily. "Let's try the manager's office," she insisted.

I didn't have much hope. "What the heck," I sighed.

"Kathleen doesn't live here anymore," the property manager told us.

"Well, do you know where she lives now?" Michele asked.

"I do," she answered, "but I can't give you that information."

"Come on, let's go," I muttered. "I knew this was a waste of time."

As we turned to leave—the lady called after us, "Who are you? Why are you looking for her?"

After sharing details with her, she had a change of heart. It turned out that she had known my mother for a long time and Mom had told her about Paul and me.

"I suspected you might be one of her sons," she said, and volunteered all the information we needed about Mom's new address. "She'll be happy to meet you!"

We parked across the street from the new address, and I took a moment to gather up the courage for take two.

"Here we go again," I mumbled under my breath.

"You can do it!" Michele chanted from the stands.

There was a man in the garage as we approached the house. "Can I help you?" he asked.

"Um, we're looking for Kathleen McGowan," I answered feebly.

"Sorry," he said, "no one here by that name."

Embarrassed, disappointed, and even a bit angry, I wanted to be able to just disappear. Unfortunately, I didn't have that magic trick up my sleeve. I still had to walk step-by-step across the street to the car.

I slammed the door behind me as hard as I could. *How many times am I supposed to go through this?*

"Wait, let's just make sure of the house number," my persistent cheerleader chimed in.

"Let's just go home. This is another dead end."

Suddenly, there was a knock on the car window.

"Are you looking for Katie?" asked the man from the garage.

"Maybe..." I said, half-heartedly.

"Well, if it's Katie Crawford you want, she's in the house. Come on in."

We followed him through the garage. By the time he opened the door, my rubber legs were so weak and shaky that I could hardly take another step. As I stumbled through the kitchen, all the stories from my childhood popped into my head like a high-definition movie running at the speed of a Formula One race car, but without the dramatic music.

"Katie, there's someone who wants to see you," the man said, standing before the very woman I had spent two-and-a-half decades searching out. There was no doubt in my mind when I looked at her face.

"Do I know you?" she asked.

"You're my *Mom*." Before the words came out she had already stretched out her arms for a hug. She recognized me, too. The resemblance was clear; I had inherited all my features from her, and looked almost nothing like my dad.

Over the next couple of hours we tried our best to catch up on the years we had missed. I'd brought along photographs and at this point we began sharing about each of our lives, filling in the gaps with photographs and stories. I met relatives I had never known existed: my half-sister and her husband, who turned out to be the man from the garage, and my half-brother. I called my children to let them speak to their grandmother, and finally, I called Paul.

I could barely choke out the words, "Paul, I found Mom." He was in shock. I handed the phone to my mom and held back the tears as I sat and listened to them reminisce and catch up.

Our emotions plunged back and forth between the hot happiness of finally meeting, and the cold sadness of the lost moments that could never be restored. As much as we wanted to soak in these moments forever, by the end of the day we were drained.

When we arrived at Uncle Ralph's for the evening, he reminded me of his request to go with us to meet my mom. There was a look of genuine disappointment on his face, and I felt terrible. It hadn't seemed like a big deal to me at the time, but now I could tell it had been important to him.

"Next time you'll come with us, I promise."

"Sure," he said with a shrug.

Even if he was disappointed, Uncle Ralph didn't let it interfere with the rest of the evening together. He and Aunt Darcie treated us to a wonderful Mexican dinner that night.

***

Not long after meeting my mom, I injured my back on a 911 call and needed surgery. Mom offered to come and visit, even though it would mean she would risk running into my dad—an idea that terrified both of us.

The surgery went well, and it was great to have my mom around to nurse me back to health. She tried her best to make up for our lost years by making me pancakes and pot roast.

It was nice having her there, but the entire time I was nervous about what Dad might do to retaliate. Over the years, he had done the best he could to keep us from meeting each other, and now he knew that we had been reunited. As soon as he found out Mom was visiting, he called and asked to speak with her. We were afraid that he might just show up, so finally she decided to pay him a visit in the park—a public place where it was easy for her to walk away if things got intense. He apologized to her and assured her that he had finally told me the truth. After that they talked on the phone a couple of times, and to my relief, nothing dramatic happened.

***

Only a week after Mom returned to L.A., a different kind of drama erupted. It started with a phone call from Aunt Darcie.

"Hey Mike," her voice was shaking, "Ralph didn't come home last night, and I haven't heard from him since."

"Did you two get in a fight or something?" I asked, hoping for the best.

"No, nothing like that at all," she said. "When he left for work in the morning he told me he'd stop on the way home to get some bait. We were supposed to go out on the boat this weekend."

I was silent. Michele stopped what she was doing and stared at me.

"This is totally out of character for him," Darcie added. *That's what I was thinking.* Uncle Ralph was usually reliable. "I've already called Sergeant Broxton," she assured me.

"That's good," I said. Sergeant Broxton from the Downey Police Department was a good friend of Ralph's. He was the same officer who had helped me years earlier by renting my Firebird for drug surveillance. I knew that he would do all that he could to find my uncle.

When I got off the phone, Michele was waiting to be filled in. I was embarrassed to tell her. I had only just introduced Uncle Ralph to her as my favorite uncle, and now who knew what he was up to. *Was he playing hooky? Had he run off with another woman?*

"Well, he must have had an accident on the way home or something," she said.

"Probably," I mumbled.

"Either that, or a midlife crisis."

"No, I doubt it," I said, reaching in the drawer for another dose of Vicodin.

Michele noticed. "Mike, didn't you already take your meds?"

"Look, I just need it right now, okay?" I said, pushing her away.

Over the next few days, we waited anxiously for news of Ralph. Christmas was coming, and with time lost to my back surgery, I still had a lot of shopping to do for the family. Sherrill came with me to look for presents for my kids, but Ralph was on my mind every moment of the day. I popped pills for the pain in my back, but also for the pain of waiting. I knew Ralph could take care of himself if he ever got into a jam; he kept a 9mm under the car seat in case he ever needed it. *Why have we not heard from him?* We were planning to head to Redding to hit some stores there, when a wave of fear overwhelmed me.

"I need to swing by my house first," I told Sherrill. I wanted to check the answering machine, but I knew that pushing the play button might bring me news I didn't want to hear. I stood in front of the machine wanting the green blinking light to go away, somehow thinking that if I didn't press play, it would have never happened.

Back in Mrs. Van Steinberg's film class in high school we had watched an old movie from 1939 called *On Borrowed Time*. The film was about an orphaned boy and his grandfather, who chased "death" up an apple tree to buy himself more time. As long as death was in the tree, no one could die. Maybe if I didn't press play on the answering machine, death would stay in the tree.

"Mike you need to call me right away." It was Aunt Darcie.

The apple tree crashed to the ground. "They found your Uncle Ralph. He's dead. He was murdered in his car. He'd been shot multiple times in the face and chest," she told me.

My head was spinning with a thousand questions. *Who could have done this and did he see it coming? Did it hurt? What was Uncle Ralph thinking as he died? Did he know how much we all loved him?*

"Where's your dad?" Aunt Darcie asked.

"I'll tell him," I assured her, "I know where to find him."

"You remember," she continued, "your dad always said that he would kill whoever was responsible for reuniting you with your mom."

It was true, he had said that more times than I could remember, and it was true that Ralph had only weeks earlier helped me find my mother, but I didn't want to think that my dad could do something so awful. I tried to put it out of my mind.

As a paramedic, I had seen many deaths, suicides, and homicides, and was all too familiar with the gory details that their families are often spared. I was able to hold myself together until I called Michele at the hospital and actually heard myself say it out loud. Then I fell to pieces; I could hardly breathe.

Instead of going to Redding, my friend Sherrill and I went out looking for Dad.

"Damn Darcie," Dad reacted immediately. "It was her, I know it. She probably got her brother to do it for her."

Ralph and Darcie had been inseparably close. Dad's theory was that Darcie wanted to get free from Ralph, but knew that he would never let her go, so she had him murdered.

I was determined to get on the next flight to Los Angeles. I wanted to be there for Ralph, just like he'd been there for me all those years. After visiting with Dad at River Park, I went to the emergency room to have the stitches in my back removed so that I could head down south the next morning. As the doctor removed the stitches, he found a great deal of puss and infection and said he would have to call the surgeon. I explained my situation to the surgeon, and though the doctor was sympathetic, he insisted that he would need to open my back up to clean out the infection. The fact that we worked together carried no weight; he picked up the phone and scheduled surgery for the following morning.

***

It was two weeks before I was able to fly down to L.A. My mom met me at the airport. It was surreal having her in my life after more than thirty years. Aunt Darcie and I had been planning a family gathering to celebrate our newfound family member, but now we were planning a memorial service for one newly lost. Mom and Uncle Ralph had not had the chance to see each other before he died.

Darcie excused herself and reappeared with a small box, which she handed to me. "Ralph would have wanted you to have this."

Inside the box was a buck-style knife that my grandpa had made for him. He made a total of three, one for each of his sons. Uncle Ralph's was the only one left—my dad's had been stolen during a burglary, and Uncle Bob's had been lost. Growing up, I had always admired that knife. Having the knife handed down from my Uncle Ralph made me feel that he had loved me like a son.

Mom and I drove to the Downey Police Department to meet with Sergeant Broxton. I wanted to find out as much as I could about my uncle's murder, down to the last detail. He told me that Ralph's car had been discovered in a residential area in Long Beach. A street sweeper called and issued a citation, since the car had been parked for five days during posted no-parking hours. Sergeant Broxton confirmed that Ralph had been shot multiple times in the face and chest. There were no leads or suspects.

How could someone be shot and killed on a crowded street and sit there in their car for five days without being noticed? I wondered. By now I was eating my prescribed Vicodin like candy.

I thanked Sergeant Broxton for all he had done and all that he was trying to do. After all, this crime wasn't even in his jurisdiction. The sergeant assured me that he would keep me updated on the status of the case.

We left the police station and went straight to Rose Avenue in Long Beach. As a paramedic, there were dozens of times that I responded to vehicle accidents involving fatalities after which family members wanted to go to the site of the accident. I never quite understood—until now. I wanted to see for myself where he had died; somehow it was like being there with him. Shards of glass were still in the gutter—a sobering reminder of the tragedy that had taken place. There was a small bait and tackle store on the corner, which must have been the purpose of his final errand, but there was also a bar, which might also have been a distraction.

The bar is what led Sergeant Broxton to his theory that Ralph might have hooked up with a prostitute, flashing the wad of cash he always carried in his pocket and tempting a pimp to shoot him for the money. The two things Uncle Ralph always had on his body were a gun and a big wad of cash, neither of which were found on him when he died.

Next we went to the Los Angeles County Coroner's office to get a copy of the death certificate, a process that took forever. Finally we went to Norwalk Toyota, where Uncle Ralph's van was being stored.

As we entered the dealership, I introduced myself. "I'm here to take care of my uncle's van," I said. The office fell into an awkward silence.

"Um, yes, ah… I'm so sorry," said the receptionist, unsure of her words. "Let me get Henry, the manager."

Henry, equally tenuous, took me aside and began to whisper, "You know, I hate to say it but *the body* was in the car for nearly a week, and, uh, well, you know, with the un-seasonably warm weather and all… let's just say that the smell is somewhat, or rather... I'd say overpowering, if you know what I mean."

The body has a name, I wanted to say. It felt so aggravating to hear my uncle referred to as 'the body', and yet I had done the same thing throughout my career when talking about newly deceased loved ones to their families.

The driver's window had been completely shattered, which accounted for the glass we had seen on the street where his car was found. I opened the side door and stepped into the van. There was dried blood everywhere, as well as brain matter splattered on both the passenger side and rear window. At work I had seen plenty of other accidents, people who had been hit by trains or cars, but this was different; this was my uncle.

The smell, as Henry had described, was unbearable. I hopped out of the van and went around to open the rear hatch. As I suspected, the nasty smell was caused by more than just 'the body'. I laughed out loud as I discovered the small Styrofoam ice chest filled with sardines that he must have purchased just prior to his death.

I got back into the van to begin the process of gathering up his personal belongings. Ralph's lunch box was also covered with the same dried blood. When I opened it I saw what remained of his lunch. Tucked next to the Tupperware container was a small folded piece of paper. It was a note from my Aunt Darcie telling him that she loved him and hoped he'd have a great day.

Ralph's blood-covered glasses were lying on the floor, one lens shattered by a bullet. I had a strange urge to put the glasses on, hoping in some weird, twisted way, that I would see something, knowing that I wouldn't. In the 1978 thriller, *Eyes of Laura Mars,* the main character could see through the eyes of a serial killer, and was able to help the police catch him. I wanted to go back in time and see through Ralph's eyes to know what had happened to him.

As I got out of the van, I noticed a bullet hole in the seatbelt. My mom went out to her car to retrieve the knife that Darcie had given me. I cut the seatbelt from the car and added it to the collection of stuff in the lunch box.

I was quickly running out of my prescription pain medicine, so I called the doctor back in Red Bluff. "I forgot my pills at home. Is it okay for me to have Michele mail them, or is that illegal?" I asked him, knowing full well what he would tell me.

"No, it's illegal. I'll just call in another prescription for you down there," he said.

He knew my circumstances, so I used that to my advantage. "I don't know how long I'm going to be needed here," I told him.

Unbelievably the doctor gave me a full month's prescripttion with unlimited refills. As soon as I got back I had the prescription transferred to a pharmacy in Red Bluff, and automatically doubled my supply.

About two months after Uncle Ralph's murder I got a phone call from Aunt Darcie. She tried her best to be sensitive as she broke the news to me.

"I've met someone," she said, "and we're getting married." Her new fiancé was a fireman and the brother of a colleague from work.

She must have met him before Ralph's murder, I thought. *How could she move on so quickly?* It felt disrespectful to his memory, but worse, it made me feel there may have been something to my dad's hypothesis, which I had otherwise dismissed.

All three theories about who was responsible for Ralph's murder seemed viable, and yet none of them could be proven. *Was it my dad, Darcie, or some unknown pimp?* Investigations never turned up any substantial evidence, and Uncle Ralph's death has always remained a mystery.

Chapter Seventeen
D.O.A.

I was doing my best to get back into a routine—putting things into perspective was difficult. I had just met my biological mom, and had said 'goodbye' to Uncle Ralph.

One cold November night, I heard the radio crackle in dispatch, "Red Bluff One, respond to a man down, vomiting blood, unresponsive." I ran to the ambulance, and we headed out to take care of the call. On autopilot, I prepared the back of the ambulance and set up the IVs, the protocols and treatment plans running through my head. My mechanical motions were sharply interrupted as the radio announced the address. I immediately recognized the address: *Dad. Shit!!!*

His condition was extremely critical. *If I don't do anything, he won't make the trip to the hospital; my problems would die with him.* My paramedic partner on that shift, who knew my situation all too well, could tell by the way I was looking at him what I was thinking and said, "Mike, this is something that you will have to live with."

As I reflect on the relationship between my dad and I, it really started to go south at Sarah's fifth birthday party. Dad had been making threats over the phone, calling Michele a pig and blaming her for the new restrictions and boundaries that we had set up. He stuck with this tactic until he got bored with it and pulled out a new trick. "Fuck you pig!" read the huge orange spray-painted letters on our driveway one morning. *I bet the neighbors loved that.*

As we were cleaning it up, my youngest son, Dustin, ran out to see what was going on. *Thank God he can't read yet,* I thought. As his quizzical young face contemplated the huge letters in front of him, I did my best to explain: "Grandpa painted something on our driveway."

"I know why," he said decisively.

"Why is that?"

"He didn't like the color of the driveway."

"You're probably right," I said, smiling at his innocence.

Over the following months, we had Dad arrested dozens of times. He was sentenced for to up to six months in jail, but each time was released after less than two weeks due to overcrowding in the jail. The more we reported him, and the more Dad was arrested, the more his aggressions continued. It was like throwing fuel on a fire. Even while he was detained, Dad's harassment and death threats never ceased, and whenever he was able, he came over with the orange spray paint.

When the Christmas season came around, he started a new tactic: cutting our Christmas lights. Michele rose to the occasion like a Christmas-light ninja. No sooner would he cut the lights than she would put them up again. We bought more than a dozen sets from Wal-Mart that year in order to keep up with Dad's incessant pranks.

By the time I had found my mom, the House of Grace had been shut down because of Dad. Since he had started drinking again, the 'sober living environment' had turned into complete pandemonium. He had been kicked out of the place several times, but, perhaps due to his initial enthusiastic participation—had always managed to talk his way back in again. By now, Dad had all the tenants drinking Pruno (fermented fruit)—also called prison wine, which he taught them to make in the shed. With his bad influence on the others, and the cops coming around constantly, the poor lady who ran the place could no longer hold things together. She decided it would be easier to shut down the halfway house.

Eventually Dad became homeless, though that did little to stop the drinking, threats and vandalism.

One evening, I walked across the street to get some milk from the corner store. On my way back, I caught sight of a strange figure lurking over my car. I noticed immediately that the windows had been smashed.

"Hey!" I called.

Just then, Dad turned to look at me from behind the up-turned collar of a comedic full-length beige trench coat, wearing a dark beanie, scarf and gloves. He was pouring on a mixture of brake fluid mixed with Drano on the car. I knew what this could do to the exterior paint job, having seen this trick before.

"Fuck with the bull, you get the horns," Dad always told me. He was never one to miss payback time, but I wasn't about to let myself get trampled in this bullfight.

"What the hell are you doing?" I screamed as he took off running. The chase was on! As I caught up to my dad I grabbed his trench coat and pulled him down to the ground. He looked so ridiculous in that cheesy Dick-Tracy-style coat, I wanted to laugh, but there was no time for that. With the coat pulled up over his head, the bull was trapped and thirty years of frustration came pouring out of me as I began to swing at him. I didn't stop until I was too exhausted to continue.

I looked down at my dad, lying in the street, defeated. Maybe in that moment he realized how pathetic he was, or maybe Dad was just hurt, but he started to cry. Suddenly, I felt guilty for what I had done. I tried to hold my composure as I turned, leaving him in a heap on the ground, but for several hundred yards toward home, tears were streaming down my cheeks.

Even though I was overcome with remorse for laying into him, the grace I had for my dad had worn thin, even though he was still homeless and living on the streets. It had come to a point where I didn't want to see him ever again. Michele was compassionate enough to bring him food and a change of clothes every week, but I didn't want to have anything to do with him. The only times I intentionally made contact with Dad while he was living among the homeless community at River Park were when he asked to see me about my birth mom and when I needed to tell him about Ralph's murder. Yet, no matter how hard I tried to avoid him, he was always there to haunt me at every corner. I couldn't even escape him at work. My co-workers on the ambulance crew had labeled my dad a 'frequent flier' as he was constantly being picked up and was in and out of the hospital for substance abuse treatment.

For some unfathomable reason, Pastor Gilbert, in spite of all Dad had done, never lost hope in him. The two of them stayed in close contact. He would visit Dad at the park, and Dad would ride his bicycle over to the church to attend Bible studies. I was frustrated with Pastor Gilbert's naïve optimism, and angry that he might judge me for feeling differently when he had no idea what I had lived through and how deceptive my dad could be.

It was probably a combination of all that was going on in my life at that time that led me to become more and more dependent on the Vicodin that had originally been prescribed for my back. After manipulating the doctor into giving me an extra prescription while I was down in Los Angeles to keep up with my ever-increasing pill-popping habit, things began to spiral.

My prescription was being Fed-Exed to me every month by a pharmaceutical company that was licensed to send drugs through the mail. Hoping to get an extra bottle of pills, I told my doctor it hadn't arrived. He had the package tracked, and found that I had signed for it upon delivery. Having caught onto my scheme, the doctor gave me a strong warning and refused to write me any more prescriptions. That bridge was burned; I needed to find another source.

My attention turned to Sherrill. I knew that she would have easy access to all kinds of pain medications due to her weight. All she had to do was go see a doctor and complain that her feet ached, or her knees, or her back, and they would write her a prescription. Sherrill was genuinely invested in our friendship, she had been there for me through thick and thin, and I knew that she needed my friendship as much as I needed hers. Since we both had an affinity for good steaks, I invited her over for a barbeque.

When Sherrill called to confirm, I was abrupt with her on the phone, "Hey, Sherrill, what's up?"

"Do you still want me to come over later tonight?"

"No," I snapped.

"I thought we were going to barbeque."

"Well, I would if I felt better."

"You took all thirty already?" she asked.

"Duh, why do you think I'm in so much pain?"

"Why don't you call for a refill?"

"It's only been two days."

Further frustrated, Sherrill asked, "So, why don't you go to the emergency room and get some?"

"You know what, just forget it, I'll just throw the damn steaks away."

"Okay. Do you still want me to watch the kids later?" Sherrill, our chief babysitter, had a soft spot for my kids.

"Forget it, I'll find someone else to watch them."

By now Sherrill was weeping, and I knew I'd be getting my pills. "If you don't care about me, then I don't want you around my kids," I told her.

"Okay, fine. I'll call you when I'm leaving the pharmacy."

"Great, I'll have the steaks ready."

I knew how to play Sherrill like a true virtuoso. I had already begun having her running around from doctor to doctor and pharmacy to pharmacy, filling prescriptions that she would never use.

Late one afternoon, when Sherrill came over to our place to help me prepare dinner, she entered the house in a panic. "Hey, your dad's walking down the street!"

We looked out the front window and watched as my dad strutted across the lawn and opened the gate to our backyard, then ran to my bedroom to peak through the blinds at the back of my house. We watched him go into the shed and pull out the lawnmower and weed eater that he and grandma had given me as a gift and dragged them back onto the street. I quickly called the police. "My dad's walking down the street carrying stuff from my shed!"

I followed my dad down the street for a couple blocks, and waited until the police pulled over next to him before I approached. The police officer was all too familiar with both of us, and was tired of dealing with our problems. "Your dad claims that the items belong to him," he told me. "It's your word against his."

I took my stuff home for the time being, but Dad decided to take the dispute to court to let the judge settle it. A few weeks later I was served with a summons. I was being sued.

Grandma called from Arkansas and encouraged me to just give him the stuff. "I'll replace it for you," she promised, but I was so enraged by the whole situation that I was not willing to budge. *I'm not going to let him just get away with this.*

Michele and I appeared in court to face my dad and defend our case. I was infuriated to discover that Dad brought Pastor Gilbert along as a character witness to testify that he was on the right path. I didn't have much of a case without Grandma's testimony, so—much to my humiliation—Dad won, and we were forced to give him the items in addition to paying the filing fees for the case.

It was around that time we also started receiving indirect threats from Dad.

One day Michele answered the phone. "Hello, this is Hoyt-Cole Chapel of the Flowers. We are terribly sorry to hear about the death of your husband."

"Excuse me?" Michele asked, looking up at me.

"We were informed this morning of your husband's death and were asked to call you to assist in making arrangements for his funeral."

Michele received a similar disturbing phone call from the Hall Bros Mortuary in Corning.

One weekend, when the kids were over for their visit, we were just cleaning up after a late breakfast when I heard a knock on the door.

"Ryan, help Sarah and Dustin pick up the toys. They're here to retexture the walls, so hurry up," I called while opening the door.

"Hi, I'm looking for Mike Casey."

"Yes, I'm Mike."

"You don't know me, but... eh... your dad hired me to help him kill you." He paused to let me grasp the meaning of what he had just said.

I stared at him. *How do I respond to that?*

"I thought he was just blowing off steam," he explained, "so I took his money, spent it, and forgot about the whole story. But I guess I was wrong, 'cause your dad showed up last night with a Taser gun, orange spray paint, a baseball bat, and a plan." The plan was to spray *dead on arrival*, "DOA" on my garage door, and when I came out of the house they would Taser me and then finish me off with the bat.

His name was Derek. A coarse-looking man in his early twenties, he was dirty enough to make me think that he was probably homeless, and that the five hundred dollars my dad had paid was quite a generous deal for him.

Dad had recently started receiving his social security checks, including back pay from two years prior, and had moved into an apartment. He still spent most of his time at River Park, where he had met Derek.

We called the police, who wired Derek up and sent him back to Dad's residence. I'm not sure if he was celebrating early or was just drunk as usual, but the recording was not clear enough for an arrest. They agreed to try again the next day. That very night, Derek called to say he was leaving for Oklahoma and wished us well.

***

Life has a way of making us face things that are difficult. A couple of weeks passed when I was back spiraling further into addiction, confusion, fear, anger, and the moment came when, as a paramedic, I could easily have let my father's life slip between my fingers. Sadly, I was tempted.

"Mike, this is something that you will have to live with."

He's right, I realized, and shook off my diabolical thoughts. Springing into action, I placed Dad on high flow oxygen via a non-rebreather mask and established two large-bore IVs running wide open. I then administered a 500cc fluid challenge and extra blankets to keep him warm and, finally, grabbed the radio to establish base contact.

"Base, this is Red Bluff One, we're in route Code 3 with a fifty-three-year-old-found-down/unresponsive patient. Has a long history of alcohol abuse. Friend states that he has been drinking all day. Patient is pale, cool and diaphoretic. Blood pressure 90/45. Heart rate is 160, sinus tachycardia showing on the monitor. Respiration's approximately 32 and shallow lung sounds are clear and equal bilaterally. Any further orders or questions?"

Unbelievably, we made it to the hospital with Dad, where he would spend the following ten days and receive another extension to his miserable life.

***

Saving Dad's life didn't change his behavior; within a week after being discharged he was back at his game. Soon he was arrested again for repeated violation of the restraining order we had placed on him. This time we managed to get my dad evaluated by a mental health specialist. A few days later, I got a call from the psychiatrist who was assigned to evaluate him. After asking me a few questions, he informed me that my dad was currently suffering from severe personality disorder with borderline narcissistic tendencies.

"Look," he told me, "I'm not supposed to be telling you this, but I would take his threats seriously." Apparently, Dad had received well over the highest scores he had ever seen for dangerous behaviors.

However, this clear information, along with other things, caused me to become increasingly worried about my family's safety. Consequently, after talking to the psychiatrist, I became outright terrified.

One day after a trip down to Monterey to see my kids, Michele and I picked up a newspaper and said to each other, "If there's a job for a paramedic or a firefighter here, we'll move." We started thumbing through the want ads and miraculously, there was a job for a firefighter.

Sure enough, there was an opening at the Carmel Fire Department. I immediately applied for the job, and before we knew it we were moving back to my childhood paradise, closer to my stepmom Geri, my sisters, and most importantly, my own children.

Life for us finally was appearing like some sun would shine.

Chapter Eighteen
Like Father, Like Son

Welcome to the neighborhood, I thought, as Michele and I stood outside in front of the rental house we had barely started moving into. The whole place was cordoned off with crime scene tape, and two police cars sat alongside our moving truck, flashing their lights out front. We all waited for the bomb disposal unit to show up and I wondered what our new neighbors would be thinking.

Earlier that day, as we had begun to unload the moving truck that we had driven down from Red Bluff, something in the garage caught my eye. The item I had stumbled upon must have been left by previous residents: a pipe bomb. Immediately I called the police department to file a report and within minutes we were being evacuated from the house. Apparently the bomb disposal unit for the county was located nearly two hours away at Fort Hunter Ligget, so we'd have to wait.

We had made the move for a number of reasons— amongst them: safety, family, and a good job opportunity. But I was also hoping it would help me break my growing drug habit. This was the mystical place where I had felt most care-free as a kid. I thought that revisiting those moments would be healing. I also figured that being away from my dad would decrease my stress. Plus, in my mind, I hoped being close to the kids would provide motivation.

Michele stayed up in Red Bluff for six weeks until she was able to find a job down in Monterey. I spent some time with my kids, and with Geri and my stepsisters, Linda and Becky, but mostly I was alone. The loneliness, alongside the dreary weather and my nostalgia, turned out to be a recipe for failure. Most of my free time was spent trying to retrace my memories, but things were different now. Cannery Row had become a bona fide tourist trap; Holman's Department Store and the movie theater were both closed. Pacific Grove had earned a reputation as *a home for the newly wed and the nearly dead*, but there wasn't much else happening there.

My plan had been simply to taper down my stash of Vicodin, and then quit by the time the prescription bottle was empty. Instead, by the time I finished the supply I had brought with me, I was already developing relationships with a number of doctors in the area, *showing off my scars* and pining for pain relief.

Visiting so many different doctors began to present a problem. For each doctor I gave myself a pseudonym and used a different pharmacy. It got so confusing that I had to start a journal to be able to keep track of all my lies. Even with all the clever steps I took to cover my steps, it never occurred to me to give a different address. Pretty soon doctor's bills started showing up in my name, and the names of my aliases. Michele was getting suspicious.

"You're using again."

"I swear I'm not." I swore on the lives of everyone I knew, but the more I lied, the more the tension built up in our relationship.

Finally, I decided to tell Michele the truth about my abuse of the painkillers, the additional physicians, and my using people by stealing their pills.

I was too much of a sissy to tell Michele face-to-face, so I wrote it all down. It felt like cutting open an abscess that needed to be drained—the confession was probably ten pages long. I finished writing it one day while she was out of the house. Still, impatiently, I waited nervously until she returned.

Giving my letter to Michele was the hard part. When she got home she headed straight for the bathroom. My inability to deal with everything caused me to push open the door. Quickly, I shoved it in her face while she was sitting on the pot.

"Read this."

"What is it?"

"Just read it."

Several minutes later Michele came out of the bathroom with a million questions I couldn't answer.

Finally, she gave up the questioning and switched tactics. "Do you work tonight?" she asked.

"Yes."

She grabbed the phone and called my work to tell them I wouldn't be coming in due to a family emergency. The next call was to the recovery center. Michele set up an appointment for the following day.

***

The next morning, as we pulled into a parking lot, I frantically scanned the area for familiar faces. I didn't want anyone I knew to see me walking inside, and I was already developing an alibi in case I'd need one.

I entered the thirty-day program to detox off the pain-killers, still working night shifts for the fire department and ambulance. In group therapy, the counselor urged us to, "dig deep and find a higher power."

"Is 'a higher power' God?" I asked.

"A higher power is whatever you want it to be."

"What the hell does that mean?"

"Just find something that is bigger and more powerful than you, and that you can begin to perceive as being a higher power.

After some deliberation, I settled on the ocean. After all, it was bigger and stronger than me and my love for the ocean was real.

Quickly I was disillusioned by the whole higher-ocean-power-thing, I quit going to required in-house AA meetings and about two weeks later, I was discharged from rehab.

Not long after that I was invited by a colleague to join a group of guys on a fishing trip in San Diego. The invitation sounded to me like a good opportunity for distraction and a chance to do something *normal* with *normal people.* Michele wasn't thrilled, but I reminded her that I'd been told to try new things.

A little more than an hour into the road trip south, the first beer was cracked open. Soon I was having flashbacks to the drunken Colorado River road trip with my dad, but I tried just to put that aside and play along. Nevertheless, by the time we got to L.A., I was feeling queasy and unsettled.

Our arrival in San Diego was followed by a day of heavy drinking before we boarded the boat. The water was emerald green and the crisp air out at sea was refreshingly cool under the beating rays of the sun. I was trying hard to focus on the moment and forget about all the memories that were standing just outside the gate of my mind canal—until someone pointed out that we were just off the coast of Mexicali. *Tijauana!* was the thought that broke the dam. All the unsolicited memories began flooding me.

I panicked. Drowning, I looked out over the vastness of the ocean and tried to call on this higher power I'd chosen to rescue me. *Nope, nothing.* It was useless. *What's wrong with me?* I thought. *Why can't I just suck it up? Maybe Dad was right, maybe I am a pussy!*

***

The rest of the trip was a blur. I came home haunted and was unable to shake it. There was only one way that I knew I might be able to cope. To use my drug of choice—for me, the thing that eased the pain the best.

I wish I could say that I didn't know what I was doing when I took up to ten Vicodin at a time, but I did. Thinking *my body doesn't even want these damn things in it*, I began to gag! Finally, able to choke them down, twenty minutes passed, and I was able to relax. *All is well with my soul,* I thought, briefly.

But the haunting feeling didn't go away. It was inevitable that I'd have to up the ante. Because as an addict I was truly powerless on my own to stop and as much as I hated going there, it was back to the methadone clinic for me. There, I knew I would find a mixture of people, those who were legitimately trying to quit and also and those who were still dabbling. Truly, it was the dabblers that I was looking to talk to and see what they might have.

While driving toward the methadone clinic in Salinas I kept asking myself, *are you really going to do this again, Mike?* I imagined myself doing a U-turn and driving back to Monterey, but I could find no willpower to stop the desperation from rolling me down into the inevitable rut that I was digging for myself.

I approached the familiar sight of the queue of addicts filing in to the methadone clinic to get their daily dose, scanning the crowd for a connection to tap. I got in line behind a harmless looking lady and struck up a conversation.

"How's it going?" I asked, simply trying to pass the time of day and feeling sorry for myself and her.

"It's okay," the rugged fifty-year-old woman said in a smoker's voice and then she pensively asked, "How 'bout you?"

I shook my head, "The clinic cut my dose," I told her, "man, I'm feeling sick."

"Where are you from?"

"Monterey," I answered. "The guy I usually score from got popped and landed himself in the county jail."

"Bummer," she answered, without really looking up at me or any others that were around.

"If you could help me out, I'll let you pinch some off."

My new friend, Beverly, quickly made a call and I followed her back to her house. She lived in a nasty little studio with a small kitchen on the east side of Salinas. The place reminded me of the Heinz hotel where Dad and I used to score.

My new relapse buddy made small talk as we waited for the connection to arrive; he was immediately suspicious of me, but Beverly masterfully began weaving a tale of our supposed ten-year friendship and recent reunion. She almost had *me* believing her. He was hesitant, but finally agreed to do business with me.

As quickly as the dealer left, I was back to performing the old cooking-and-shooting-up ritual, alongside Beverly, like any other pious heroin-addict. Nine long years had passed since I'd attended Duane's intensive detox program and it all vanished in the blink of an eye.

Beverly was having trouble hitting a vein, so I stepped in to be of some aid to get things moving along and for me to be able to get my bump over with for the time being, anyway. Many of her veins had collapsed due to multiple injections, forcing her to be more creative in locating unused veins. Being a paramedic, I knew all the possible sites.

"What are you, a fucking doctor?!" She was impressed with my skills.

My plan to stay away from Salinas lasted only two days. I was back at Beverly's in no time, where I was able to quickly score. When she saw me walking down the driveway she stuck her head out the door and called, "Be there in a minute."

A few minutes later, the door opened again and a couple of guys walked out. Beverly said goodbye and invited me inside.

She sat down on the couch and lit a cigarette. "I hate doing it," she said.

"Doing what?" I asked, stopping myself as I realized what she meant.

"I wanted to be a teacher," she said, "but shit, everything just went wrong, you know what I mean?" She'd been to prison several times for various crimes and eventually gave up on the dream. She needed money, and selling her body seemed like the only feasible option.

We had little in common, but shared devotion makes for quick friendships. I started paying her visits three to four times a week, spending more time in Salinas with Beverly than at home with Michele. Beverly and I would call her connection and then sit around talking about our plans to quit. We would hit up, each time resolving that this would be the last time, both knowing that we were full of it, yet hoping all the same.

There's a certain allure that an addict and a dealer have with one another. It's a bond that is hard to understand unless you've actually been in this type of relationship.

***

Things at home were getting worse by the day. Michele was constantly suspicious of where I was spending my time and what I was doing, and I was constantly making up excuses and denying accusations. It was harder and harder for me to hide my other world from Michele. The tension and distrust was building a wall of fire between us.

Michele finally found her own drug: church. Since we'd moved to Monterey, Michele had decided that she wanted to attend church. At some point I had hoped that the *Big Guy* would help me out with the quitting thing, so I tagged along. It didn't seem to make any difference. *He must be too busy*, I thought. *He's no better than my dad. Father in heaven— what a bunch of crap!* Rather than finding support, I just felt like an outsider. I knew that I was one of those 'sinners' and it made me squirm in my seat, wondering if anyone else had noticed.

Of all the churches that Michele chose to stick with, it had to be Calvary, the same one that my ex-wife Shelly and our kids attended.

"Fine, go to church," I told Michele, "just don't preach to me." But the very fact of her attending made me furious.

Then, one night Michele announced to me that she had become a Christian, and I immediately flew into a rage. "This is my house and I'm in charge, not God." I wanted to break something. I kicked the chair next to me and sent it tumbling.

"You broke the chair!" she cried out. "What's your problem? You're the one with the Bible collection. Why do you have so many Bibles?"

I had been collecting Bibles for years, whether gifts from friends, churches, or Gideon Bibles I'd snatched from hotels; my growing Bible collection followed me everywhere I went. I never bothered to open them up and look inside, but somehow I considered them a treasured possession.

Still, something inside me was raging and I didn't know how to shut it off. Now my wife, ex-wife, and all my kids were going to church and talking about God. I felt totally alienated. Michele had even asked me to go with her to see the senior pastor, Bill Holdridge, for marriage counseling. There was no way I was going to let the church meddle in my marriage. I felt I was losing control of my family and didn't know what to do about it, so I did what I did best: avoided the issue and buried myself deeper in my addiction.

Even though I was making good money at work, I needed more to be able to afford my habit. I began to collect clothing, furniture, dishes, jewelry, or anything I could find to sell to a local pawnshop or trade with the dope man for drugs. I even stole from Geri, who pretended not to notice. I pawned Michele's wedding ring three times, each time feeling so guilty that I returned to buy it back, paying an additional twenty percent. I wasn't as lucky when it came to my own ring; when I went to buy it back, it had already been sold, so I had to buy a new one. I was used to buying myself new rings, though—for all the times I'd smashed it with a brick, flushed it down the toilet, or thrown it out the window in the heat of an argument with Michele.

Eventually, Michele lost the diamond in her ring, so she had the setting removed and replaced it with a cross. This only confirmed for me that she was more committed to her new relationship with God than she was to our marriage, and that made me angrier.

Something else that infuriated me was that Michele was giving money to the church. I needed every penny I could get, and I couldn't bear the thought of her giving it away. I did my best to convince Michele that the church was scamming her, but she wouldn't listen. Finally, I realized she wasn't going to budge and decided to try a different approach. *If I give her the whole church thing, maybe she'll leave me alone.* I decided to go to church with her to make her happy, and at the same time I resolved to find a way to get the money back.

One Sunday, I brought an empty backpack with me to church with the intention of snatching ladies' purses, but I couldn't bring myself to do it. Instead, I kept my eye on the offering bag, and then followed the ushers back to the church office where the money was kept. Still, I couldn't find a way to get to it. Finally, during the week I called the church and complained to the assistant pastor, Steve Braselton.

"You're conning my wife into giving you money," I accused him.

"Okay," the pastor replied, "I'll write you a check for whatever she has given."

But Michele overheard the conversation and stepped in to stop things from going further.

Of course that incident just stoked the fire between us even more. Realizing that I was in danger of losing my wife—who I loved—I made every attempt possible to repair things between us.

I made a plan to spoil Michele, hoping to take her focus off of my drug habit. I called dispatch and told them I was sick and was replaced on the ambulance by another paramedic. Afterward, I bought a bottle of wine, picked up some intimate apparels from local shops and surprised Michele at work. I gave her the package and told her that I had a romantic evening planned for the two of us. She reluctantly agreed. When Michele got home, I turned on some music, lit candles and served her a homemade dinner. For those few moments we forgot about our differences and enjoyed each other's company. All of a sudden the phone rang. It was my stepsister, Linda, and she was frantic; Geri had been rushed to Natividad hospital, unresponsive.

"Where was she?" I asked.

"At home," Linda said. "She was complaining of a headache and just stopped talking."

I jumped up and raced to the hospital. Geri was pronounced brain dead and died soon after.

The ambulance that had picked her up that night was the one that I was supposed to be working on. If I hadn't called in sick, I would have been the one doing CPR. *What a relief,* I thought, but that was the extent of the emotion I felt. I willed myself to cry, but couldn't even do it. There were so many things to cry over at that point in my life, and yet the numbing effect of the drugs in my system completely shut me off from any sensation or tears.

I knew that I couldn't continue life as it was going. My addiction was affecting my work and my relationships, and it was becoming increasingly difficult to hide the habit from those around me. I didn't want my kids to think I was a loser. Determined to get clean again, I tried to pull myself together. I tried to quit on my own, and when that didn't work, I tried to get help.

***

It was back to rehab, where I met Dr. Goldman.

"You're suffering from a disease," he told me after my initial intake evaluation, which had only confirmed what I already knew and had learned in all the meetings: that I was hopelessly addicted to opiates. Dr. Goldman lifted a huge weight off my shoulders. *I'm suffering from a horrible disease!* I was beginning to feel better already as my self-esteem returned, bringing color back to my paled ego. *It's not my fault!*

I couldn't wait to tell Michele.

"Not your fault," she said sarcastically. "You have a disease, huh?"

"Why do you have to be so damn skeptical?" I snapped back her. "What do you want me to do?"

"Well, I think you should go talk to Pastor Bill."

"Fine, I will."

I'm not sure if I was expecting him to pat me on the back and say, "You poor guy, you have a disease," but I was certainly expecting him to be sympathetic.

"No, Mike. What you are suffering from is a problem with sin," he told me.

"So this is all my fault?"

Michele kept silent. I wasn't about to admit it, but I knew he was right. When I was young, my dad used to refer to his addiction as a disease, which always felt to me like a poor excuse for inexcusable behavior. Sadly enough, I now had found myself in the same trap. I didn't want to think that this was my fault, but if it was, I had no idea what to do about it.

All the recovery programs say that you have to call on a higher power to help you find freedom from addiction. I decided that I had better take this idea seriously and I began to focus on discovering my true higher power. My dad had always praised Khalil Gibran's book, *The Prophet,* so I gave that another read. It was good, but didn't give me the answers I wanted. I looked into Buddhism, Hinduism, and Mormonism, Wicca and Scientology. I ordered a copy of *Dianetics* by L Ron Hubbard; the commercials had promised all the answers, but the book delivered none. I looked into acupuncture, vitamins, and Chinese medicine. I even did my best to recall some of the concoctions Duane had whipped up for me. I made a few calls trying to track him down, with no luck. I looked deep within myself. *What am I missing?* I repeatedly asked myself.

After unsuccessfully searching for an alternative, I turned back to the ocean. I found myself constantly standing in the freezing waters at Lovers Point, shivering and trying desperately to make some kind of connection with my higher power. *Is there anyone out there?*

Someone told me that when acclaimed motivational speaker Tony Robbins spoke he would have plants placed around the stage so that he could draw life energy from them as he spoke. I was inspired. At home I gathered up all our plants in and around our house until I had turned the bathroom into an overstuffed greenhouse. Then I gathered all the salt I could find, shakers and jars, and poured it into the bathtub to simulate the ocean. I jumped in expecting nothing short of a healing miracle. A couple hours later, I crawled out of the tub looking like a prune and feeling like a fool.

None of my attempts at finding a higher power were successful. Meanwhile my kids, their mother, and my wife were all nagging me to come to church and consider the Christian God. I'd seen so much hypocrisy in churches; I just *knew* that the whole thing had to be a delusion. I had a list of inconsistencies that I felt would be able to disprove the religion, but I needed to get some questions answered before I would be able to publicize my findings. I imagined myself being interviewed by Oprah and bursting the big bubble on national TV. At the same time, I wasn't sure I really wanted to burst the bubble. *Even if it is false, it seems to be working for some people. Why would I want to take that away?* Michele had been super nice to me lately. It was irritating because it made it harder to put the blame on her when we fought.

I found out later that the change in behavior for Michele came after a church picnic when she'd had a talk with Pastor Bill. She told him that she was planning to leave me, hoping to get his blessing. She got a rather different response. "You need to stick by him," he told her, "God's not done with him yet." My wife was furious, but submitted to his guidance. "Win him over with a gentle and quiet spirit."

Michele really did take the challenge seriously. She stopped confronting me and stopped begging me to come to church.

Occasionally, I did come to church, and I eventually even agreed for Michele and I to go to marriage counseling with Pastor Bill. This gave Michele a speck of hope that I might change. I wanted to change, but I didn't have any idea how. The distance between A and B seemed like the Grand Canyon. I knew there was something wrong with me, but I was paralyzed, too terrified to admit any fault. So, I continued to maintain my innocence to those around me. Once I complained to Pastor Bill that Michele was accusing me of using, when I was really clean.

"Well, why don't you just take a drug test to settle things once and for all?" he asked. Cornered, I stormed out of his office. "If you want a drug test so bad, you pee in the cup!"

One afternoon, I was tired of arguing with Michele. I reached into my pocket to get my keys, and out flipped a gram of heroin neatly packaged in a brightly colored balloon. It bounced across the floor as we both scrambled to reach it. Michele snatched it up, putting it in her mouth to keep it from me.

Having never used heroin before, I knew that if she bit into the balloon, she would be dead long before an ambulance could arrive. Anyone who had never used before would be dead if they swallowed a full balloon. At this point I was so scared for her that I honestly no longer cared about the heroin, but I wanted to get that thing out of her mouth. Michele was not about to surrender without a fight. She kicked, punched, and bit my fingers as I tackled her to the ground and dug the balloon out of her mouth. I finally wrestled it away from her—I grabbed it and stormed out of the house, slamming the door behind me as if she had done something wrong.

***

As much as Michele wanted to help me, she needed backup. So she staged an intervention. I sat there, my knees awkwardly knocking, sitting in the living room of my ex-wife and her new husband's house, being confronted by the two of them and my wife. I wanted badly to say, *Yes, you're all right.* But I couldn't. I couldn't admit that I was hurting the ones I loved the most. It was easier to just listen, deny everything, and walk out feeling angry and justified.

"How dare you drag Shelly and Don into this!" I yelled at Michele when we got home. "It's like you want them to think I'm a total loser."

"Well, you sure are acting like one!"

"I'm so sick of you judging me. You think you're such a saint ever since you started believing in fairy tales."

"Mike, the people who love you are trying to help you."

"What happened back there was not loving. Ganging up on me like that—that was fucking nasty."

"Why can't you just admit you have a problem?" Michele yelled at me.

"Why can't you just leave me alone?" I yelled back.

"Well, if you want to be left alone so badly, maybe you should just go away and give us some peace around here."

"Maybe I should just move out then."

"I think you should."

"Then I will."

"Do."

Reluctantly, I packed my things and left.

Chapter Nineteen
Downward Spiral

After living in my own apartment for about a year, Michele had only recently agreed to give me another chance and let me return home. I had lost my paramedic jobs as well as my job as a firefighter...due to dishonesty and carelessness—though the root cause was always addiction—and I was now working as a plumber with a local plumbing company. I was trying hard to be responsible and prove to Michele that I could change.

For a few weeks, things looked somewhat hopeful. I had managed to convince her that I was doing well enough that she could trust me to take care of her daughter for a couple hours.

Michele had been just on her way out the door when the phone rang.

Michele's cheerful face turned sour as she listened to the voice on the other end of the phone, and I knew my reprieve was over.

"Well, my husband is a heroin addict," she said, glaring at me. "Sure, he's right here."

It was Detective Johnson. "Mr. Casey," he started, "we raided the house of a suspected drug dealer this morning. Can you explain why he would be in possession of your personal checks, drawn on your account and made out to him?" I tried desperately to think of a possible explanation.

"Before you answer," he went on, "your wife let me know that you're an IV drug user." I kept my mouth shut. "A bit of advice, Mr. Casey: stay the hell out of Salinas. We're watching you."

The message came through loud and clear, but I took the risk anyway and found myself back at Beverly's within the next couple of days. I bought myself a quarter ounce of heroin before heading to my current employment. Shortly after getting to work on a backed-up toilet, the customer came in and asked, "Did you do something wrong? There are cops swarming the house."

I quickly left what I was doing and walked around the side of the house to my work van. I managed to get the door open and pop the quarter ounce in my mouth and swallow the balloon before being stopped by police.

"Freeze! Put your hands up." I stood there with my hands in the air, while watching about a dozen or so police officers approach me from every direction. There was nowhere to hide, and there were enough spoons and syringes in the van to land me in jail. Oddly enough I felt relieved, like I had the afternoon I handed Michele the letter confessing my sins.

My arms were cuffed behind my back, and Detective Johnson looked me right in the eyes. "I told you to stay the hell out of Salinas, didn't I?"

As he escorted me back into the house to collect my things, I heard the customer talking to my boss on the phone. "Can you send someone who's not a criminal, please?"

***

My experience in the Monterey County Jail was less than pleasant. The red-and-white striped jumpsuit was okay, but I was shocked to find out that I wouldn't be given a pillow or a blanket, and was expected to sleep under bright fluorescent lights that produced a constant, irritating hum. Most inmates stayed up all night playing spades. When I had a moment alone, I stuck my finger down my throat and threw up my stash, carefully unwrapped it, bit off a piece, and then swallowed it again. This was a trick I had learned years earlier from my dad at the methadone clinic. The quarter ounce didn't last long, and soon I was faced with the challenge of detoxing in jail.

In court, I was sentenced to Deferred Entry of Judgment, which meant that I could go free, but would need to complete some classes and stay clean. I was able to complete all that was required of me in order to have the charges dropped, except staying clean. I overcame that obstacle by purchasing clean urine, pouring it in a condom, and hiding it in a dark, warm place.

After getting out of jail, I lost my job as a plumber. A wealthy and generous customer who believed in second chances bought me my own van, and I still had a good rapport with enough customers to keep myself busy. I was grateful for that van, but it sure didn't keep me out of trouble.

***

The final chapter of my despair turned into an epic that lasted well over a year and could fill the pages of a book on its own, but would be too tedious to print and too horrific to remember. Ahead was a long, drawn-out cycle of moving in and out of Michele's until I ended up living in my van, trying to come clean and blowing everything all over again. Dad always said, "If a frog had wings, he wouldn't bump his ass every time he hopped." I think it was his attempt to quiet my inquisitive nature, but it kept me feeling like I'd never get out of that rut. I was born a big hairy frog. If I wanted to stop bumping my ass, I would need to change my nature. The trick is: *How can a frog stop being a frog?*

That fall, a new Christian high school was opening up in town and a pastor was coming all the way from Australia to run it. Shelly decided to enroll our kids, and they were all super excited for me to meet their new principal, Pastor Skip. Everyone talked him up so much that I started to share their anticipation. When I finally met the man, I had to admit I was impressed. He was an extremely animated character and had an intriguing personality.

Skip seemed to take me on as his mission, undoubtedly after hearing about me from Shelly and the kids. He gave me a little booklet about the path to God and invited himself over to explain it to me. After that, Pastor Skip came over a couple times a week to chat about God. He lived just down the street from us, so he would just show up on our doorstep. I saw it as my opportunity to trip him up by pulling out some of my clever questions that would invalidate the entire Christian faith. I interrogated him about cavemen, dinosaurs, UFOs, and aliens, but he didn't seem shaken by anything. Still, he wasn't able to convince me that there was any truth to the Bible and Christianity.

"How are you supposed to trust someone you can't even see?" I asked.

Calmly looking me in the eye, he answered, "Well, that's where faith comes in."

"I don't even trust most of the people I know, and I can see them." This had been ingrained in me as a child, and reinforced as a paramedic, where I had learned the acronym ACT: 'Assume nothing, check everything, and trust no one'.

I was always especially suspicious of the motives of men who tried to get too close, but Skip managed to win me over with his good humor. I genuinely liked the guy. He asked deep and insightful questions, which made me want to let my guard down, even if I wasn't able to relax at all yet.

It was because of Skip that I started to attend church services with Michele on my own initiative. One particular Sunday, they announced an upcoming men's retreat.

"Why don't you come?" Skip asked.

"What do you do there?"

"Well," he said, thinking for a moment. "We pray, we sing, we have Bible studies, we eat, and we just hang out and have fun."

Suddenly, I felt extremely uncomfortable and found a quick reason to excuse myself from the conversation. Part of me wanted to go, and part of me felt like I wasn't good enough to go. Still, I couldn't seem to get the idea of having a chance at a different life out of my head. Later, when talking with Michele, I mentioned the possibility of going to the conference and, of course, she was extremely excited and encouraged me to go. Part of my dilemma, probably the biggest part, was *Can I go to this men's conference and still continue to use? How will I pull it off? Will God strike me dead?*

Well, I'll go for Michele, I thought.

The first thing I did at the retreat, after locating my room assignment was to find the nearest bathroom to shoot up in. *If God's gonna strike me dead, here's his chance.* I sat in the bathroom searching for that perfect vein, which could sometimes take me hours since so many of my veins had collapsed. Sweating with frustration, I thought, "*This is not the life I want for me or my family. What happened to me? Have I given up on my dreams? Am I okay with this?* Suddenly, I was in the vein. That familiar warm feeling took over once again. I was okay... *for now.* After the usual time it took to nod off, I headed outside to play basketball with Skip and the guys.

When all was said and done... I had attended several retreats in this manner. I don't remember much about the Bible studies; I spent most of that time nodding off. *Learning by osmosis,* I'd hoped. What I do remember was having the other guys banging on the bathroom door while I struggled to locate a vein, "Are you all right?" Every time I went into the bathroom to get my fix, I felt worse.

Looking around at the other guys from the church, I was impressed: one owned a large construction company, another had a good job in agriculture. There was a lawyer, a teacher, and a doctor. They were clean-cut and had nice families. It totally baffled me. *Either they're all living a lie, or I'm the one that's totally out of my mind.*

It was in front of an entire congregation at Calvary that I finally publically admitted my addiction. Michele had invited me to a Wednesday night service, and I had agreed to follow her there. I jumped in my van and began to drive. That night it was raining heavily and the wind was howling like the twilight zone. About half a mile from the church, my van began to lug.

"Shit!" I yelled as I pulled over. I was out of gas. Because of the rain, Michele couldn't see I had pulled over, and I didn't want her to think I was playing hooky. *Not this time,* I told myself.

I was determined to get there, so I jumped out of the van and began to run along the highway in the pouring rain. I was out of shape, and my lungs were burning. Cars were whizzing by me, and with limited visibility, they probably couldn't even see me, but still I pressed on, convinced to try even if I never got there. I truly wanted a new life.

When I finally arrived at the church, fifteen minutes later, I could see the relief on Michele's face. At the end of the meeting, Pastor Bill asked if anyone needed prayer for anything. Without thinking, I stood up. A man ran over to me with a microphone and it came out, unfiltered. "I'm a heroin addict and need help." There was a palpable gasp. The next moment a middle-aged woman, Suzy, jumped out of her seat and announced that she too had been trapped in addiction for years, but had now been clean for over a decade. Before I knew it, I was surrounded by a crowd of praying people.

The prayers didn't seem to help, and neither did the baptism, which I received later. I had two reasons for signing up to get myself dunked for the second time since being cajoled into my foster-home conversion. First of all, I knew it would make Michele happy, but there was also a part of me that genuinely hoped it would make a difference. By this point I didn't have a lot of faith in a magical cure-all, but there was no harm in trying.

Skip took advantage of my voluntary baptism, and tried to follow up by 'discipling' me. He got a book on the beginnings of Christian growth, and invited me to go through it with him.

One Tuesday afternoon, Skip knocked on the door.

"You free this afternoon?"

"Yeah."

"Let's go for a walk."

The weather was beautiful that day and so we decided to walk the two miles it took to get to the farmers market in downtown Monterey. Conversation was light, no discussions about God, religion, or my addictions. It was good to feel like a human being, if even for a few moments. Together we tasted strawberries and peaches, paused to listen to some street musicians playing jazz, bought flowers for our wives, and sat down on the curb to eat a late lunch. Among the sights, sounds and smells of a carnival, we laughed and joked like old pals. By the time we got home, I felt safe enough to open my heart to him.

"Skip, why do you spend so much time with me?" I asked.

"Because I love you." I felt he was sincere.

"How can you love me? You hardly know me, and I am totally strung out."

"God loves you no matter what you do."

"I don't get it. I spend most of our time together trying to prove you wrong and yet you keep coming back. My own father never spent this much time with me."

Skip repeatedly told me that he was praying for me, and reminded me that his wife, Terry, and Michele were also praying for me constantly. It frustrated me that everyone thought I was so messed up that they had to pray for me with such fierceness, but I couldn't deny that he seemed genuine.

***

It was a visit from my brother that had sent me out of the house the final time. Paul and his then-wife, Karen, were living up in Red Bluff at the time. Grandma had also moved back there from Arkansas to be close to Dad. I wanted so much to visit, but I didn't because I didn't want her to see me strung out. Instead, Paul came down to visit me.

When Michele heard Paul was coming she announced that she would be going to stay a few days with her mother. I found out much later that she actually stayed at a friend's house and spent their days there driving around in her car, knowing that a visit from Paul would bring nothing but trouble.

Paul's use of heroin was recreational; he didn't have the same problems as I did with addiction, and seemed to be able to start and stop whenever he wished. Still, by the time Michele returned from her 'visit', Paul was in the hospital from an overdose. When Paul woke up after several days on a ventilator in the ICU he asked me, "Where's the stuff?"

"I was so scared you would die, I flushed it."

"That was dumb," he said. "Go get some more."

After a quick trip to Beverly's, I searched around the hospital to find some syringes. And, as insane as it sounds, Paul and I cooked up right there in his hospital room.

When Paul was discharged, my brother and I decided to stay together in a motel, since by now we were definitely not welcome at Michele's. Neither of us really were ready to get away from what now seemed 'our way of life'—so we spent our days working and looking for ways to get ahold of some extra cash, and our nights in whatever seedy motel we could find. So many of my veins had collapsed that I gave up trying to find them and started skin-popping. There wasn't as much of a rush that way, but at least it kept me from getting sick and from having to face the heavy weight of my emotions un-squelched. The real drawback was that I was developing abscesses, which I had to cut open with a hobby knife to drain out the thick, brown, foul-smelling pus. There were times that my legs were so swollen I wasn't able to put my pants on. I would wear the same pair of sweat pants for several days in a row. If that wasn't bad enough, I was smoking three packs of cigarettes a day and living on ninety-nine-cent double cheeseburgers from Burger King. They say addictions lead to hospitals, institutions or death. I was well on my way to all three—settling for a substandard way of existence. *What in the hell is happening to me?* At this point I had completely given up on myself. Being numb was the only thing I really knew. I considered moving to Salinas to be closer to my connection. I realized I had become comfortably numb and this scared the hell out of me. I wondered how I could ever be comfortable living like this. This is when I realized I needed to get it together at all costs.

***

When Paul announced he was going home, I didn't say a word. I totally understood why he needed to leave. Two strung out addicts trying to live together was unbearable by any standard. Fighting over cigarettes and arguing about money for what little food we ate, much less the arguments about the drugs just got to us both. Even though I could barely swallow the thought of being alone, I just told myself, *Suck it up, you pussy.*

At times, right after Paul left, I thought about suicide, but I wasn't quite sure how I would do it. I knew that I was not willing to keep on living my current way of life, but didn't have any idea how to stop the things over which I had no control. I had always thought of suicide as a permanent solution to a temporary problem, but now I wasn't so sure. There seemed to be nothing temporary about my situation; it had been going on for years. I was killing myself slowly. *Wouldn't it be so much easier to just get it over with?* I was beginning to regret that I had pawned my guns for dope. *Or,* I almost didn't dare to think, *was someone looking out for me?*

With Paul gone, I could no longer afford even the cheapest hotels, so I spent my nights parked in front of Calvary, sleeping in the van. It was the only place I felt safe.

Even though we were separated at the time, Michele did her best to look out for me. One night she invited me to come over for dinner. Exhausted, I found myself nodding off at the table. Suddenly, out of the corner of my eye, I saw Michele reaching for my keys. I quickly jumped up and chased her out the door to my van. She hopped in and locked the doors behind her.

"What's this?" she hollered from inside the van, holding up my newest $700 stash of dope while I pounded on the doors and windows. Michele sat in the driver's seat and started the engine.

"Please stop!" I screamed as she shifted into reverse and started to back out of the driveway.

"I'm taking this to James' house!" she yelled. James was a local cop she knew from church. I was not about to let that happen; I was not going back to jail again.

Clinging to the side mirror, while watching Michele jump the curb, she headed into a small park next to our house, throwing me to the ground. I leaped right back up again and onto the front bumper, hanging onto the windshield wipers and pounding on the front windshield as hard as possible. Michele took a sharp turn, and I fell onto the grass. She stalled, and I took the opportunity to grab a large rock, smashing it into the side window. It bounced off, but I picked it up again and jumped back onto the bumper, holding on with one hand and striking the windshield as hard as I could with the other. I was spewing every threat I could think of, but Michele was not fazed. The back wheels got stuck in the lawn, and she was doing her best to get the vehicle out, while I ran around the van trying to smash each window. As a fireman I had broken my share of car windows, but for some reason these wouldn't break. Since it was in the late evening hours, fortunately there were not a lot of people milling about for us to worry about them calling the police.

Finally, she gained enough traction to get the tires loose, and off Michele drove, jumping the curb and heading down the street. All I saw were the taillights as she sped out of view.

I fell to my knees in the street. I wish I could say I realized the error of my ways, but my only concern was where I would get another seven-hundred bucks to replace two days' worth of dope she'd found.

Returning to the house I sat on the couch, waiting to be arrested. The following morning I woke up to find my keys on the kitchen table. Michele never went to see James; she just threw away the dope.

Later, I tried to apologize for my life-threatening rage. "If you had only left my van alone, this never would have happened. I could have killed you."

"It's not up to you to decide when I die," Michele answered, giving me a look that said, *God is protecting me.*

On one night, after a huge fight, Michele—in what she refers to as an act of God—found herself at another local church for an evening prayer meeting. There she heard the testimony of a Salinas pastor who had overcome heroin addiction and was now running a rehab home. It was Pastor Herb from Victory Outreach.

"Good for him," I said flatly, after her heartfelt retelling of his story. Still, I was interested in hearing more and agreed to attend their Friday night service. The church looked nothing like the spacious and well-groomed Calvary. The whole place was lively and filled with a sense of excitement. Michele said it was the Holy Spirit. When Pastor Herb began to share, I felt like I was the only person in the room and that he was talking directly to me. *How can another man know the pain in my heart?*

The recovery program sounded like a good idea, but I wasn't willing to commit an entire year of my life. Thirty to forty days was my limit.

Meanwhile, I was still living the low life in my van, skin popping, dealing with abscesses, and barely scraping by. In my desperation one night, I even tried to borrow money from my teenage daughter, Sarah.

"Psst," I called out as I tossed a couple small pebbles at her bedroom window.

"Dad! What are you doing?" she whispered.

"I'm sick and need to get a motel room," I answered. "Do you have any money I could borrow?"

"No, I wish I did."

Then I stooped even lower. "What about your piggy bank?"

"No," she answered, stifling tears.

I'm such a dirt bag, I realized. It was so hard to believe my low had even included me asking my daughter for something that would have in the end been so little money and only helped for such a short time.

"Sorry to bother you, sweetie. Go back to sleep."

"I love you, Dad," she called out as I crept back to my van.

I had used up all my finances and destroyed the bank account that Michele and I still shared. I had found a way to trick the ATMs by depositing empty envelopes at night and immediately withdrawing cash. Back then, banks would accept envelopes and confirm the deposit on the next business day. Eventually, one of the bank clerks, who went to Calvary, warned Michele about what I was doing. Michele confronted me and demanded I pay back what I had overdrawn. "The bank's going to close the account, Mike. Did you really think you could get away with this?"

Until that point, Michele had begun letting me into the house for meals and showers, on the condition that I would sit down with her and listen to sermons on tape. I actually borrowed several of the tapes and listened to them in my van, too. Secretly I was hoping that something would rub off on me. But after I had jeopardized our joint bank account, Michele banned me from the house. "You're on your own," she said. "You need to get some help." One of the things that comes with being as addicted as I was is the ability to manipulate all systems—that sadly included my wife.

One morning, when I knew Michele would be at work, I crawled into the bathroom window to take a shower and grab some breakfast. I found Michele's paycheck from both jobs sitting on the table, so I grabbed them on my way out. As usual, I told myself I would use the money to get well and then try to borrow some cash to pay back the bank. Instead, like a dog returning to its own vomit, I easily cashed the checks since our first names were so similar, spent all the money, and returned to Michele with my tail between my legs.

"I am tired of this, Mike. I can't help you anymore. You need to get help," she told me from behind the fence.

A moment in time occurred which I have no recollection of—hence the next thing I knew I ended up knocking on Skip's front door. He called Pastor Herb, who suggested I talk to Pastor Charlie Reyna, who was in charge of the rehabilitation program.

"This is a year of your life. Are you sure you're ready?" He asked me over the phone.

"I have no other option." I surrendered, still having no idea how my future would evolve.

Chapter Twenty
Victory Outreach

It was about 8:30 p.m. when we pulled up in front of the old Victorian-style house. The sign posted on the front lawn read, "Victory Outreach," another rehab. This would be my fourth. *Doing good, Mike,* I laughed to myself. *It looks as though you're following in Dad's footsteps after all.*

This one was a stark contrast to the shiny new rehabs I had been to previously. It was part of a network of Christian recovery homes and churches that were all started and run by graduates of the program. The building in Salinas was a large residential home, which seemed ancient with its old wooden floors, rusty, dripping pipes, and weary staircases. The house itself was once an R&R Army station during WWII. As one of Salinas' preserved historic homes, renovations had been kept to a minimum.

What did you expect? I asked myself. *It's free.* All the other rehabs I had attended cost anywhere from $700 to $1,000 a day.

This program was also an entire year rather than one or two months like the others had been, but the thing that made this rehab stand out the most was its distinctly Christian approach. There would be no option to seek help from the ocean or to choose my own higher power here; it was already decided. In addition to group therapy and counseling sessions, there would be prayer circles and Bible studies.

***

Earlier that morning, it had been business as usual. As I drove my white van down Highway 68, from the lush Monterey Bay toward the plain fields of the Salinas valley, I thought about the previous night's conversation with Michele, unable to shake the foreboding sense that this was fast becoming the end of the line for our marriage.

I rolled down the window and threw out a challenge to God, "If you really do exist, why don't you help me? You seem to be willing to help everyone but me." And then, for good measure, "You suck!"

I tried to put all this out of my mind as I arrived at my first client's house to replace a water heater in South Salinas. I worked fast that morning, and had finished with my third client slightly after midday with two hundred bucks in hand and an appetite for a greasy lunch. As I returned to work for a final client after lunch, I eagerly anticipated a stopover in the east side of the city for one last fix before checking into rehab. Trying to cover all debts and all these drugs had finally taken me down.

As I arrived at East Market Street, in desperation, I stopped at a phone booth to call my old connection, 'Moppa'. I dialed his pager number off the top of my head and waited until he called me back. Juan would be there soon, I dared to believe. Within seconds and with a smirk, I climbed back into my van in the parking lot of the Hot Stop Food and Liquor, waiting for my runner.

Juan pulled up to my window in silence to make the transaction.

"I'll bring the money later tonight, and an additional fifty bucks for you," I said. Juan trusted me because I always paid him extra for his cooperation.

"You'd better pay up soon," he warned, and with that he left as quickly as he came. I had already maxed out my $500 credit limit with my dealer and this extra $200 was a favor on his part. I could have given him the money, but I wanted to have something to give to Michele.

No sooner had he left than I was cooking up my last ration in the back of the van. I pulled out my tools: the spoon, the water, the cotton, the lighter, the syringe. I straightened out my jeans and stuck the needle straight through, penetrating my thigh and injected it with the familiar fluid that made everything okay. *I will certainly miss this warm feeling.*

I went directly back to Michele's and she let me in. I handed her the money I had made that day. She helped me pack a huge bag for my year-long stay, and we headed back to Salinas together.

As she drove, I sat in silence.

"I hope it works this time," she said.

I thought about the other failed attempts at rehab. *Would this be any different?*

"I talked to your sister, Becky," Michele broke the silence again. "She will come to see you next week." I already knew where this was going.

"I'll be leaving for Redding soon." It hurt to hear those words. I had known that our marriage was over, but Michele going to her mom's made things feel worse.

When we arrived at Victory Outreach, Pastor Charlie wasn't there, so his wife, Marlene, met us and passed me off to one of the other guys to show me to my room on the second floor. As we went up the staircase we passed by a group of about a dozen or more guys sitting in the living room having a Bible study.

I was assigned a top bunk in the room I was to share with five other guys. Quite humiliating for a heroin addict who wakes up frequently throughout the night with screaming diarrhea. As soon as I had unpacked my belongings into the cabinet assigned to me, I went back downstairs and stepped outside to light up a smoke. Immediately all the guys inside stopped what they were doing, turned, and snapped at me, "No smoking!"

"This is going to be interesting," I thought to myself as I put out my cigarette. None of the other rehab places I had been to banned cigarettes. They were more like high-class resorts. This place was worn out, but had a good feeling about it.

A few minutes later, I was called back into the room to meet the guys and to be initiated into the house by prayer and the 'laying on of hands'. This kind of prayer was common practice in the house. I sat in the middle of the ring and was quickly surrounded by sweaty bodies and heavy hands were placed all over my head, shoulders, back and arms. All at once they started to babble gibberish. As they spattered out incomprehensible sounds and consonants, one voice came through in plain English, passionately praying to God for my stay at Victory Outreach. He prayed that the spirit of God might come in and heal me from my addictions, and he prayed against the power of the evil one who might try to thwart God's plan for my life. A chorus of 'Yes, Lords' and 'Amens' flew out like sparks in the fiery circle.

I sat there thinking, "How the hell am I supposed to survive these crazy, non-smoking Pentecostals?"

By the time I had the chance to go back up to my room I was crazy for a smoke. I found myself alone in the bedroom and saw my window of opportunity. They had confiscated my cigarettes, but I thought I might be able to find some if I could just get out. I snuck through the back door across the hall from my room and found myself on a landing; I climbed down the back of the roof and jumped to the ground.

Just down the street there was a car dealership where I found several cigarette butts in an old nasty ashtray. The butts had lipstick on them. *Beggars can't be choosers*, I thought. I got a light from a stranger and then used one to light the next, until I had smoked through all that I could scavenge. It wasn't enough to get me high. *I need a real fix,* I thought. So I walked down to the Rodeo Inn, where I borrowed a stranger's cellphone to page my connection. We waited for the call back, but after about ten minutes the phone owner started getting impatient. I grabbed him and begged him to stay just a little longer, but he threatened to beat me up and pushed me away.

Feeling totally demoralized, I headed back toward the house. As I approached, I found the whole crew walking toward me like a herd bringing in the stray.

Later that night, Pastor Charlie arrived and met me before going to bed. He said he would give me a few days to recover from withdrawal. He understood what I was going through because he'd been a heroin addict as well. Even just listening to the sound of his voice comforted me.

The following day, I woke up feeling like I had just died. *So much for God's help.* I was sick, shaky, weak, and desperately in need of a fix. *I would do anything—and I mean anything—for just one more fix.* Instead I had to put up with the morning's charismatic prayer and worship, which just felt chaotic to me.

During the morning chores I found my moment to sneak out. I told the lady at the Salvation Army across the street that my wife was in a terrible accident and I needed to use the phone. This time the return phone call came quickly and Juan said he'd be there soon. I waited for a while, but he never showed up. Before long someone back at the house spotted me from across the street and the game was over. They called Charlie at work and he came straight over to pick me up and take me back with him.

On his way back to work, Charlie pulled up in front of a convenience store. He watched as I jumped out of the car and started collecting cigarette butts off the ground and going through the ashtrays at the front entrance.

Charlie was cool. He had been through the same thing, he told me, so he knew what it was like. I was jittery and nervous. The cigarettes helped a bit, but I needed something hard.

Over lunch, Charlie shared his story in more detail. It gave me some hope to know that someone had been in my situation and was able to turn around and help others, but I still didn't see how that could ever happen to me. At the end of the day he bought me ice cream and energy bars. He totally understood what was going on inside of me.

After dinner that evening I made another attempt at sneaking out. I returned to the Rodeo Inn and this time I called Beverly.

"Moppa is pissed at you," she said. "You owe him $700."

She told me she'd try to come and help me out, but I knew she wouldn't make it. I turned back, defeated. My body was aching and every step took effort. On the way back I stopped on the overpass and climbed up onto the railing. I lay, face down, my stomach pressing into the cold hard metal railing and my chin on my hands, staring down at the freeway below, trying to gather the strength to roll off. I was a hopeless case. Clearly, I was not cut out for this rehab thing. In spite of Charlie's kindness, I wasn't able to resist the temptation to sneak out. I just couldn't take it anymore. *If I'm not going to be committed, what's the point? I can't handle disappointing Michele and my kids once again. Why don't I just give them all a break and end this thing right now?* But I didn't have the courage, so I trudged back to Victory Outreach, feeling doomed.

I knew that if I left the recovery home, I'd never get Michele back, but there was no way I was going to pull off sobriety. *If I could only find a way to keep using while I'm here,* I thought. The solution came to me just a few minutes before my entrance interview with Pastor Herb: the guys at the home did odd jobs here and there to bring in a little income, but they didn't get a lot of work. *I could easily hook them up and keep them busy with referrals from my business. They'll be so happy with the income—they can finally make renovations—and they won't even notice when I put some of the money aside. I could easily put some guys to work and then slip off to get my high.* All I had to do was convince Pastor Herb that I would come clean, become a model citizen, and provide the perfect solution to all their monetary problems.

Pastor Herb didn't buy into my pitch. He just smiled and said, "Mike, the only way you will ever truly be free is at the hand of God. You need to be delivered." *Maybe that worked for him*, I thought, *but it's not going to work for me.*

The next day, I woke up with an awful feeling. I'd been feeling horrible constantly, but this was worse. I had a sharp headache, I wanted a fix more than ever, and I was entertaining the idea of withdrawing from the program. Worse yet, I had huge abscesses on each of my legs where I had injected too many doses of heroin. That's when my desperate mind began scheming; these abscesses were my ticket to relief. As a medic I knew that the hospital would give me morphine for the pain. I ran downstairs and showed my wounds to Marlene.

"I need to go to the ER," I told her.

***

As I waited my turn at the hospital, I started to think about how morphine had started this cycle with heroin twice before. I had been clean now for three whole days, but this would put me right back where I started. *Do I really want that?* I thought to myself.

I went up to the window to ask when it would be my turn. "You're up next," the nurse told me. I started pacing. *No!* I decided, *I don't want to stay.* I turned to the guys who had accompanied me from Victory Outreach: "Let's go."

On the way back I explained to them that I had really had just wanted the morphine they would give me in the hospital. We talked about how it's not uncommon to get abscesses from heroin injections, and they could heal just fine on their own. I was proud of myself for making the right decision. This was the first time that I had managed to resist the temptation of drugs all by myself. *See*, I thought, *I am victorious.*

Sister Marlene, to my surprise, was indignant. "This doesn't smell right; I think you should go back to the hospital," she said, and started talking about 'spiritual warfare'. She figured I wasn't strong enough to say 'no' on my own, and reasoned that it must be the devil's game to keep me away from the hospital. "Go back," she insisted. "Your life might be at risk."

This 'spiritual warfare' talk was new to me—although I had heard Pastor Bill talk about it a few times before—but her decisiveness was hard to argue with in my condition.

When I got back to the hospital the doctor recognized that these were no ordinary abscesses. It turned out that the last time I had shot up, I had been infected by a flesh-eating bacteria, called necrotizing fasciitis that had bored through both my thighs, requiring immediate surgery.

"I'm sorry to tell you this, Mr. Casey, but this is very serious," the doctor warned, suggesting that I notify Michele. "I have to inform you that you may not survive the surgery."

Chapter Twenty-One
A New Beginning

As I opened my eyes, all the sights, sounds and smells were familiar to me. After all, I had been a paramedic for seventeen years; I was intimately familiar with hospitals and hospital rooms. It was the Christmas tree in my room that was puzzling. I could vaguely remember coming to the hospital from Victory Outreach the week before Thanksgiving.

I felt a strong desire to get out of bed and stretch. As I tried to get up, I realized that my left arm and leg had fallen asleep. *I must have slept wrong. I'll just give it a minute, and then I'll get up and go see what the heck is going on.* After numerous attempts to get up, I pressed the call button for the nurse.

"What's going on?" I inquired anxiously.

"Relax," she said with a smile, and then a reply that left me even more worried. "I will call the doctor to come and talk with you."

The doctor informed me that the infection in my legs had required not one, but ten operations over a period of nine days.

"Unfortunately, during your recovery time you suffered a massive stroke and had to be placed on life support." I had been in the hospital for a total of thirty-five days, and in a coma for twenty-five of those. "I'm afraid that the damage caused to your brain is very severe."

Massive stroke. Coma. Life-support. Brain damage. The words gagged me. I looked down at my arms and legs, under the starch white hospital sheets, and held my breath for the rest.

"In fact," the doctor continued, "the lack of feeling you are having in your left arm and leg actually affects the whole left side of your body. You have little to no function in your left hand and arm because of the severity of the stroke. There will be a lot that you won't be able to do." Fear filled what was left of my veins as the reality began to sink in. "The simple fact is that, more than likely, you won't walk again."

I struggled to come to grips with what had happened as the doctor, and then Michele, tried to fill me in on what my memory could not grasp.

It had been around two in the morning on November 27, 2001, when Michele had received a call from Natividad Medical Center telling her that I had suffered a stroke and was on life support. She left immediately for the hospital. By the time she arrived, I was breathing well enough to have the breathing tube removed, but every breath was a struggle. My brain had begun to swell and my speech had become slurred.

In the fog of my mind, as I listened to the story, I started to recall a distinct dream-like memory of having been stuck in a bathroom in the basement of a furniture store. I had been shopping and needed to use the toilet, but somehow got locked in the stall. I couldn't get out and no one would help me. There was a small window from where I could see the sidewalk, with people walking up and down. I banged on the window and yelled, but no one seemed to hear me. This went on for days, and I was exhausted.

Michele had stayed with me as long as she could that night but then had to leave for work. Early the next morning she returned and met with the doctor. Things had gotten worse, the doctor said, and it was time to call the family together. My kids were pulled from class and told they were going to the hospital to say *goodbye* to their dad. Paul and Sherrill drove down from Red Bluff. My mom, Katie, came up from Los Angeles. Friends and family gathered around me as I lay in bed, struggling for every breath. Michele tried to coach me to breathe. As the swelling increased, my body was shutting down and I would soon have to be put on life support, with no chance of recovery.

Meanwhile, I was in a different, even stranger world. I awoke in my hospital bed, lying on my back, but instead of being in the hospital I was in the center of a boxing ring encircled by red velvet ropes, with a spotlight directly over the bed. I could hear the muffled sounds of the announcer. Just outside the ring, directly in front of me, was a red 1955 Chevrolet Bel Air. The hood was open and there was a man in a mechanic's jumpsuit, a red rag hanging out of his back pocket, who was bent over and looking under the hood.

The reality of my situation was getting much worse. I had developed an antibiotic-resistant infection and my body, thrashing, was put in a four-point restraint. Apparently, I punched my nurse in the face and spat on her. Maybe that explained the boxing ring. As a paramedic, I used to hate it when patients were unruly.

As my brain-damaged mind tried desperately to make sense of what was happening, I stayed in the *land of make-believe*. This time I was stuck in my hospital bed on an enclosed porch. I could hear the doorbell ringing and ringing, and was hoping that someone would come in and find me.

As my crazy dreams repeated themselves over and over, my family continued their vigils. The men and pastors of Victory Outreach and Calvary Chapel joined in, and others, all praying for me to get well and still have a chance to change my life. There were several close calls in the ICU and I continued to get sicker and sicker. By the time I came out of my coma, a couple of weeks later, I was considered 100% permanently disabled. My driver's license would be permanently revoked, and the medical world said that I would be reliant on care for the rest of my life.

I certainly had hit rock bottom. I had always thought that there was plenty of time ahead of me to make different choices, but meanwhile, each of my past bad choices that I had made was adding drops of water to the bucket until I had almost drowned in it. *I did this to myself.* What a horrible realization. There had been plenty of warnings. My mind flooded with memories of all the times my wife and kids had begged me to turn my life around, of all the interventions that I had refused.

Everyone had been telling me that God loved me. *Well, if that's true he certainly has a funny way of showing it,* I thought. I had gone from independence to total dependence. I couldn't do anything for myself. I was on oxygen, and I had a tube feeding me nasty-looking grub, a rectal tube to remove it, and a Foley catheter because I couldn't pee properly by myself.

I was totally dependent on my family. *Poor Michele,* I thought. *Just when she was about to bail, this happens.* I had lost everything, except for my family. For some reason, in spite of everything, they were still hanging on for me. Again and again, I had turned my back on everyone who tried to help me. Now, I had no choice but to surrender—and there they were, right by my side. If they hadn't been around, I'm not sure how I would have survived.

Growing up there were so many times I had felt scared, but this time, stripped of everything but a strong sense of being loved, it was different. Somehow, as terrified as I felt, I had a deep sense of peace that I couldn't explain.

I spent my days tooling around the hallway pushing my wheelchair with one hand while my other one hung lifeless, deriding myself for all the past mistakes I had made that had led me to this point. The only break I had from my thoughts came during the refreshing moments of visiting hours with my wife and kids.

Besides my family, there were several other visitors who proved to me that they cared by showing up at the hospital to see how my recovery was progressing. Pastor Steve, his wife, Nora, and Pastor Skip all came to visit the day after I woke up.

"We've come to encourage you," Steve said, sitting on the foot of my bed. "God is clearly watching out for you, Mike. The Bible says, in Joel 2:25—that the Lord will restore the years that the locust have eaten. God can do that for you, I believe it."

I wasn't so sure what the locust stuff was supposed to mean. *But that's okay, I like this guy,* I thought. Steve's jolly outlook was enough to cheer anyone up.

Skip must have perceived my inability to decipher the cryptic scripture reference, because he tried to explain it to me. "All the years that you've spent as a slave to drugs, letting your addiction rule and ruin your life, God can make up for them by giving you better days ahead," he said. The poor guy had been trying to interpret the Bible for me so many times over the last year, his words mostly falling on deaf ears. This man had had the whole high school praying for me.

While at the hospital I had to face the painful reality of skin grafts. According to the plastic surgeon, it would be the largest one he had ever performed, as well as one of the larger he had ever seen. Massive amounts of tissue had to be removed from my legs due to the infection that had brought me to the hospital in the first place. This was by far the most painful thing I had ever experienced in my life, and the daily dressing changes made me wish each day that death would be the outcome, as healing felt much more ominous.

***

When I got out of the ICU, I was put in a room with a view: I could see the helicopter pad. For some, the daily drama of incoming crises might have been depressing. For me, they brought back moments of glory that played in my memory like a film of someone else's life:

"Trauma activation" is announced on the radio. It's the golden hour, which is the critical time, for intervention, between life and death. The whirling blades descend over night-time city lights onto a traffic accident. Time has stopped, as has the traffic; all eyes are staring up in hopeful anticipation.

What a stark contrast between my life then and my life now—lying in bed, helpless, unable to take care of myself. Soon the tubes started coming out, the Foley catheter, the feeding tube and, best of all, the rectal tube. Partial recovery felt good. I lay back in the hospital bed watching the sunset and wondering what tomorrow would hold for me.

The nurse poked her head in the room, "Mr. Casey, the ambulance will be here in about five minutes." I would be going to a different kind of rehab. Instead of trying to overcome addiction, I would be learning how to walk, talk, read and write, eat solid foods and brush my teeth. As a grown man, I was reduced to the state of a child who doesn't even know how to take care of his own primal needs.

To add to my embarrassment, the very ambulance company that I used to work for would be transporting me to Santa Clara Valley Medical Center. Just as I feared, both the EMT who was driving the ambulance and the paramedic who sat in the back to tend to me were familiar faces.

Are you kidding me? This must be some sort of cosmic joke or something, I thought. I wondered how much they would know about what I had been through. I had kept up the façade for so long, acting like everything was okay, while on the other side of that smile I was falling apart inside.

Lying on my back, weaving through the Northern California Mountains in the rattling ambulance, connected to various monitors, I thought about how the doctor had told me earlier that I would not be able to walk. It was bizarre not to be able to feel the entire left side of my body, and I couldn't imagine having to live like this for the rest of my life—in complete dependence on others.

"Hey Mike, remember me?" my former colleague asked. "We worked together."

I remembered him, sure enough. This was the guy who was known for his remarkably strong memory, and I was not necessarily pleased with the coincidence. I had been in his place hundreds of times, and I knew exactly what he needed to do, but this time I was in the position of the helpless patient. Mine was the body that had to be carefully lifted onto the stretcher and loaded into the ambulance. I felt pathetic. I was supposed to be the champion who saved lives, not the one drowning who needed to be saved. For the first time, I was forced to realize that I wasn't bulletproof.

"Oh yeah," I said, trying to sound enthusiastic, "you were an EMT student!"

"What happened to you?" he asked, holding my chart.

He didn't have to ask me that. It was clearly described on the chart he was holding in his hands. "IV DRUG USER" was splattered all over those pages. For some reason I lied anyway, "Aw man, I cut my leg and had to go to the hospital, then I got an infection…" At least the rest of the story was true.

He changed the subject. "How are Michele and the kids?" Much to my surprise, but true to form, he remembered all of my family members by name. While working together he and I had hardly talked; *where on earth did he get this information?* I certainly didn't feel like having this conversation, so I closed my eyes, pretending I had gone to sleep.

In paramedic school we were told of this little black box where we could stuff all of our feelings about the senseless tragedies we would encounter—the dead kids, the drunks walking away without a scratch, and so forth. "You need to hold onto your senses and keep your feelings at bay," they told us, "so that you can think clearly, get the job done, and ultimately save lives."

That little black box was only designed to hold so much. The funny thing was that my black box was already full—long before I had become a paramedic. With "suck it up" as the motto I had inherited, I had never learned a healthy way to deal with things. Drugs became the overflow receptacle for my bursting-at-the-seams black box—the only hiding place I could find.

At the rehab center, I had to be put in isolation due to a Methicillin-resistant Staphylococcus aureus (MRSA) infection, since contact with others would put me at greater risk of a flare-up.

Soon I was introduced to a whole cadre of therapists that would be working with me. There would be physical therapy, occupational therapy and speech therapy. The pace would be brutal, but I would have to battle the clock if I was to get better.

In a conversation with the doctor, I was asked to describe my hopes. "Pick three."

Chapter Twenty-One

"Walk, work and maybe someday run," I answered.

My expectations were too high, I was told, and I was promptly referred to a shrink who wanted to put me on anti-depressants, which I refused.

***

Only a couple of nights after entering rehab, joyful noises of New Year's Eve celebrations echoing right outside my window made it impossible for me to sleep. Since I couldn't join in the festivities, I instead threw myself a great big lonely pity party as I lay there in the darkness. I thought through the events of the past year: the way that I had carelessly let my life, money and relationships sift like hourglass sand, each chance I'd been given to flip things around slipped away. The next morning, I woke from the noise of a nurse walking in with my breakfast tray. She repeated the instructions she had already given every other time she had served me about the size of the portions of food I should take in, and how I should make sure my food was well chewed before swallowing it. It seemed kind of obvious, but because I had no feeling in the left side my mouth, I would have to stick my finger in to feel the food, which usually made quite a mess.

At least I am eating regular food, I told myself. I couldn't stand the tube feeding any longer, and I wasn't a fan of baby food, either.

Great, I thought, *the first day in the year 2002 marks me growing out of baby food!*

After breakfast, a nurse had to accompany me to the bathroom to shave. It was humiliating but I tried to joke, "What? Do you think I'll cut my throat?" I would have never thought that brushing my teeth could be such a chore, but showering was the worst; they would hose me down while I sat in my wheelchair. I was always freezing or burning up. Since the stroke, my body wasn't able to balance its internal ther-mometer, especially in the shower. Not knowing where to put the soap and washrag, much less how to manipulate the rag around my reachable body parts was a circus act. At least, though, I was getting clean.

My goal was to get dressed on my own, but the task wasn't easy. I knew what a shirt was, but I didn't understand how to put it on. Even worse, if it was inside out I couldn't figure out how to turn it right side up again. After some fifteen times trying to put on my underwear, only to still have them inside out and backwards with one leg in and one leg out, I succumbed to accepting help. Mustering up that smirk instead of the prideful scorn was called for when asking for aid, but often I found no other way to move forward with my recovery.

If you drew a line down the middle of my body, I had lost feeling in the entire left side. The challenge was to figure out how to send messages to those parts of the body I couldn't feel, to make them function. The wires in my brain had been crossed and jumbled up into a pile that I had to untangle each time I wanted to perform a new task. I would stare at my thumb and tell it to move, and my ring finger would respond instead. As these results came it was hard to feel I was making headway but it was also certain the fatality of my prognosis was off the table, at least for now.

After the bathroom ordeal, I was exhausted (as usual), largely due to my troubled sleep the night before, and so I took a nap. The smile from my dream faded as I woke up. I usually had dreams of being normal again, back at work doing what I loved—responding to a full-on house fire, a traffic accident, or working a Life Flight call, which was one of my favorite things to do. The contrast between my dreams and the reality I found myself in when I awoke was quite painful.

Suddenly, the physical therapist knocked lightly on the door and pushed it open.

"Are you ready for some exercise, Mike?" he asked.

I nodded my head and said 'yes' with a slur. He moved the wheelchair closer to my bed and helped me to sit in it. The exercise consisted of moving my arms and legs in a circular motion. This really frustrated me because I wanted to walk, not 'exercise' in a wheelchair.

When he left, I was so annoyed, I just had to get out. I had always used running as a way to release my fears and frustrations, but now I was stuck in a wheelchair. I wasn't going to let that stop me, so I just wheeled myself out of the room, out of the building, and with the sun on my face, down the street into the neighborhood where I had heard the New Year's celebrations the night before. I watched cars driving up to stop signs and strangers passing by as if I was sitting in front of an IMAX screen for the first time. After being claustrophobic indoors for almost three months, I absorbed the life-giving sunlight and natural breeze like a dying plant brought back to life. I stayed outside until I felt better and then returned to a frantic nurse who had been searching for me.

"You are not allowed to leave your floor!" she scolded.

As a consequence of my little 'outdoor fun' the staff had an alarm placed on my wheelchair that beeped whenever I got close to the elevator.

After my little adventure, lying back in isolation, I had nothing to do but grab the TV remote control and shuffle between channels. They were all in Spanish. Finally, I landed on the local access chaplain channel. It was not exactly my hobby to watch Christian channels, but I'd seen this film about the life of Jesus several times. Every other time I had been rather indifferent about the film, but this time I was drawn to the story like a moth to a flame. At the end of the film, a narrator explained how, through Jesus, I could find freedom from the guilt of sin and shame. All of a sudden, everything in Jesus' life made sense to me. I understood that my own actions were separating me from my creator, but that Jesus died and rose to reconcile me to God. For the first time, I found myself submitting to God, and weeping as I joined in the prayer saying, "Lord, make me the person *you* want me to be."

By the end of the film, when the presenter invited the viewing audience to repeat a prayer, I was ready. *What do I have to lose?* I thought. *I've done things my way for forty years and it's gotten me nowhere.*

I'd spoken this prayer before, preceding both my baptisms, which had each for their own reasons been a total hoax. This time I meant it. In that moment, the events in my life made sense. With this revelation I was able to understand a bit more the reason I had never died from overdose, and the way that Michele had become a Christian and still stuck with me, even with the misery I had put her through with each catastrophe, all began to click. For the first time in a very long time (if ever) I felt humble. Hope grabbed ahold of me and I prayed it would never let go.

"I feel clean." I voiced this realization to myself as the new feeling engulfed me. All of a sudden I felt satisfied and more hopeful with each moment, even though I was lying there alone.

As my revelations began to sink in I wanted to pick up the phone and call Michele, but the number pad didn't make sense to me. *She'd be so happy for me and with this thought even more hope flooded me.* I'd have to save my excitement for the next time my family visited and I could share my experience with them. My family and so many others had been praying for me, telling me that I needed to give my life to God and allow him to change me. I finally understood what they were talking about and was eager to tell them so that they could share in my happiness.

When the day came, I spent the entire morning staring at the clock in anticipation of visiting hours. There was really no point in looking at the clock, since it was just a jumble of numbers to me and I hadn't any idea how to read it, but I stared at it all the same. My family finally showed up, all masked, gowned, and gloved to maintain a sterile environment and to keep me from infection. I told them about my New Year's Eve experience and about the Jesus film I had watched. They stared back at me with blank faces and a distinct lack of enthusiasm.

After a short pause, Michele reached out to pat my arm and said, "We'll see. Time will tell." She wasn't a cold person, but all her years with me had taught her to doubt my transformation stories. None of the others seemed anymore hopeful that I had changed. The elation I felt was not shared—not this night anyway. Still deep down inside of me—I knew something was 'brand new' and things were going to be different for me...and since they were going to be different for me, I was certain I could make things different for the rest of my family as far as their relationships with me.

My daughter, Sarah, who had been listening quietly, went over to the whiteboard where my therapy schedule was neatly drawn out. She picked up the eraser and wiped clean half the board, proceeding to scratch out a Bible verse in red marker. "Count it all joy, my brothers, when you fall into various trials, knowing that the testing of your faith produces patience," it read.

I was annoyed. "Sarah, the doctor's not going to be happy about that," I said, deflecting my frustration. I liked the orderly chart telling me what I would be doing that day, and I did not like the verse. I had hoped for a positive reaction from my family, but I did not want them to start preaching at me about how this suffering I was going through was somehow meaningful. It seemed ludicrous that anyone would expect me to be happy about my situation. Despite the change that I felt taking place in my heart and the new joy I felt in my spirit, I was still disappointed with the progress I was making health-wise.

The next morning, unlike the previous mornings, I put on my own shirt victoriously, then brushed my teeth and was ready for the physical therapy session.

"Who wrote this?" the physical therapist asked, standing in front of the whiteboard.

"Oh, that was my daughter," I replied, apologizing.

"That's one of my favorite verses," he said. "You Christian?"

"I actually accepted Christ here," I told him, eagerly.

"Wow, I've been a believer since I was as young as your youngest child," he smiled. "So you came to believe here? Tell me about that."

Quickly, I started to tell him everything, even about the drugs, which he surely knew already from having read my chart. He sincerely listened while I told him about my long struggle with Michele, my work as a paramedic, and my life with my dad.

"The best is yet to come, Mike," the physical therapist replied after listening to my story.

"If only I could move my body. I'm not seeing much progress," I conveyed.

"You're already better than when we started. Maybe tonight, if you're okay, we can do some more exercises together."

Together, Scott and I began a more rigorous routine, adding extra sessions in the evenings. With this Olympic determination, we started to see progress. In one evening session a couple of days later I reached up, grabbing the parallel bars, my whole body shaking violently. I was using every ounce of strength I could possibly muster. *I can do this,* I thought. With one final pull, I let out a scream and stood up by myself.

"Walk! Walk!" my coach shouted.

Holding onto the bars as tight as possible, I awkwardly put one foot in front of the other.

"Oh my God, I'm actually walking!" I shouted.

Scott quickly moved the wheelchair around to the other side and I gladly collapsed into it.

"I'm ready for bed now," I slumped, totally exhausted.

"You're doing great, Mike," Scott encouraged me, "but we still have a long way to go."

"Just let me enjoy this victory," I said.

As the hours turned into days, he continued to push me, and I continued to respond. Getting up in the morning was easier, but getting dressed was still a struggle. When I was feeling down, Scott reminded me that I'd be getting a day out on Sunday, when I could go to church and spend time with my family. To me that sounded better than winning the lottery. Finally, I was beginning to understand Michele's eagerness to go to church.

"How can I get out of this place permanently?" I asked.

"Well," Scott said, "I suppose if you let the doctor see you walking, he'll probably send you home."

The next morning during rounds, I slipped out of bed and began to walk toward the bathroom. "Hey," the doctor said, "how long have you been walking?"

"A couple of days."

"Then you don't belong here anymore," he commented, just as Scott had said he would.

"You misunderstood him," Michele insisted on the phone. "They told me that they'd send you home for a day on the weekend. I'm sorry Mike, but you're going to be in rehab for a while."

When I had arrived at the rehab center, I was told that it would be weeks, more likely months. Each hour brought more and more recovery and more and more strength. Contrary to everyone's expectations, I was discharged before I even had my first home visit. Before I could go home, Michele had to take a safety-training class and meet with my therapists to understand my requirements for home care.

My first car ride after being in hospital environments for so long was a bit difficult, but it felt like a sign of normalcy to me to go through the Taco Bell drive-through on the way home. Unfortunately, being discharged from rehab didn't mean that I had fully recovered. In spite of all my high aspirations and tenacity, apparently I still didn't have the eating thing down. By the time we got home I was covered from head to toe in burrito matter, bits stuck on my face, my hair, and smeared all over the passenger window. *How humiliating.* Michele was in hysterics. I felt like a two-year-old who still hadn't figured out how to use his spoon.

My wife, now my caregiver, was thinking the same thing. "It's kind of nice having a toddler in the house again," she teased. "Don't worry, I'll clean you up." Her smile eased my frustration a tiny bit. Clearly, I had no choice but to let her mother me, at this point.

All my anxiety disappeared the moment we arrived home and I saw our lawn covered with close to fifty smiling faces waving balloons and *welcome home* signs. Still spattered with the innards of my upturned burrito, I carefully reached for my cane and made my way slowly but steadily across the yard, surrounded by love and full of gratitude.

When the crowd finally cleared, Michele asked me, "What do you want to do tonight?"

"It's Friday," I said, eagerly. "Let's go to the service at Victory Outreach."

Chapter Twenty-Two
A Long Road to Recovery

Michele was stuck. She had planned to move while I was at Victory Outreach and get as far away as possible. After my stroke, she was obliged to take me in and look after me. It wasn't going to be an easy job, either. Even though the doctor had discharged me from rehab, I still needed as much attention as a newborn baby... only I was a measly 130 pounds heavier than an infant and a lot more awkward.

The morning after I had returned home, I woke up foggy-headed, reflecting on the fanfare that had surrounded my return home: the smiling crowd, pats on the back and shouts of "Praise the Lord, brother!" *I guess I'm saved now,* I thought. *I said the prayer and meant it—that is, unless God's going to make me earn it this time.*

The real gravity of the situation hit me in the face as I tried to spring out of bed, landing splat on the floor. *Oh yeah, I have to remember to use my cane.* It was discouraging, but I was still thrilled to be home.

Michele was understandably still skeptical about my full recovery, but looked after me dutifully nonetheless. The progress of my recovery was slow. At first, I could not be left alone; I needed someone to bathe and dress me, and take me to the toilet. After just minutes of activity, I would collapse with fatigue. Michele struggled to keep me awake until noon. Shelly let our son, Dustin, who was thirteen at the time and still being homeschooled, stay with us as much as possible to help with all that needed to be done.

When Michele started to leave me home alone for short periods of time so she could go to work, I was given instructtions not to cook or go outside. Still, oftentimes she would return home to find the sink running, burners on high, refrigerator and cupboards open with food, cans, and containers scattered on the floor. My *real* memory of all this is still as dim now as it was then.

One afternoon while waiting for Michele to return home, I got my foot caught in my recliner and was unable to free it. Therefore, I had to sit there for several hours, feeling mortified while I watched the puddle of urine on the wooden floor grow larger and larger until someone came home to rescue me.

***

Deep in my heart, I knew that my new faith was real. After resisting God for so long, I was now surrendered to a solid conviction no longer deniable. Instead of Skip pursuing me, I was now tracking him down—after all he only lived a few doors down and I could get there by walking with my cane. I showed up on his doorstep like he had shown up on mine, and dropped by his office at the high school. Sometimes I called him up on the phone with thoughts to share and questions to ask. Skip and I continued to study the Bible and other books together. I was eating it up. The difference was that now, instead of asking questions to stump him, or prove him wrong, I was genuinely seeking answers and wanting to understand scripture and spirituality.

Skip told me to read a passage in the Bible, write down what I understood it to mean, and then read a couple different commentaries to find out if I had it right. It was so exciting for me to see that I could actually make sense of what I was reading. The fact that throughout my life collecting bibles had become a hobby was also beginning to make sense.

Though, as sincere as I was, discovering how to be a Christian was still a struggle. I had thought that everything would just automatically be better if I believed in Jesus. It didn't work that way. I was forty, permanently disabled, and applying for social security. I received notice from the DMV that the revocation status on my license was permanent. It was a blow to go from driving firetrucks and ambulances to having to taking public transportation—and we were so broke... I had to apply for a handicap discount card to ride the bus. There was nothing I could do to fight what was happening to me, so essentially I was forced into humility—but with God as the center of my life, there was no need for me to be kicking and screaming. Taking things in stride and patience was becoming a forced way of life for me.

Riding the bus proved to be harder than I thought. The routes and times were a mystery to me. Not only could I not tell time, but I didn't even understand the concept. There were times I would go from bus to bus, never getting closer to where I wanted to go. Regardless, I was too proud to ask for help, which made every day an unwelcome adventure.

I remember one particular day I ended up on the wrong bus in Salinas and found myself close to my old stomping grounds. For just a moment I contemplated getting off that bus to score. *I would feel better in an instant, and no one would know.* I immediately snapped out of it. The thought made me uneasy. *I would know, and God would know. There's no way I'm going back there.*

Quickly my thoughts jumped to Beverly and the gang. I wondered how they were doing. I somehow felt guilty for being sober when they were most likely still down in the dumps.

***

That night it felt good to get home. I walked into the house to find Pastor Charlie waiting for me and was so excited to see him that I gave him the biggest hug ever.

"Have you been smoking?" he asked.

"No."

Pastor Charlie turned to Michele, "Is that true?"

"I don't think he's been smoking," she shrugged.

He continued to investigate with his nose, sniffing my hands and collar for any looming tobacco odor. It was such a relief to have nothing to hide.

"What's the big deal about smoking?" I wanted to know.

"Once you start to compromise on the little things, it becomes easier to compromise on all the others," he explained. For once in my life these were the types of things that were beginning to ring true to me.

It didn't feel like I was being frisked by the moral police; instead it felt good to have someone looking out for me. *Maybe there are people that truly care.* As usual, my dad's voice came back, "No one does something for nothing!" But this time, I stood up to him in my head. Saying to myself—*That's not true,* I told myself. For the first time ever, I was developing my own voice. At that moment I realized that I had spent most of my life agreeing with everyone else. Now, I would have to develop a moral compass to help me know when to say yes or no.

***

Pastor Charlie continued to minister to me. He visited me regularly and asked straightforward questions to help keep me accountable. Whenever I was tempted to turn back to drugs, I would stop myself, knowing that I would have to give an answer for my actions.

Now that all my lies were out of the bottle, I was in no position to be defensive and had zero leverage for the manipulation of others. Instead, Michele held all the leverage in our relationship, and she used it as best she could. She insisted on transparency for all my actions. I had to account for every penny I was given, which was difficult for someone who can barely count, let alone add and subtract. There needed to be an explanation and a reason for every place I went and there could be no deception or sneaking around.

The one area where I did allow compromise to sneak into my life, and which Pastor Charlie never asked me about, Michele was quick to discover. At home alone, for hours at a time with nothing to do, I still often felt depressed and hopeless. With drugs and alcohol out of the picture, I tried to escape into a different kind of high: pornography. With my mental challenge from the stroke, I was useless at covering my steps.

Michele found the videos I had downloaded and swiftly put an end to it.

"You're going to have to figure out for yourself that this is wrong," she told me. "I've stuck around through thick and thin, but I *will* leave you, if this continues."

It had been hard enough for me to admit my heroin addiction out loud, but the dirty dark secret of pornography seems to carry even more shame. I didn't want Michele to leave me, and I definitely didn't want anyone else to know the things that I had been watching. Neither potential reality was worth it, so I quit without debate. Still, it was months and months before I really understood how pornography could be as damaging an addiction as heroin.

***

The Friday night meetings led by Pastor Herb in Salinas were also a big help in building me up. Pastor Herb always took the time to check in, see how I was doing, and offer a word of encouragement.

It had seemed like a gigantic commitment to give up an entire year of my life to attend the recovery program at Victory Outreach before my stroke, but instead I was forced to give up everything. Although I'd only been a resident at Victory Outreach for less than three days, they would eventually award me an honorary graduate certificate.

In order for me to move forward, I felt that I needed to make amends with the past. I needed to confront Dad, tell him that I was making a new start, and forgive him for his role in leading me down such a destructive path. I was also anxious to see Grandma, Paul and Sherrill. So clearly, a trip to Red Bluff was in order.

***

The long road between Los Angeles and Red Bluff was a landmark at so many points in my life. This was the first time I'd taken the trip by Greyhound since I was fourteen and was forced to leave the safety and security of my grandparent's home to live with my dad. The other time I'd left their home to live with Dad was when I got caught in the heroin trap. I prayed that the speech I had been preparing to confront Dad with this time would be more effective than the one that had failed miserably back then.

But what this trip reminded me of most was the time I escaped both Dad and heroin, taking a month-long detour at Duane's in Berkley before returning to Grandma's house. I remembered how I had celebrated my freedom by playing loud music and shouting out the window. At the time I had felt so empowered. *What happened? How did I get back into that snare?* I was struck by the sharp contrast between the victory I had felt then, and the total humiliation I was experiencing now. Technically, I was free from drugs, but instead of being victorious, I had been defeated. This time, the drugs had won battle after battle until they had destroyed me completely. I was given a second chance at life, but only as half a man. With no feeling in my left side, I felt like a shell of my former self.

In Redbluff, Paul met me at the bus stop and took me on a little trip down memory lane to visit Sherrill at Francisco's and to eat some of my favorite chips and salsa.

"I can't believe you're sitting here; you were supposed to be dead!" she began crying as she reminisced. "I remember the day Paul and I came to say goodbye to you in the hospital, knowing I would never see you again."

Her tears were out of joy, but I just felt guilty. I was ashamed for the ways I had misused our friendship, and for having put all my friends and family through such anguish surrounding my addiction, my stroke, and now, my recovery.

Sherrill didn't want to see me in such distress, and she tried to cheer me up.

"I'm okay," Sherrill nodded fighting back tears.

"The way I see it," I paused, "I actually got what I deserved. This has been a huge wake-up call for me. I abused and misused everything in my life that God had entrusted me with...my ability to work and to be a husband and a father the way I see it—I took it all for granted and it was all taken away.

If I want trust, respect and good relationships back, I need to do the right thing. I'm sure I'll get back just exactly what I need to get back and nothing more. It reminds me of the story of Jacob in the Bible in Genesis 32. He wrestled all night long with the angel and in the morning, he touched his hip and put it out of socket. His affliction was a reminder of his encounter with God. My affliction would be a reminder to me of my encounter with God. I feel like this whole thing will always be a testament to me of what I had, what I lost and will be getting back.

"You have no reason to be ashamed," she said. "Instead, be grateful to have a second chance at life! See, God has finally answered all our prayers for you."

Sherrill encouraged me to share my story with the guys I had worked with at the fire station and the hospital. But I wasn't up for it. I knew their mentality, they wouldn't understand my faith, but would see it as a sign of weakness, a crutch. They would think the stroke had done something to my mind and I had gone off the deep end. *Get over it, Mike. Just go,* I tried to convince myself. But I couldn't stomach facing them with a dangling left arm—and my lack of courage just made me feel worse.

Other than Sherrill, I kept the visit to just to my family. Grandma was next. Just the sight of her and the smell of her home-cooked food was a comfort to me, but it also reminded me of another reason for remorse. I had only come to Red Bluff to see her a couple of times since she had moved back. If I had not been so drugged up and stuck in my selfish world, I'd definitely have visited her more often.

Grandma hugged me so hard, I could hardly breathe. "God must have something special in store for you," she said.

I passed by to see Pastor Gilbert, who was still an active part of my dad's life, helping him to stay organized, write checks, and pay his bills.

"Your dad's filled me in on your situation," he said. "There were a lot of people praying for you. Praise God you made it through." In that instant, I understood Pastor Gilbert and his role in my dad's life. He was to my dad as Skip had been to me. He was trying to protect him, to mentor him, to connect him to Jesus. I felt bad for all the times I'd been angry with Pastor Gilbert for defending Dad. Suddenly, I was overwhelmed with gratefulness.

"Thank you for looking out for my dad," I told him. "God bless you."

***

The next morning it was time to face my demons. I was terrified, but determined as I stood before Dad's apartment door, working up enough courage to knock.

"Come in," Dad called from inside.

I took a deep breath and entered. He was slouched on his all-too-familiar green furnished-apartment couch. Before I had the chance to open my mouth and utter a greeting, Dad broke down in tears.

"Oh my God, what have I done to you!" he wept.

I had seen him cry plenty of times before, but this was different. He had heard about my addiction and my stroke, and seemed paralyzed with grief.

I immediately abandoned my prepared speech. "It's okay, Dad." I did my best to sooth him.

"Show me your legs, Mike," he insisted.

"No, you don't want to see them," I answered.

"Yes, I do."

So, I showed him my legs. He was overwhelmed, "It's much worse than I imagined."

Dad and I talked well into the evening, and this time there was no reminiscing about the past. When I was getting ready to leave, Dad led me into his room.

"Look," he said proudly, pointing.

My eyes filled with tears. Sitting on a table next to his bed were two radio-controlled planes that he had recently finished.

Chapter Twenty-Two

"I thought maybe we could go flying sometime," he said.

Doesn't he know that all I ever wanted was to be able to do things with him?

"Yes," I replied, both of us knowing it would probably never happen, "I'd love to."

Chapter Twenty-Three
Public Transportation

I studied the big digital watch on my wrist, capturing the picture in my mind, before looking up at the bus stop sign to search for a matching image that would somehow tell me when I could catch a bus back to Monterey. Even though my stepdaughter Lindsey had been coaching me on the bus system, I had already missed my bus in Salinas and subsequently my doctor's appointment. The numbers made no sense to me. In desperation, I stopped a lady with two young children to ask the time.

She gestured to my watch with a quizzical look.

I tried to cover my embarrassment, "Uh, I just want to make sure it's right."

"Oh," she said; "it's right." She must have caught on that I still needed the answer because she continued, "12:45."

"Mommy that man doesn't know how to tell time!" her oldest noted as they walked away.

As I got off the bus in Monterey, a young man approached me with his arm extended and handed me a flyer.

"Would you like to come to church?"

"What church?" I asked.

"Victory Outreach," he replied.

"I was in Victory Outreach men's home in Salinas!"

"I'm in the men's home in Seaside," he extended his hand, "I'm Robert."

I had no idea that there was a Victory Outreach home in Seaside, a small town between Monterey and Salinas, and I was thrilled. That night, Michele and I went to the mid-week Bible study Robert had invited me to attend. It was a much smaller ministry than the one in Salinas; the meeting was held in a garage that was transformed twice a week to accommodate the Bible study and church service.

It was a no-frills church service with worship accompanied by a cassette tape played over a boom box, but I felt right at home. Pastor Mario, like all the other residents, had been down that same hard road, as the tattoos that covered most of his body suggested. His wife, Rosanna, had lived a life of addiction as well. The small garage was packed with people who had been in bondage to drugs, gang life, and/or prostitution. They understood my struggles because they each were battling their own demons.

Michele was excited because Pastor Mario agreed to let me spend most of my days over at the home in Seaside. I still needed a lot of supervision, and there were plenty of people there who could keep me company and help out with my recovery. It also provided a good environment for my spiritual growth.

Robert and I became friends and I had the chance to learn a bit about his background. As a juvenile, he had been tried as an adult for second degree murder and had served over seven years in prison. During his time at Victory Outreach, Robert had totally reformed. My measly experience in jail was nothing compared to the time he had spent in prison, but I was able to understand him and where he was coming from.

I was still receiving calls from old customers asking me to help with their maintenance issues. Although, I was physically incapable, it suddenly occurred to me that I might be able to use Robert as my hands and feet. The plan worked well and Robert and I were able to pull it off as a team.

When it was time for Robert to move out of the Victory Outreach home, Michele and I decided to invite him to come and stay with us. Most people thought we were crazy to bring an ex-convict into our home. I didn't care. *It's not as if he's going to kill me in my sleep. What's there to be afraid of?* It just seemed like the right thing to do.

Robert had had a rough childhood and had never known his father, so I stepped into the role and took him under my wing. It was fun to introduce him to new foods and take him places he had never been. He had been in prison since he was seventeen, so he had never had the chance to get his driver's license. Michele and I helped him get his permit and taught him to drive. Robert had never had any sort of job or job training, so I gave him a job and trained him.

My son, Ryan, graduated from high school and took a year off to work with Robert and me. The two of them quickly became the best of friends. By the end of the year, Ryan went off to Bible College. The time came when Robert had earned enough money to move out on his own. He found a place just down the street, so he could still visit us frequently. For a few more months Robert continued working with me just until he was able to start a business of his own with the skills he'd learned.

***

My recovery was slow, but I was doing better than the doctors ever thought I would. At the very least, I wanted to be able to take care of myself, and I hoped that someday my disability wouldn't be so obvious. I knew that if I waited for Medicare to come through to get physical therapy covered, I would lose my crucial window for recovery. If I were to regain independence, it would require determination and lots of effort. I threw away my handicap sticker and told Michele to park at the other end of the parking lot so I would be forced to walk. I requested that Michele, or one of the kids, sit down with me to drill me on telling time or dialing phone numbers. My cognitive abilities never returned to full capacity, but I learned how to function. I never regained feeling on the left side of my body, but I learned how to dress myself, walk, run, drive, and, eventually, ride a bike. It took me a year and a half before I was able to eat without drooling or having to stick one of my fingers in my mouth to make sure all the food was chewed properly.

By the time Ryan went off to college, I was able to do some odd jobs by myself. Then, after Robert started his own business, I was offered a job as a janitor at Calvary Chapel. I was hesitant to accept the job because I didn't, particularly, want to spend all my time there. *Me working at a church – how strange?*

It was already a difficult transition for me when Michele had left her job at the Community Hospital to take a secretarial position at Calvary, because I knew it meant we'd need to be more committed to the church.

Michele felt right at home at Calvary, but I felt out of place. Everyone was proper and well behaved. We had to always dress nicely and make sure no one noticed what car we were driving. We were still trying to fit in. Still not sure of ourselves whenever we visited people in their homes, we would park a couple blocks away, and not only so that I could get some exercise. *If only they would take the time to get to know us, they might understand what we've been through,* I thought. Instead, I felt the pressure to act like I had it all together, even though I certainly didn't have anything together.

***

At Victory Outreach meetings I could be myself; there was no pretending, no one was judging me. *Isn't being a Christian supposed to be all about helping those who are struggling?*

One of Shelly's neighbors, who attended Calvary, tried reaching out to me. I had usually ignored him back in the days when I was going to men's retreats and shooting up in the bathroom, and I continued to ignore him after becoming a Christian. I had no real interest in having someone else giving me advice; Skip was my go-to guy and that was enough. But Bob Stewart was a big man with a huge heart, and though he was soft spoken, he simply would not give up.

"Let's go get a burger and talk," he suggested, and before I knew it I was telling him my life story.

I think Bob wanted to shock me and prove that there was no topic off-limits for him, because he came right out and asked me, "What do you know about relationships and sex?"

I chuckled, "Do you really want to know?"

"Yes, I do."

"Well, for a start, my dad used to tell me that a woman is just a life support system for a vagina."

I apologized for the expression, but Bob wasn't intimidated. I had never been able to speak so candidly with my dad; with Bob—I never had to worry about saying the wrong thing or making him angry (after all, I wasn't worried about Bob's opinion). We spent the next three or four hours parked in front of the In-N-Out Burger while Bob helped me totally reframe my way of thinking.

In the In-N-Out Burger in Salinas it felt strange being with Bob in my old stomping grounds. I had scored in this very parking lot many times and I can't believe how many times I had shot up in their restroom. *Thank God that's in my past.*

It was a kind of conversation I had never been able to have with my own father, but the way things had gone the last time I'd seen him made me optimistic. Later that night, I called Dad to give it my best shot. I tried to steer the conversation, but within a few minutes, our communications degraded to our old pattern of reminiscing about the past. As usual, Dad managed to parade my most miserable memories as glory days. I resorted to my habitual polite chuckle and wrapped up the conversation as soon as I could.

Since I clearly wasn't going to be able to get the kind of interaction I longed for from my own dad, I surrendered to letting Bob father me. He took it as his personal mission to 're-parent' me.

After that, Bob and I talked on the phone several times a day. We often went out to lunch together as he helped me learn how to live a practical Christian life, navigate decisions, and cultivate healthy relationships. The contrast between Bob and my dad was profound, and seemed to appear at every juncture.

Sitting across the table from Bob at Chef Lee's Chinese Restaurant I stared blankly at the menu. "Why don't we order two dishes and share?" Bob asked.

"Sounds good."

"What would you like?"

"Whatever you want."

"You pick something and I'll pick something. How 'bout that?"

"Um," I fumbled.

"Why the hesitation, Mike?"

There was a reason for my hesitation. If I chose the wrong thing with Dad, he'd go off his rocker. It wasn't easy for me to get it in my head that Bob wasn't like that.

Dad usually didn't even bother to ask what I wanted; instead he would tell me. Even at a buffet, Dad would tell me exactly which items to put on my plate. I'd have to finish it so I could go back for seconds and get what I actually wanted. I remember one time I asked him, "How come you always order my burger with no pickles?"

"'Cause you don't like pickles on your hamburgers," he informed me. I have no recollection of ever having even tasted a burger with pickles. For years, I ordered my own Burger King Whopper exactly the way Dad always had: "No tomatoes, no pickles, extra ketchup." It wasn't until long after I'd married Michele that I mustered the courage to try a burger with pickles, and I liked it.

Now, it was a lot easier for me to just let Bob do the ordering. Once I finally admitted I wanted the Mongolian Beef, and we had placed our order, Bob could see that there was a lot more on my mind than chow mein.

"What's going on in that head of yours?" he probed.

"What's wrong with me?"

"What do you mean by that?" he smiled.

"Everything I do always seems to be wrong."

"Like what?"

"Well, Michele and I had a huge fight this morning. She's really upset because I bought a pair of running shoes and spent too much money. I bought them in faith because I want to start running again soon, I feel like she doesn't believe I can do it."

"Well, it's tough to feel that she doesn't share the same faith you have in your recovery," Bob sympathized, "but don't you have a deal that you're supposed to ask Michele before you buy anything?"

"Well, I did, and she even gave me the credit card to buy shoes."

"So, why is she so upset?"

"She kind of thought I was going to spend $19, but I spent $125."

"That's a big difference. Where did she get that idea from?"

"We had seen a sales ad, advertising running shoes for $19, so I asked her if I could buy a pair and she approved. I tried them on, but I didn't like how they fit, so I went to a shoe store in Carmel and found a better pair. Today, she saw the bank statement and blew up."

"So, you lied to her."

"That's what she says, but I didn't lie. I just didn't tell her how much they actually cost."

"That's lying, Mike."

"No, I was really careful not to lie about it. I never specifically said where I would buy the shoes. When I got home, she just asked me if I had bought a pair and I said, 'yes.' She even told me they looked great."

"You were being deceptive and dishonest," Bob explained. "Leaving something out is the same as lying."

"Whatever, I'm not going to sit here and argue with you about this. This is totally ridiculous."

Bob looked me in the eye, knowing the ball was about to drop. "It's called a lie of omission."

"What the heck?"

"You may not have downright lied, but you left out enough of the facts to make it sound like you were being honest, when you weren't."

"See that's what I mean. What the hell is wrong with me?" I groaned. "I think I'm doing the right thing, and then I find out I'm not. I didn't tell her I spent more on shoes because I didn't want her to be mad at me."

"So you let her believe a lie."

"Yeah, so I guess it was a lie." I was feeling totally frustrated, but was beginning to understand what he was explaining and helping me to process.

Bob explained to me that while some things are black and white, there are also many shades of gray. "For example, it says in the Ten Commandments, 'thou shall not commit adultery', but Jesus goes on to say that if you even lust after a woman you have committed adultery. We all know that murder is wrong, but Jesus goes on to say that if you're even guilty of calling someone an empty head it is like you have murdered them in your heart."

By getting to the root of my depravity, Bob helped me to strip down my façade and become a genuine person, a better husband, father and friend.

In Bob, I saw someone who was completely transparent because he had nothing to hide. He wasn't embarrassed by his weaknesses because he found his strength in God. His advice, and the example of his life, helped me to see that I needed to deal with the deeper issues of my heart in order to become a new man.

Chapter Twenty-Four
The Man with the Devil Tattoo

One day I was out doing errands when I accidently pocket-called Dad on my cellphone. He answered before I had the chance to hang up.

"Hey Mike, so glad you called!" He was unusually cheerful, but I didn't have time to talk.

"Hey Dad, I'm right in the middle of something. Can you call me back tonight around 9:00 p.m.?"

I didn't always feel like talking to Dad in those days. We had been through another saga with him, and I'd just about had enough. As with most addicts, it was a tedious and grueling cycle of attempting to turn his life around followed by sliding back into habitual behaviors.

He had even been drunk at Grandma's deathbed and funeral. When I showed up in Red Bluff to visit her in the hospital, I had found him sitting in his room halfway through a second bottle of vodka and surrounded by Mickey's Big Mouth bottles full of urine. *Just like the good old days.* I had to clean him up and take him to visit his mother, who was suffering from kidney failure. "It's just a matter of time," the doctor told us.

Grandma was true to her nature, telling us all to be strong as we gathered around her bed. Uncle Bob, Aunt Sandy, and their girls were all there, along with Paul and myself. She motioned me over and whispered in my ear. Grandma wanted me to have a few of her treasured items, namely the coffee set from her wedding. "Go right now," she insisted.

She must have known better than to leave her most treasured possessions to the vultures, because as soon as she died they were at it. Uncle Bob was already removing her jewelry before her lifeless body was moved off the hospital bed onto the coroner's gurney.

Dad was a sight at the funeral. He showed up late and disheveled wearing jeans and a stained polo shirt; his face was cut up and bruised, and he reeked of booze and cigarettes.

A couple of months later, he reached out to Michele and I for help. We got him checked into a program in Payne's Creek near where he lived, but he didn't like it. So, we found Dad a program associated with Calvary Chapel called U-Turn for Christ, not far away in Camino. After his initial enthusiasm, the complaints started rolling in. They made him get up too early, there wasn't enough to eat, there were too many guys, etc. Finally he quit the program.

Michele suggested that we let Dad come down to our area and check into a nearby Victory Outreach men's home so we could keep our eyes on him.

"Are you kidding me?" I said, "After all we've been through with him?"

So Michele and I compromised and set up some clear boundaries. We found him a Victory Outreach home a safe distance away in San Jose, where we could easily visit but where we would have no chance of running into him accidently.

When Dad arrived in Monterey he was carrying a small lock box with his entire inheritance from Grandma in cash. He did great for a couple of months. We visited regularly for services on Sundays or in the middle of the week. At one midweek service, Dad responded to an altar call. My first thought was that he was working some sort of angle, *what could he be up to?* But when I watched him raise his hands in the air in an act of submission, I could tell it was genuine. I pushed my way through the crowd and kneeled next to him. "I've made my peace with God and accepted Jesus," he told me later.

Only a couple of weeks later, he was in trouble again. He left Victory Outreach and the next we heard from him he was drunk and holed up in a hotel in Salinas. Michele picked him up and put him on a Greyhound back to Red Bluff. Michele stopped by our house to pick up a few things, and I looked out the window to see Dad standing outside by the car, smoking a cigarette. I couldn't bring myself to say goodbye—instead I stayed at the window and watched them drive away. The moment they were gone I broke down crying. "I just want my dad!" I shouted. *I really hope you're working on him,* I prayed.

Two weeks later, I received a collect call from the Tehama County Jail located in Red Bluff. *At least I know where he is,* I thought. I reminded him of the commitment he had made at Victory Outreach, encouraged him to keep up with Pastor Gilbert, and told him about another Christian recovery program called The Well Ministry of Rescue in Chico. He promised that he and a friend he knew from the jail would both go and check it out as soon as they were released.

A month later I got a call from Dad, saying that he had gone to the Well, his friend had been accepted into the program, but he had been rejected due to restrictions on the meds he was taking. He decided to move to the retirement community where Grandma had lived when she passed away.

It had been a while since he and I had talked, but I was so disillusioned with his shenanigans, I had little hope he could change.

It was 9:00 p.m. and I was just settling down to watch a new episode of *Law and Order* when the phone rang. *Oh crap,* I thought. *I told Dad to call me.*

Reluctantly I answered the phone. I had been avoiding this conversation for some time, because I still hadn't told him that I was running a recovery ministry. It was Bob who put me up to it, even though I had resisted the idea for some time. People had been hearing my story and asking me for advice, but I had no idea what to tell them. Skip just told me, "Tell them the truth and continue to share your story."

Bob was convinced I had a calling. "God clearly has a plan for your life," he would say, echoing Grandma's reaction when she found out I'd become a Christian.

Suzy, the recovered addict who had backed me up when I had first admitted my addiction at a Wednesday night meeting, was also convinced. She kept submitting prayer requests asking the church leaders, "Pray that Mike Casey will start a recovery meeting at Calvary."

Are you kidding? I thought. It like felt everyone around me was convinced except me.

Bob finally persuaded me to go to a recovery ministry training conference in San Diego. "Just check it out," he offered, "you don't have to commit to anything." The conference was called "The Most Excellent Way" and was run by two former alcoholics, Glen and Judy Wright, who had also written a book with the same title. They had turned their lives over to God and were now helping others.

"Sorry, I'm not the guy. I can't do it," I told Bob while handing him a stack of notes and materials from the conference. As I drove away from his place, I felt a rubber band wrapped around me, which tightened the farther I went. Literally. *What the heck?* When you have a strong physical sensation, you don't ignore it. That was the only time in my life I ever experienced something like that. I turned the car around and found Bob standing outside his house, waiting.

"I knew you'd come around," he said.

Pastor Bill was as hesitant as I was. "This whole thing would certainly attract a different class of people than the current congregation!" he would say. In the end he agreed to let us try it, so long as Bob was closely supervising and attending all the meetings.

An announcement was placed in the church bulletin to invite anyone interested in supporting a recovery ministry to attend a meeting at Bob and his wife Carolynn's house. *I'll do this for a couple weeks or months until it fizzles out,* I thought, never imagining forty-five people would show up to that initial interest meeting.

We kicked off the ministry with a Monday night meeting. Bob was there every week to unlock and lock the church—

there was no way they were trusting me with a key, not this ex-junkie who had spent much of his time trying to figure out how to rob the place.

Week after week, I grappled with the Bible and tried hard to relate it to the struggling addicts. Before long I began to develop some trust; I was even given a church key and the alarm codes. The last time anyone had trusted me with a key was when I was leading the 10:00 p.m. meeting for AA, fixing in the bathroom prior to the meeting, then telling everyone how well I was doing. I was no longer defining my higher power standing in the cold waters at Lovers Point. For the first time, I felt at ease with who I had become.

A major turning point came when I was given the opportunity to share a morning devotional at a men's Bible study on a Saturday morning. It was after Pastor Bill had moved on and Pastor Roger had taken his place, with Bill's son, Nate, as an associate pastor. I was just starting to gain confidence in my abilities, and felt I had a stellar message to share with the group. The following Monday morning I was anxious to get feedback from Pastor Roger. I kept passing in front of his office door, which was propped open, hoping that he would call me in to pat me on the back and say, "Great job, Mike!" Eventually, he did call me in.

"I've got two words for you, Mike," he said, "vague and erroneous."

That was not what I was expecting. I had to sit down and bite my lip to keep from crying as he challenged me. "It's time to lose the training wheels and get serious, Mike. Teaching the Bible is not a joke."

He opened up the Bible and showed me how James warns, "Not many of you should become teachers, my brothers, for you know that we who teach will be judged with greater strictness (3:1)."

"If you are a teacher, people will be influenced by what you are saying. It's a big responsibility, and you need to really think about whether you're up for it."

I left his office feeling discouraged. *Maybe I'm not cut out for this after all.*

Pastor Nate's office was open. *Maybe he'll cheer me up*, I thought.

He opened up the book of Proverbs, "If you faint in the day of adversity, your strength is small (24:10)."

My pride was crushed. I took the rest of the day off. As I was leaving Michele, who was working in the office, asked, "Are you crying?"

Embarrassed, I went straight home to cry alone. When the tears dried, I spent some time in prayer, and self-examination. *What Roger said was dead on,* I realized. It was time to grow up. Those words changed my life.

After that dose of humility, I was able to see things in a new light. I began to find my confidence in God, rather than in myself. As I grew in reliance on him, my calling and commitment were solidified. In a matter of months, Pastor Roger had me ordained and in the years that followed, the recovery ministry had taken on a life of its own, and there was no shortage of people looking for help. This was truly a blessing being a part of the solution rather than a part of the problem.

***

The day came when I decided it was time to share what was going on in my life with my mom. I wasn't quite certain how she would react to the whole *God thing* not to mention her son being a pastor. We had done our best to stay in touch since reuniting. I realized she carried a lot of guilt and regret over the past and I wasn't quite sure that she would see God working in my life the way that I did. My conviction was that 'what was meant for evil, God could use for good'.

I was no longer the victim of my life and I had a purpose and was ready and willing to explore this new life to the fullest. Hence, I gave her a call and began sharing some of the things that I was doing. Mom seemed happy that I was able to help others. Next, I shared with her that I had been ordained as a pastor. As fate would have it, at that very moment, the call dropped. I think it was God's sense of humor as I immediately called Mom back and told her that she could go to hell for hanging up on a pastor. The two of us laughed, which broke the ice and we were able to share a lot of what was going on. I explained how happy I was being able to help others. She seemed to understand that things had turned out the way they had for reasons not evident to everyone. *Sure I often wonder what life would've been like growing up with my mom rather than my dad.*

I no longer want my life to be filled with regrets—looking back, I have decided I now choose to look forward and to move forward only.

***

My stepsister Linda was just about as excited. She still lived in Pacific Grove, and we saw each other quite frequently, but she avoided the topic like the plague. On the other hand, Becky was supportive and happy, but had never seen any relevance it might have to her own life. Micky, who was in the middle of serving a fourteen-year prison sentence for selling meth when we spoke on the phone, seemed happy to know I was doing well.

My brother, Paul, had never shared the same qualms I had with God and religion. He had attended church off and on since we were kids and was supportive and perhaps a little envious of my new life.

But for some reason, in those early days of my ministry, I was the most terrified about telling my dad. I could hear his voice in my head telling me that I was just another bleeding heart who needed to grow some balls. Even though he had attended his share of these meetings himself and had even made a profession of faith at some point, it was still impossible to read him. So, I kept putting it off until that night when he called me at nine.

"That's awesome, Mike," he had said, "I'm so proud of you!" Dad told me that he had been leading a small group of folks where he lived.

Chapter Twenty-Four

"What?" I replied.

"We're going through the book of Proverbs in the morning. It's something that I enjoyed doing at U-turn for Christ."

I was dumbfounded. I guess God had been answering both of our prayers. We spoke for nearly two hours—the kind of conversation I had always longed to have with him. I smiled as I hung up the phone.

Going to bed that night, I felt totally peaceful. *You finally reached him, Lord.* This time I was confident that his heart had really changed.

The next morning at around four I was startled awake at the sound of the phone ringing. *It is never a good thing to receive a call this early,* I thought.

Michele answered the phone, "It's the Tehama county Sherriff."

I was crushed. "What the heck did he do now?" I groaned, grabbing the phone.

"Is this Michael Casey?"

"Yes."

"Are you related to Leslie Paul Casey?"

"Yes, he's my dad." I prepared myself to hear about another incident.

"I'm sorry to inform you that he was found dead in his home earlier this evening."

In just a few short hours I was standing in the viewing room of the Hal Brothers Mortuary in Corning. Dad was wheeled in on a gurney, covered in a layer of plastic with his shirt open, exposing the electrodes from the electrocardiogram machine that was used by the paramedics to verify his lack of cardiac activity.

My brother Paul, his wife Karen, Michele and I all stood there staring at him in complete silence.

"I need to be alone with him," I said. I had always told Michele that if my dad were to die, I would need to see the tattoo on his arm to be sure it was him. In the days when he used to torment us, I was paranoid that he would try to fake his own death, simply to be able to catch us off guard.

When everyone had left, I peeled back the plastic and pulled his shirtsleeve down off his shoulder. *Yup, that's him,* I thought, as my trembling finger traced the outline of the devil on his arm, *the meanest son-of-a-bitch in the valley.*

I stepped back and pointed my finger at the tattoo and smirked victoriously, "You didn't win!"

Saddened by the fact that Dad died at the young age of sixty-five, I ran my hand through his hair. Tenderly, I kissed his forehead and stated, "I love you, Dad. I'll see you soon!"

Epilogue

By the time I finally made the journey to Hogsback Road to scatter Dad's ashes, I was ready to let go. I was about a year into writing this book and it was so hard for so many reasons. The place I chose to write the majority of the book was at BookWorks, which was a quaint little coffee shop/bookstore that had a friendly vibe. The coffee shop was located in downtown Pacific Grove, California and also was just a few doors down from the house on Park Street where we lived with my stepmom. Sitting there staring out the window it was easy to get lost in the memories of what seemed like a different life. I was ready for the next chapter in my life and I was hoping for a miracle.

By this time, I was a seasoned Christian, and I had seen my share of miracles, so I knew it was possible. I wanted all those years of pent-up pain to dissolve as his ashes drifted from my fingertips down the ravine. It didn't happen. There is still so much pain.

Opening the box of ashes that afternoon was like opening Pandora's Box; every emotion came flooding out. It was more than I could handle. I felt happy, sad and angry moments. The guilt and heartache was stronger than ever. *Did I try hard enough? Was I a good son?* There was no magical answer. No happy ending. I just felt empty.

All I had ever wanted was a normal relationship with my dad. I'm not even sure what that would have looked like, but it probably would not have included the intimidation, the dishonesty, the sex and the drugs. I wanted to laugh with him, hang out and talk—without the sinister side that always came out to spoil everything.

In the twelve years I had been clinging to his ashes, I never lost that longing for a father—a relationship that I have perhaps always idealized as paramount to my own identity. There has always been a tacit understanding that finding my wholeness would be dependent on healing the brokenness in my dysfunctional relationship with my earthly father.

In a lot of ways Bob met that father-need for me. I was able to laugh with him, ask questions without fear of retribution, and have normal conversations with him. Bob cared about me in a genuine way, and he took interest in the things I cared about. He understood me and accepted me unconditionally, just as I was, while encouraging me always to be better. Bob was also a good role model. He talked a lot about helping people, while my dad would talk about how he planned to screw somebody over.

Still, no matter how much I loved Bob, he could never fill that deep ache I had for a relationship with my father. When I started my ministry with recovering addicts, I was calling Bob three or four times a day for advice. He knew that I was completely dependent on him and would tell me, "There will come a day when I'm not here." I didn't want to hear it. I finally had someone I could turn to. "You're not going to really be able to grow until I'm gone," he said. "Then you'll have to lean on God instead of me."

***

The only other friend I had in my life that I could count on like that was Duane, whom I always missed. Duane and I were buddies; we could finish each others' sentences. The last time I'd seen my old friend was shortly after Michele and I had first moved in together. Duane contacted me to see if he could borrow some money. I went out of my way to get it to him, though it quickly became clear that he was wasting it on a serious drug problem. I knew that he needed help, and I wished I could be the one to rescue him the way he had helped me to come clean so many years ago, but I had been swept away by the same current. Now that I had recovered and was beginning to help others, I had no idea how to find Duane. Eventually I hired an online service to help me in my search, and we were able to locate his sister. Duane had passed away homeless in Hawaii, she told me. I spoke to his mom on the phone and she told me that Duane had also found faith. "He always had his Bible with him."

Bob wasn't the same kind of friend as Duane, but we were tight. When he finally did pass away—in a hospital room surrounded by his family and a couple of us who were privileged enough to be considered honorary family members, it was hard. There was no one to call anymore. I would still reach for my phone, and then remember. I finally understood what he had meant. Now I had to figure out the answers to my questions on my own.

I had never wanted Bob to replace my father. No matter how angry I was for all Dad had done in my life that hurt me, or how much I blamed him for my problems, I still loved and respected him. The yearning for that broken relationship to be restored continues to haunt me. To my disappointment, letting go of his ashes didn't change the clinging in my heart. It took writing down the details of my life for me to realize that the tugging in my heart will only be quieted when I can surrender to my Heavenly Father's gentle invitation to adopt me as his son.

I have a lot to learn about what that means. It has been a long struggle in my life. While I understand in theory that God is my Father in Heaven, that He loves me and will never leave me nor forsake me, it is hard for me to accept it. My father is the man I feared most. God's not like that, *but what does it mean to call him Father? As a Christian, shouldn't I be able to sit down and have that kind of father-son conversation I've always wanted with God?* It's something I have desired for so long.

Writing this book has been the most painful, and yet the most healing thing I've ever done in my life. As I write these final words, I am only beginning to see the depth of the relationship that God is calling me to share with him. Just a few days ago, with only the epilogue to finish, God literally spoke to me, saying, "Let it go." He wants me to let go of the fear, the pain, the regret, the disappointment. "Let it all go, and allow me to be your Father."

Not all people need the same type of changes to occur before a trauma becomes a miracle. Everyone has their own story and their own ups and downs that transform them. My hope is that by sharing my story and these events with you, my readers, that you, too, will be able to find recovery in your life.

Afterward – September 2016

Two years after his stroke in 2002, Mike Casey started a recovery ministry called Most Excellent Way, now known as 'Regeneration'. Regeneration is a weekly support meeting for those in addiction or other life dominating struggles, those coming out of addiction and the friends and family of those struggling with addiction.

In 2004, Mike was ordained as pastor at Calvary Monterey. This allowed him to further his ministry and begin visiting inmates in local jails and prisons.

Mike and Michele Casey felt led to open a home for men who were also struggling with addiction and desiring to lead a life of recovery. In 2006, with the encouragement of Bob Stewart, and the help of many others, The Bridge Restoration Ministry was opened in Seaside, California. It's a year-long faith-based recovery program that started out with just two residents and soon expanded to six residents.

In May 2008, The Bridge moved to a larger location in Pacific Grove, California. This new house was a historical eight-bedroom, eight-bath Victorian home previously known as The Gatehouse Inn. This move allowed the program to expand from six to twelve, and then eventually to 22 residents.

The residents of The Bridge began serving the public with community service projects. They also have regular Bible studies, weekly reading, counseling, mentoring, small-group discussion, accountability and job training.

In 2012, The Bridge opened Second Chance Thrift Store. Its mission is to provide job training, serve as an outreach service to the community, and as a way to fund The Bridge's residential program. It's also a connecting point for those wanting to know more about the program.

A men's transitional housing program was added in 2012, known as second phase. It allows successful graduates to have a place to live while completing their transition back into society.

In 2014, The Bridge opened a women's home, which can house six ladies at a time. This addition has proved to be a blessing in many ways.

The Bridge Restoration Ministry desires to change the lives of men and women. One of the graduates, Jordan Jeske, is now working with Prison Fellowship and ministers to inmates at various local prisons. He currently runs his own hauling and gardening company and was just recently ordained as a pastor in August 2016.

The Bridge opened a second thrift shop location in Monterey earlier this year. Second Chance Thrift Store in Monterey had its grand opening on March 1st, 2016. Their mission is the same as the first one – to serve the community and help men and women recover from addiction and lead productive lives.

After his stroke, Mike Casey rediscovered his passion for running. After being told he would never walk again, he has since gone on to complete six marathons. Mike can often be found running alongside members of The Bridge enjoying the recreation trails in Pacific Grove, California. Occasionally you may even find his wife, Michele, out there as well.

Mike and Michele continue to love on and minister to men and women every day. Through their efforts, lives are being changed on a daily basis. Mike can often be found running alongside members of The Bridge enjoying the recreation trails in Pacific Grove, California. Occasionally, you may even find his wife, Michele, out there as well. God's mercies really are new each morning and Mike continues to be reminded and grateful for that.

Please visit http://www.tbrm.org/ if you are wanting
to know more ... or if you are struggling with addiction
For more information, contact:
P.O. Box 113
Pacific Grove, CA 93950
mike@calvary.com

Author's Bio

After a downward spiral into heroin addiction, Mike Casey found himself living in his van, without his family, jobless, and in a recovery program. Before heroin, Mike had been a successful firefighter and paramedic with a wife and kids who depended on him. But over time, he fell into a deep addiction, desperately seeking to ease the pain from a troubled childhood. His addiction led to an aggressive flesh-eating bacterial infection accompanied by a massive stroke, both of which should have killed him. Based on all that has happened in Mike's life, he should not be capable of doing all that he is doing today.

While in the hospital, and contemplating all the things he could no longer do (which included feeding himself, writing, and walking, among others), Mike finally came to terms with the message of Jesus. His life turned around as he surrendered to God. Mike is now the founder and director of the Bridge Restoration Ministry in Pacific Grove, California, a nonprofit addiction recovery program, and a pastor at Calvary Monterey.

Michele and Mike Casey